WHO ABOLISHED SLAVERY?

EUROPEAN EXPANSION & GLOBAL INTERACTION

GENERAL EDITORS
Pieter C. Emmer, *Institute for the History of European Expansion, Leiden University*
Seymour Drescher, *University Professor, Department of History, University of Pittsburgh*

It may be said that the question of how the technology, languages, institutions, and even pastimes of Western Europe came to dominate global civilization— even came to create that civilization—is the greatest historical question of modern times. Yet scholars have paid relatively little attention to this veritable monumental phenomenon. This new series is designed to offer a forum for debate and bring new research to light.

WHO ABOLISHED SLAVERY

SLAVE REVOLTS AND ABOLITIONISM
A DEBATE WITH JOÃO PEDRO MARQUES

Edited by

Seymour Drescher
&
Pieter C. Emmer

Berghahn Books
New York • Oxford

First published in 2010 by

Berghahn Books
www.berghahnbooks.com

©2010, 2021 Seymour Drescher, Pieter C. Emmer, and João Pedro Marques
First paperback edition published in 2021

Library of Congress Cataloging-in-Publication Data
Who abolished slavery? : slave revolts and abolitionism : a debate with João Pedro
Marques / edited by Seymour Drescher and Pieter C. Emmer.
    p. cm. — (European expansion & global interaction ; v. 8)
Includes bibliographical references and index.
ISBN 978-1-84545-636-8 (hbk. : alk. paper)
    1. Slaves—Emancipation—America—History. 2. Slave insurrections—
America—History. 3. Antislavery movements—America—History. I. Marques,
João Pedro. II. Drescher, Seymour. III. Emmer, P. C.
    HT1050.W47 2010
    326'.809—dc22   2009025448

British Library Cataloguing in Publication Data
A catalogue record for this book is available from the British Library

ISBN: 978-1-84545-636-8 Hardback
ISBN: 978-1-80073-005-2 Paperback

CONTENTS

PART III. AFTERTHOUGHTS

PREFACE

Seymour Drescher and Pieter C. Emmer

During the past 50 years, the study of slavery and of the Atlantic slave trade has provided us with many new insights. It is difficult to find another field in history in which the advance in our knowledge has been so rapid and so comprehensive. We now know that African, not European, slave traders dominated the supply of slaves in Africa and that the staggeringly high mortality during the voyage was mainly related to the physical condition in which the slaves embarked. We now also possess more precisely measured frequencies of slave ship uprisings and their cost to and impact upon the slave trade, both in African waters and on the high seas. Other research has given us new insights into the family life of the slaves, slave demography, the profitability of the plantations, manumission, and emancipation. And that list of topics can easily be enlarged.

In addition, the past half-century has also produced a mass of information regarding slave resistance on land, ranging from small, individual acts of disobedience to massive uprisings such as the slave revolts in Saint-Domingue and elsewhere. Many of these acts of rebellion and resistance have been studied extensively, yet the ultimate goals of the insurgents—if at all known—remain open for discussion. Were the slaves simply interested in escaping the factory-like discipline of the plantations, the limitations of their freedom of movement, and the social confines of the slave quarters, or was their resistance ultimately aimed at overthrowing the institution of slavery *an sich*?

Recently, several historians have suggested that by resisting slavery, slaves achieved their own freedom. That would decrease the importance of the groups that have hitherto been seen as the prime movers behind slave emancipation such as "the saints" (Wilberforce, Clarkson, Schoelcher, just to name a few), abolitionist pressure groups of both whites and blacks, parliamentarians, and the governmental and anti-governmental armies of the various slaveholding empires. The idea that rebellious slaves were the prime agents of slave emancipation is also endorsed by the UNESCO web page on the slave route project, where you will be able to read, among other things, that, "the first fighters for the abolition of slavery were the captives and slaves themselves."

Now, the easiest thing to do would be to play down these different interpretations by arguing that both groups helped to bring down slavery, each in their own way. In any case, it seems nearly impossible to measure carefully the effectiveness of the anti-slavery actions of one group against that of the other. Would the slave rising in Saint-Domingue have met with success had there been no revolution in France? And would the discussion about slave emancipation in Britain not have lasted longer had there been no slave rebellions in Barbados in 1816, in Demerara in 1823, and in Jamaica in 1831–32?

Yet, the question remains of whether the ideological content of slave rebellions and abolitionism is indeed one and the same. Is it possible to speak of a black anti-slavery movement, in addition to the classical anti-slavery movement in Europe and North America? And if so, were the aims of these two groups in any way similar? Or should we distinguish between slave resistance and rebellion on the one side, and abolitionism, on the other? Did some of the slave protests include the demand for abolishing the institution of slavery wherever it existed and replacing it with free labor? And if that is not the case, should we then limit the use of the word abolitionism to describe only those protests and actions that can be categorized as attacks on the universal institution of slavery, which thus did not occur before 1750 and emanated from some parts of Western Europe and the New World until late in the nineteenth century?

The starting point of this volume is the text by João Pedro Marques, which stresses the ideological cleavage between Western abolitionism on the one side, and slave protests, rebellions, and insurgencies, on the other. As he writes at the end of chapter 1:

> It is quite wrong, therefore, to suppose that behind grand marronage and rebellion there necessarily lays an anti-slavery attitude. As a rule, runaways and rebels sought merely to escape a system in which their prospects were grim, but they had no intention of reshaping it. Clearly, slaves objected to their own enslavement, but rarely to the practice of slavery. In other words, they were not against the system of slavery itself but against the position they occupied within that system. It is equally wrong to imagine that in those societies where revolts took place, they led to any sort of emancipatory impulse or vocation.

In Part II of this volume, we have assembled a series of comments, written by some of the outstanding historians of slavery and its abolition. In the wake of their comments, we asked Dr. Marques to respond briefly to their comments and the degree to which they challenge or enhance his thesis.

Last, but not least, our thanks go to Dr. Marques for agreeing to have his work published as part of this volume, to the authors of the comments who all spontaneously agreed to contribute, and to our publisher, Marion Berghahn, who immediately agreed to our proposal to publish a debate rather than a monograph.

Pittsburgh/Leiden, December 2008

Part I

Slave Revolts and
the Abolition of Slavery:
An Overinterpretation

João Pedro Marques

Translated from the Portuguese by
Richard Wall

Introduction

***

A t the beginning of the nineteenth century, Thomas Clarkson portrayed the anti-slavery movement as a river of ideas that had swollen
over time until it became an irrepressible torrent. Clarkson had no doubt
that it had been the thought and action of all of those who, like Raynal,
Benezet, and Wilberforce, had advocated "the cause of the injured Africans" in Europe and in North America, which had ultimately lead to the
abolition of the British slave trade, one of the first steps toward abolition
of slavery itself.[1]

In our times, there are several views on what led to abolition and they
all differ substantially from the river of ideas imagined by Clarkson. Ironically, for one of those views, it is as if Clarkson's river had reversed its
course and started to flow from its mouth to its source. Anyone who, for
example, opens the UNESCO web page (the Slave Route project) will
have access to an eloquent example of that approach, so radically opposed
to Clarkson's. In effect, one may read there that, "the first fighters for the
abolition of slavery were the captives and slaves themselves".[2] Indeed, the
UNESCO web page considers that the insurrection of Saint-Domingue
(Haiti) was the event that led to the abolitions, and that is why August
23rd—the day on which, in the distant year 1791, the largest slave revolt
in history broke out—was chosen as the International Day for the Remembrance of the Slave Trade and its Abolition.[3]

The tendency to over-emphasize the role of the resistance to slavery
in its abolition, so clearly evident in an organization as important and far-
reaching as UNESCO, is even more pronounced in the discourse of jour-
nalists, political activists, and the so-called remembrance groups, large
associations which devote a fair amount of attention to the memory of
slavery, a memory that they seek to reconstruct primarily as the outcome
of slave resistance everywhere—in Africa, on the slave ships, on the plantations in the colonies where slavery was practiced—and only secondarily
the result of the anti-slavery movement, which emerged and developed
in the Western world.[4] Although this approach occurs most frequently in
the mass media, this is not simply a case of popular mystification, extra-

neous to the academy. This book addresses a type of discourse at least partly to be found in the academy itself.

A major gain for scholarship has occurred in recent decades. There has been a welcome surge in the number of studies on slaves' resistance to their masters. In those studies, historians have investigated cases of insurrection, conspiracy, escapes, the withholding of labor, and sabotage. They have built up a complex and surprisingly full picture of the way in which an anonymous and often brutalized mass reacted to their bondage. Often, the different forms of slave resistance—especially armed revolt—have been seen as the manifestation of a hitherto unsung heroism and of a spirit valuing liberty and refusing to be restricted by the brutality of the masters. Many aspects of this resistance had remained hidden by the age-old stereotype of Negro docility.

Some historians, however, went further and replaced the stereotype of the docile slave with the counter-stereotype of the always-rebellious slave. For a number of these historians, the slave as rebel was the first, and the main, agent—or at least the most significant one—in the abolition of slavery. In the words of Nelly Schmidt, "Overcoming slavery was the aim of those primarily concerned, i.e., those who had been captured in Africa and deported to the Caribo-Americas between the end of the Fifteenth Century and the end of the Nineteenth Century. *Subsequently,* it also became the aim of the Western abolitionists who sought to convince the European governments of the need to put an end to the slave trade and to the system of slavery" (author's translation).[5] To illustrate the notion that African slaves were the first opponents of slavery, Schmidt adopted a cumulative and teleological conception, lumping together revolts on the plantations and on slave ships, poisonings of masters, escapes and suicides, infanticides, and even the slave's daily, stoical survival itself. All of these phenomena are conflated as forms of the struggle against slavery and as actions which undermined the colonial slavery regime for centuries, so that it eventually collapsed.[6] In other words, for Schmidt, the purpose of all of these manifestations, whether of resistance, rejection, and despair, and whatever form they took, was to end slavery itself. Hence, slaves were the historic precursors of the movement that would take on its visible political form—abolitionism—at the end of the eighteenth century.

There are obvious difficulties with this thesis. To group together the manifestations of slave resistance as if they all derived from the same motivation and had only a single objective is tenuous to say the least. Even aligning such closely related phenomena as conspiracies and revolts raises a number of difficulties from the point of view of historical analysis. It should always be recalled that the confessions of those allegedly involved in conspiracies generally were obtained under torture. It seems likely that whites invented some of the conspiracies. Many historians refer to outbreaks of paranoia and persecution, which take us beyond the issues of slavery. Trevor-Roper, for example, demonstrated how people under torture confess to whatever their interrogators want to hear, denouncing their friends and neighbors or involuntarily exaggerating the importance of harmless episodes or non-events.[7] Another problematic posture is equating all slave revolts with anti-slavery, but only from the sixteenth century onward. This excludes Antiquity and the Middle Ages, both Christian and Muslim. If Schmidt had not excluded them, she would have had to acknowledge that resistance to slavery and the anti-slavery attitude supposedly deriving from it had their origins in very ancient times, and would have had to explain why that anti-slavery attitude did not lead to abolition in those times. Of course, as an alternative, she could always regard the revolts, conspiracies, and escapes that took place before the sixteenth century as not being expressions of anti-slavery. In that case, however, she would have to explain why they were not similar expressions of antislavery.

Despite these and other problems, a number of historians have developed the thesis that the struggle of the slave masses both preceded, and had a significant effect on, the final decision to abolish the institutions of slavery. In addition to Nelly Schmidt, the theory is also to be found in the writings of Elikia M'Bokolo, Hebert Aptheker, Hilary Beckles, Richard Hart, and several others.[8] I examine these in greater detail in chapter 4. Regardless of the differences between them, all of these historians see the actions of slaves in revolt as having led to abolition. They supposedly did so directly, in that successful insurrections produced an area of freedom that undermined or destroyed the fabric of slavery, and indirectly in that those actions, helped to instill generalized fear amongst whites, and thus eventually force them to abolish the system. In other words, these historians have helped to encourage two persistent misinterpretations: first, that revolts were always ways of fighting slavery; and secondly, that the decision to end the system of slavery in most Western nations was for the most part the outcome of such revolts. As Schmidt concluded, "Every emancipation act, whether it concerned French, English, Spanish, Danish or Dutch colonies, was preceded by a more or less extended slave rebellion which precipitated the decision" (author's translation).[9]

This statement is biased, because it does not consider what happened in the majority of Western countries. And it is also misleading because, unless one ascribes a meaning to the verb "to precede" so widely that it covers events that took place several decades or even centuries before abolition, the emancipation decrees in most countries were not preceded by slave revolts. On the contrary, it is generally impossible to establish a direct, necessary or sufficient correlation between slave uprisings—which are an integral part of the history of slavery in various epochs and latitudes—and the emancipation laws enacted in the West, which were all highly localized and specific events in human history. On the rare occasions when such a correlation can nevertheless be established, those who dub the slave as the main agent of the abolition of slavery have generally placed the cart before the horse. It is precisely this thesis that I will seek to demonstrate.

The first of this book's four chapters deals with events prior to the end of the eighteenth century. It provides a general picture of the various forms of slave resistance and it explains what usually happened as a result of resistance in terms of its threats to the prevailing systems of slavery. Chapters 2 and 3 analyze the main revolts that occurred during the Age of Abolition, between the end of the eighteenth and the end of the nineteenth centuries. It further asks whether and to what extent those revolts deviated from the usual pattern, and if it is possible to establish a correlation between violent slave agitation and the decision to end slavery—and, if so, what sort of correlation. Finally, in looking at the close relationship between history and ideology, chapter 4 seeks to identify the origins and nature of the theory that views emancipation as something which was primarily the result of the struggles of the slaves themselves.

Notes

1. Thomas Clarkson, *History of the Rise, Progress, and Accomplishment of the Abolition of the African Slave Trade by the British Parliament* (London, 1839; 1st edition 1808), 47ff.
2. http://portal.unesco.org/culture/en/ev.php-URL_ID=27519&URL_DO=DO_TOPIC& URL_SECTION=201.html.
3. http://www.unesco.org/focus/newslett/newslet8.html.
4. By way of illustration only, see the web page of Le Collectif des Antillais, Guyanais, Réunionnais (http://www.collectifdom.com).
5. "vaincre l'esclavage fut l'objectif des premiers concernés, les captifs d'Afrique déportés aux Caraïbes-Amériques entre la fin du XVe et la fin du XIXe siècle. Ce fut *ensuite* et aussi celui des abolitionnistes qui, en Occident, cherchèrent, du XVIIIe au XIXe siècle, à convaincre les gouvernements européens de la nécessité de mettre un terme à la traite négrière et au système esclavagiste"
   Nelly Schmidt, *L'abolition de l'esclavage. Cinq siècles de combats (XVe-XXe siècle)* (Paris: Fayard, 2005), 7 (my italics).
6. Schmidt, *L'abolition de l'esclavage*, 49. For a critique of Schmidt's book, see João Pedro Marques, "Terão os escravos abolido a escravidão? Considerações a propósito de um livro de Nelly Schmidt," in *Africana Studia*, 8 (2006): 249–273.
7. H.R. Trevor-Roper, *Religion, the Reformation and Social Change* (London: Macmillan, 1967) (I used the Portuguese translation by Maria do Carmo Cary, *Religião, Reforma e Transformação Social*, ed. Presença (Lisboa, 1981), 73ff.). For examples of conspiracies that were the result of white fear, see Winthrop D. Jordan, *Tumult and Silence at Second Creek: An Inquiry into a Civil War Slave Conspiracy* (Baton Rouge: Louisiana State University Press, 1993); and Matt D. Childs, *The 1812 Aponte Rebellion in Cuba and the Struggle against Atlantic Slavery* (Chapel Hill: The University of North Carolina Press, 2006), 138.
8. By way of example, see Herbert Aptheker, *Abolitionism. A Revolutionary Movement* (Boston: Twayne Publishers, 1992), xiii.
9. "chaque décret d'émancipation, qu'il s'agisse des domaines coloniaux français, anglais, espagnol, danois ou néerlandais, fut précédé d'un soulèvement d'esclaves plus ou moins long qui précipita la prise de décision."
   Schmidt, *L'abolition de l'esclavage*, 326.

1

SLAVERY AND RESISTANCE: AN OLD RELATIONSHIP

The African slave has often been represented as someone always ready to revolt against slavery, but it is wrong to think that the inherent injustices and violence of servile institutions—of Africans and other peoples—necessarily or frequently gave rise to such rebellious outbursts. Slave labour was widely used in Antiquity, but as far as we can determine from the available sources, sizeable revolts were uncommon both in the Near East and in Greece. The same can be said for the Roman Empire where, with the exception of the servile wars that ravaged Sicily in the final third of the second century BC, and later Spartacus' famous revolt, there were no major slave-originated rebellions.[1] Nor were the Middle Ages particularly troubled by slave uprisings, either in Europe—where slavery, moreover, declined—or in Asia. It is true that in the Islamic world, there was a major insurrection in the ninth century (which will be examined in greater detail below) and that between 1182 and 1232, there was a period of slave revolts in Korea, where the number of slaves may have reached the equivalent of a third of the total population, in the context of a civil war and the Mongol invasions.[2] These were exceptional periods, however, in a generally more peaceful story. Available data on sub-Saharan Africa is scarce, or too widely dispersed to allow us to make any categorical statements about the sub-continent as a whole. But up until the nineteenth century, in areas documented by Europeans, there do not seem to have been major slave rebellions, notwithstanding the advent of the transatlantic trade. Despite its high concentrations of slaves, both resident and transitory, no open revolts ever took place in Luanda, for example.[3] In sum, it seems clear that slave revolts were much less frequent than violent resistance on the part of the free or half-free disadvantaged classes.

In fact, slaves' attitudes to the actual conditions of their bondage depended on the interaction of multiple factors, and there were various ways of responding to the injustice and brutality of the masters' world, one of which was acceptance. Strictly speaking, the history of slavery reflects not only exploitation and resistance, but also acquiescence and even collaboration. In that history, the counterpart to the figure of the rebellious slave is the slave who remained faithful to his master even in the context of a revolt.[4] It should be recalled that, in the Afro-American and Atlantic colonial settings of concern to us here, many slaves, attracted by the promise of enfranchisement, objectively supported slavery as a social system, fighting beside their masters against internal and external threats; and that some of those trusted slaves were armed, on occasion forming small armies or militarized corps;[5] it should also not be forgotten that throughout colonial America—and also in São Tomé and other Portuguese colonies—many Africans, whether emancipated or not, were enticed to catch fugitive slaves by the rewards offered.[6] In sum, the range of responses to the slave society, despite its intrinsic violence, was varied, and did not necessarily involve resistance, let alone direct confrontation. This is understandable, given the obvious imbalance of military force available to the exploiters and the exploited. In these circumstances, rebellions were extremely risky and were mercilessly repressed. For these reasons, recalcitrant or insubordinate slaves usually preferred alternative forms of passive or more indirect resistance, such as sabotaging their work or escaping.

Let us ignore the different forms of sabotage and concentrate for the moment only on slave flights, which, in certain circumstances, could be a threat to the slaveholder society. The French used the term *marronage* to describe all slave secessionist movements. The term derived from the Spanish *cimarron* (which in turn went back to an Amerindian word) and meant fugitive, savage, a man of the mountains. However, unlike the British, who used the term *maroon* only for those who tried to escape for good, the French made a distinction between *petit* and *grand marronage*. The former term applied to the temporary absences of those slaves who, having escaped, came back to the place they had left.[7] The term *grand marronage* could apply to the more extreme cases of those who openly rebelled, but it generally covered slaves who had escaped to regions on the periphery of the slave society that were inhospitable or easily defensible, in order to sever their ties to their masters for good. There, they would establish villages and encampments of variable sizes and types, according to the area and the epoch: *cumbes, palenques, rochelas, magotes, ladeiras, mocambos,* and *quilombos* (a label I shall hereafter use in a general sense).

The problem of *grand marronage* was a feature of the colonial slave system from the beginning, and by the mid-seventeenth century, there were hundreds of communities of fugitive slaves, both in the plantations and in the great mining regions. These were mostly small communities, sometimes of no more than half a dozen people. But they could also be very large, and their existence might be disruptive to colonial societies. Fugitive slaves attacked travelers, kidnapped women for reproduction, and stole from the nearby plantations, searching for men, provisions, and weapons.[8] The most famous *quilombo* was Palmares, which arose at the end of the sixteenth century following an escape from a sugar-mill in the port of Pernambuco. Other Africans, Indians, and ordinary criminals fleeing the arm of the law soon joined the founding group and in such numbers that, at its height, Palmares may have had a few thousand souls in several villages spread over a wide area.[9] During the Dutch occupation, the *quilombo* was a kingdom with an administration and a capital— Macaco, about 110 kilometers from Pernambuco—and had an army equivalent in size to that of many African *sobados*. It offered prolonged resistance to the punitive expeditions of the colonists who, despite having destroyed villages and recaptured fugitives, were unable permanently to eradicate the threat. Thus, in 1678, the Portuguese authorities suggested a truce to Ganga Zumba, the supreme leader of Palmares, offering him freedom for all of those born in the *quilombo,* the grant of lands, and the assurance that they would be able to trade freely with neighboring villages in exchange for peace, which was accepted, but which lead to disagreements among the Africans. Under the leadership of Zumbi, the dissidents poisoned Ganga Zumba, and the kingdom of Palmares embarked on a period of factional war, which weakened it until it fell apart in 1694. Zumbi was captured and executed in the following year, with his head being exhibited in public.[10]

Even though Palmares was to some extent untypical, by reason of its size and longevity, the basic pattern it so well embodied was endlessly repeated. There were hundreds of *quilombos* in Brazil throughout the colonial period. In the eighteenth century, there were more than 110 in Minas Gerais alone. Fugitive slave encampments had existed in parts of Mexico since the sixteenth century, and, at the beginning of the next century, at least one of them—San Lorenzo de Los Negros—was able to ensure its survival through a non-aggression treaty with the Spanish authorities.[11] During the seventeenth century, the *quilombos* around Cartagena (in modern Colombia) grew in number, size, and threat potential for the white population, despite non-aggression treaties. They were finally destroyed in various military campaigns by the Spanish authorities. In Jamaica, during the last thirty years of the seventeenth century and the early part of the eighteenth century, the British colonial authorities sent various punitive expeditions against the maroons, but were unable to wipe them out; in desperation, and in order to safeguard the plantations, which suffered frequent attacks, they made treaties with the fugitives, acknowledging their freedom and ownership of a territory. In Suriname also the problem of the maroons persisted, since neither the British nor the Dutch (the colony changed hands several times) were able to deal with it. Thus, between 1760 and 1793, various peace agreements were signed with groups of former slaves, recognizing them as free peoples and allowing them to live in the lands they then occupied. None of this was specific to black slavery in the Americas. *Quilombos* also existed in the mountainous island of São Tomé, on the outskirts of Luanda, and in other regions of Africa, such as Mombassa, for example. Similar processes occurred in the Antiquity, in Calabria, during the fourth century BC, and on the Greek island of Chios in the following century. Here, the slaves who had fled *en masse* to the mountains, whence they occasionally descended to attack the properties of their former masters, eventually accepted a non-aggression pact in exchange for recognition of their freedom.[12]

Although the *quilombo* was the most common form of collective slave resistance, the revolt was obviously what was most feared. Strictly speaking, the concepts of escape and rebellion are not entirely separate. There is—or there may be—an area of overlap. Even though many *quilombos* took shape gradually, others arose as a result of collective flight following a revolt. Having said this, the fact that we acknowledge these cases does not mean that, as is frequently the case, one then subscribes to a kind of conceptual amalgam in which flight and rebellion are seen as being equivalent. In overall terms they were not, nor did they have the same meaning. It is thus impossible to go along with João José Reis when he states that, "the very existence of the *quilombo* and above all its military defence and incursions into enemy territory, may be regarded as revolts."[13] In fact they cannot be—or should not be—just as desertion is not to be confused with revolt in military terms. Essentially the *quilombo* is the result of an escape, a desertion. A revolt is something else.

One particular form of revolt was that which could occur on board a slave ship. As a rule, this was an action driven by despair and its aim was to go back to Africa. It therefore happened more frequently when the ship was at anchor or during the early days of its journey, while it was still conceivable to turn back. Revolts on board ship were one of the greatest risks of the slave trade, and there were a number of cases where complete white crews were slaughtered or where the rebels blew themselves up with the ship. Data collected by Eltis show that there were 383 on-board slave revolts, the majority of which took place in the second half of the eighteenth century; only 23 of those revolts were fully successful, enabling those responsible to land as free men at various points in the Atlantic basin.[14]

It was on land, however, in areas with large concentrations of slaves such as mines and plantations, that the revolts could, by reason of their scope and form, become more troublesome for the white community as a whole—and sometimes for the creole community as well. Portuguese and Brazilian legislation held that meetings of 20 or more slaves constituted an insurrection, and Texas legislation made the same judgment of a meeting of 3 or more armed slaves.[15] If we adopt this and other definitions enshrined in the legislation of the time, and if we categorize as an insurrection any meeting of armed slaves seeking freedom by force, then we must conclude that up until the end of the last decade of the eighteenth century, there were several dozen insurrections in the colonial world, from the island of Reunion to Peru and from New York to Argentina. Some historians have attributed great significance to this scattering of small insurrections, basically for two reasons: either because they over-estimate their scope or impact; or, more frequently, because they believe that this, along with escapes, conspiracies, and workplace sabotage, was one of the factors involved in achieving a slow but persistent erosion of the slaveholder societies, leading them ultimately to the suppression of slavery. But this theory is not convincing. As Freehling correctly emphasizes, sabotage, at worst, might make slavery "less damaging, more endurable."[16] As for violence, one should not exaggerate its revolutionary potential. The history of the frontiers of the Roman or Chinese empires, for example, shows that human societies can deal with low to medium-intensity conflict for many centuries, with peaks of great violence and destruction here and there, without altering their behavior in any fundamental way. In addition, and specifically in the context of the modern colonial world, we should remember that some of the earliest states to abolish slavery were precisely those where such resistance was insignificant; by contrast, areas where there were many conspiracies, minor revolts, or escapes were the last to emancipate their slaves. If we are focusing here on slave actions that might bring about change in the political and economic destiny of a slave state, then we shall have to refer to revolts involving a minimum number of rebels of around three hundred (the number of slaves on a medium to large-size sugar plantation).

Revolts on this scale were less common than is often stated. The first of them occurred in 1595, on the island of São Tomé, when a self-styled "king Amador" led an uprising of some four thousand slaves, destroying 70 sugar-mills and various buildings; "Amador" was imprisoned and quartered in the following year. In 1598, a revolt involving thousands of insurrectionists erupted in the gold mines of Colombia. Thirty years later, there was another uprising, started by a group of 40 slaves, which grew rapidly until it was suppressed by the colonial armed forces. In the same period, in 1735, Mexico went through its greatest revolt, in the Veracruz province, involving perhaps a thousand slaves. In 1673, Jamaica had to deal with an uprising of around 300 slaves, and seventeen years later, an insurrection by another 400 or 500. In 1760, there was another major uprising on the island—the so-called Tacky's rebellion—which involved thousands of slaves and lasted for months, eventually being put down with the help of the maroons. Three years later, there was an insurrection by thousands of slaves in Berbice, a part of Guiana. This lasted for over a year, and almost led to the establishment of a rebel state. Finally, in 1774–75, a new revolt broke out in Demerara.[17]

Nine major revolts in total occurred, none of them as extensive as similar events that had taken place elsewhere in the past. It should be recalled that in Roman Italy, for example, the first Sicilian revolt lasted at least four years and involved some seventy thousand slaves; and that

Spartacus' revolt lasted three years and may have involved even larger numbers, ten legions being required to suppress it completely.[18] Small-scale slave revolts were nevertheless more frequent in the Atlantic colonies than in the Antiquity and the Middle Ages, a fact which may be related to the way slaves were used in each time and place. In fact, many of the rebellions occurring in the colonies erupted in the plantations, especially the sugar plantations, where working conditions were, as a rule, particularly inhuman. By contrast, and if we exclude work in the mines or certain forms of exploitation of farm labor in Roman Italy, the way slave labor was used in the Antiquity and the Middle Ages did not produce concentrations of many slaves in one place, but rather produced their being dispersed in their masters' houses, where they were required generally to perform domestic duties. It should also be noted that there was a huge, often suicidal imbalance between free men and slaves in many Atlantic colonies. In a number of cases, slaves accounted for 90 percent of the population or more. In the middle of the eighteenth century, Berbice, for example, had 11 slaves for each European. Imbalances of this magnitude were unknown or unusual in the history of slavery. Even at the height of the Roman Empire, no more than 40 percent of Italy's population, for example, was made up of slaves.[19] In addition, these disparities in the Atlantic colonies were not always counterbalanced by minimally adequate military or police garrisons. The Danish island of St. John, where some 150 slaves revolted in 1733, had a small, ineffective militia and a military garrison of just 8 men, at a time when slaves outnumbered whites by 11 to 2.[20]

These and other reasons go some length in explaining why insurrections in the colonial world were relatively more frequent. Even so, it should be noted that insurrections did not affect equally all regions. Away from those colonies that were particularly prone to rebellion—like Jamaica, where there were as many insurrections as in the whole of the rest of the British Empire[21]—many others generally were spared slave agitation. The case of Luanda has already been mentioned; but Brazil also remained relatively calm; and the same goes for the large island of Hispaniola (or Santo Domingo), which went through 270 uneventful years after having experienced the first black slave uprising in America in 1522.[22] Similar considerations apply to Cuba and Peru, and to Barbados and other Caribbean islands.

In the light of these comments, and having outlined the main revolts that took place in the first three centuries of the colonial world created by the Europeans in Africa and America, let us move on to the key issue: were these revolts forms of anti-slavery? Were they ways of combating slavery? These questions demand that we ask what were the aims of the rebels. In some cases, nothing is known because, as with a small revolt in South Carolina in 1739, the rebels were killed before they could say anything.[23] In most cases, however, once the rebellion had been put down, survivors were taken to court, and we can therefore reconstruct what they wanted either through their statements to the courts or by what they actually did in the field. In yet other cases, the temporarily successful rebels imposed their will on a given territory. They were able to stake their claims and, for better or worse, implement their political plans. Thus, in overall terms, the most common objectives were flight, retaliation, and restoration; in other words, the aim was to reconquer freedom, kill the whites, destroy the sugar-mills and other facilities, and, depending on the balance of forces on the ground, to escape or subjugate the region, where modes of social organization of African origin would then tend to be restored.[24] In this context, and as a general rule, the rebels' aim was not to suppress slavery, which they often were prepared to perpetuate, albeit with a reversal of roles. The aims of Tacky's rebellion in Jamaica were to kill the whites and takeover power on the island, where they intended to carry on producing sugar by enslaving those blacks who refused to follow them. The same thing occurred with the revolt on the Danish island of St. John in 1733, where the rebels were even prepared to sell slaves in order to buy the powder they lacked. The rebels who took over Berbice in 1763 also enslaved some whites, half-breeds, and blacks; and of course, if they allowed slavery in their midst, they would be all the more ready to allow it outside. As Coffy, the leader of the revolt, stated in one of the letters he sent to the Dutch governor of the colony, his men did not want to continue being slaves, so they had rebelled; but the governor could make up the missing numbers by importing other Africans: "Let the blacks you have on your ships be your slaves."[25]

Successful escapes had similar outcomes. In actual fact, no *quilombo*, regardless of its size and duration, should be seen as an attempt to destroy slavery, nor even as an absolute rejection of that system. The *quilombo* no doubt created areas of freedom, but those areas of freedom neither undermined nor dissolved slavery as a social system; in one sense they complemented it, operating as a safety valve, which, in allowing relapsed or insurgent slaves to withdraw to the periphery, lessened the tensions at the heart of the system and prevented it from exploding.[26] Moreover, it should be emphasized that the maroons obtained freedom for themselves, but were not generally or necessarily opposed to slavery. For that reason, the non-aggression treaties between colonial authorities and those fugitive slaves who had not submitted generally provided for their collaboration with the whites in capturing and returning other runaway slaves, in exchange for the recognition of their own freedom.

This method had already been used in the Antiquity—the authorities on Chios, for example, made a treaty with the rebellious slaves that also provided for the return of future runaways[27]—and was repeated several times in America while slavery lasted. It was thus in Panama, New Granada, and Mexico, where the former slaves of San Lorenzo de los Negros, in exchange for recognition of their freedom, committed themselves to helping the Spanish authorities catch runaway slaves;[28] the same happened in Dutch Suriname.[29] The maroons of Western Jamaica, for example, bought, sold, and owned a considerable number of slaves, and were bounty hunters, that is to say, they hunted runaway slaves not only on the island itself but also in any other place their services were called upon. In addition, they helped to combat slave uprisings on the plantations—such as Tacky's rebellion, for example, which is why they were hated by part of the slave population and appropriately known as "the King's Negroes."[30] In southern Bahia, in 1806, dozens of runaway slaves established the *quilombo* of Oitizeiro on the lands of a farming community they had befriended and for whom they grew manioc; when the *quilombo* was dispersed, it was ascertained that the runaway slaves had used the labor of other slaves in the production of that food crop.[31] In Palmares as well, slavery was not eradicated; on the contrary, those who joined the runaways of their own accord would be free; but those who were caught in a raid were regarded as captives and would be put to work in the *quilombo*.[32] Identical practices were followed by other fugitive slave communities, such as, for example, some on the island of Santo Domingo.[33]

This means that also in the *quilombos* were there people who were not free, and who sometimes tried to escape. In such cases, the reaction of their new masters was not substantially different from normal practice in the white community: the head of the *quilombo* would send out a group in pursuit of the fugitive. If the fugitive were caught, he would be executed quickly, in exemplary fashion.[34]

In sum, the main concern of slaves who achieved individual freedom by escape or rebellion was not to free other slaves, and they often ended up creating a social structure that involved the enslavement of other Negro and half-breed population groups—which is hardly surprising, given that this was the custom of the time in both Africa and America. It was not only in the Atlantic basin slave system that those who had just escaped from slavery recreated it. In 869 AD, the many thousands of black slaves who worked in southern Iraq started a major revolt. They fought the Caliphate's armies in the canals and swamps of the area, and in 871 AD, they even took Basra. Only twelve years later were they defeated and crushed. What is significant in the context which interests us here is that during the rebellion and the years of independence which followed, right up until their final defeat, the rebels did not abolish slavery. On the contrary, they rebuilt the system to their own advantage, enslaving prisoners of war, women, and children captured during their conquests of the towns and cities of Iraq. The same thing happened in Roman Italy, in the revolts that marked the final phase of the Republic.[35]

It is quite wrong therefore to suppose that behind *grand marronage* and rebellion there necessarily lies an anti-slavery attitude. As a rule, runaways and rebels sought merely to escape a system in which their prospects were grim, but they had no intention of reshaping it. Clearly, slaves objected to their own enslavement, but rarely objected to the practice of slavery. In other words, they were not against the system of slavery itself but against the position they occupied within that system. It is equally wrong to imagine that in those societies where revolts took place, they led to any sort of emancipator impulse or vocation. It is true that the revolt in Iraq in the ninth century had an impact on the Arab world, discouraging similar agri-capitalist undertakings, which were dangerous and volatile by virtue of the high number of slaves they required. But they did not lead that world with a view to abolition, nor did they prevent the continued importation of slaves for domestic, military or other purposes. The same thing occurred in the Roman Empire before, and in the Atlantic world thereafter, where, despite the occasional revolts that here and there sprinkled further violence on the already violent domain of colonization, slaves continued to be imported in ever-increasing numbers. Revolts on board ship did not prevent the continuation of the trade either, nor did they have a significant impact on the Western decision to abolish it.

In sum: in the first three centuries of existence of the Afro-American world, colonial slaves rebelled, just as Roman slaves had done before them. Their struggle was for revenge, for land, and for individual or group freedom. But they did not seek freedom for all, a goal that is indispensable in the anti-slavery conception of human relations. Contrary to what is often asserted or suggested, slave rebellion is not synonymous with anti-slavery.

Let us now examine when, why, and in what circumstances there arose a tendency to knit these two issues together so that they began to be seen as part of the same equation.

Notes

1. See in this connection Keith Bradley, *Slavery and Rebellion in the Roman World, 140 B.C.– 70 B.C.* (Bloomington and Indianapolis: Indiana University Press, 1998; 1st ed., 1989), 46–101. For the revolts in Greece, see Yvon Garlan, *Les esclaves en Grèce ancienne*, ed. La Découverte (Paris, 1995), 184–191.
2. Ellen Salem, "Slavery in Medieval Korea," (Ph.D. diss., Columbia University, 1978).
3. Joseph C. Miller, *Way of Death. Merchant Capitalism and the Angolan Slave Trade, 1730– 1830* (Madison: University of Wisconsin Press, 1988), 270–271. Beatrix Heintze, *Asilo ameaçado: oportunidades e consequências da fuga de escravos em Angola no século XVII* (Luanda: Museu Nacional da Escravatura, 1995), 8, mentions some slave revolts in the Angolan markets, which were not referred to in correspondence sent to the Crown because they were of little importance and took place outside the Portuguese area.
4. Laurent Dubois, *Les esclaves de la Republique. L'histoire oubliée de la première émancipation, 1789–1794* (Paris: Calmann-Lévy, 1998), 115; Edward A. Pearson, "A Countryside Full of Flames: A Reconsideration of the Stono Rebellion and Slave Rebelliousness in the Early Eighteenth-Century South Carolina Lowcountry," in *Slavery and Abolition*, 17, 2, (1996): 39.
5. On armed slaves in Minas Gerais and in Jamaica see Stuart B. Schwartz, *Slaves, Peasants, and Rebels. Reconsidering Brazilian Slavery* (Urbana and Chicago: University of Illinois Press, 1996), 118, and Michael Craton, *Testing the Chains: Resistance to Slavery in the British West Indies* (Ithaca, NY and London: Cornell University Press, 1982), 125, respectively. For the identical situation in Portuguese Africa see James Duffy, *Portuguese Africa* (Cambridge, MA: Harvard University Press, 1959), 143. For a comparative his-

torical approach see also Orlando Patterson, *Slavery and Social Death. A Comparative Study*, (Cambridge, MA and London: Harvard University Press, 1982), 287–293; for the military role of slaves in defending slave regimes, against other slaves as well, see David B. Davis, *The Problem of Slavery in the Age of Revolution, 1770–1823* (Ithaca, NY and London: Cornell University Press, 1975), 73ff.; Eugene D. Genovese, *From Rebellion to Revolution. Afro-American Slave Revolts in the Making of the Modern World* (Baton Rouge: Louisiana State University Press, 1992; 1st ed., 1979), 18; and especially Christopher Leslie Brown and Philip D. Morgan, eds., *Arming Slaves From Classical Times to the Modern Age* (New Haven and London: Yale University Press, 2006).

6. Décio Freitas, *Zumbi dos Palmares* (Luanda: Museu Nacional da Escravatura, 1996), 7. See also Kátia de Queirós Mattoso, *Ser escravo no Brasil*, ed. Brasiliense (São Paulo, 1988), 162ff.; and Emília Viotti da Costa, *Crowns of Glory, Tears of Blood. The Demerara Slave Rebellion of 1823* (New York: Oxford University Press, 1994), 57 and 81.

7. Hilary Beckles, "From Land to Sea: Runaway Barbados Slaves and Servants, 1630–1700," in *Slavery and Abolition*, 6 (1985): 82–83. Laurent Dubois, *Les vengeurs du Nouveau Monde. Histoire de la Révolte Haïtienne* (Rennes: Les Perséides, 2005), 84ff.

8. See, for example, Gabino La Rosa Corzo, *Runaway Slave Settlements in Cuba. Resistance and Repression* (Chapel Hill and London: The University of North Carolina Press, 1988), 136–137.

9. João José Reis, "Quilombos e revoltas escravas no Brasil," in *Revista da Universidade de São Paulo*, 14, 39 (1995–96): 16.

10. Décio Freitas, *Palmares. A Guerra dos Escravos* (Rio de Janeiro: Graal, 1978); Stuart B. Schwartz, "Mocambos, quilombos e Palmares: a resistência escrava no Brasil colonial," in *Estudos Económicos*, 17 (1978): 40; Schwartz, *Slaves, Peasants, and Rebels*, 122ff.; Ronaldo Vainfas, "Deus contra Palmares. Representações senhoriais e ideias jesuíticas," in *Liberdade por um Fio. História dos Quilombos no Brasil*, eds. João José Reis and Flávio dos Santos Gomes (São Paulo: Companhia das Letras, 1996), 60–80.

11. Luz Maria Martinez Montiel, "Integration patterns and the assimilation process of negro slaves in Mexico," in *Comparative Perspectives on Slavery in New World Plantation Societies*, eds. Vera Rubin and Arthur Tuden (New York: The New York Academy of Sciences, 1977), 453.

12. Garlan, *Les esclaves*, 181–184. For *quilombos* in colonial America see Schwartz, *Slaves, Peasants, and Rebels*, 106–108 and 119ff.; Edgar Love, "Negro resistance to Spanish rule in colonial Mexico," in *Journal of Negro History*, 52, 2 (1967): 89; Maria del Cármen Borrego Plá, *Palenques de negros en Cartagena de Índias a fines del siglo XVII* (Sevilla: Escuela de Estudios Hispano-Americanos de Sevilla, 1973); Craton, *Testing the Chains*, 67ff.; Silvia W. de Groot, "The Maroons of Surinam: agents of their own emancipation," in *Abolition and Its Aftermath. The Historical Context, 1790–1916*, ed. David Richardson (London: Frank Cass, 1985), 56–65.

13. Reis, "Quilombos e revoltas," 16.

14. David Eltis, *The Rise of African Slavery in the Americas* (Cambridge: Cambridge University Press, 2000), 232.

15. Herbert Aptheker, *American Negro Slave Revolts* (New York: International Publishers, 1993; 1st ed., 1943), 162.

16. William W. Freehling, *The South Versus the South. How Anti-Confederate Southerners Shaped the Course of the Civil War* (Oxford and New York: Oxford University Press, 2001), 26.

17. For "Amador's" revolt, see Arlindo Manuel Caldeira, "Rebelião e outras formas de resistência à escravatura na ilha de São Tomé," in *Africana Studia*, 7 (2004): 132ff. For an overall view see Genovese, *From Rebellion to Revolution*, 33ff. Some writers include among the major revolts the so-called Andresote revolt, which occurred in Venezuela between 1731 and 1733. In fact, this was not a slave revolt but a social and military disturbance in which the *maroons* under Andresote, supported by the Dutch, played a part (see Angelina Pollak-Eltz, "Slave revolts in Venezuela," in Rubin and Tuden, *Comparative Perspectives on Slavery*, 440–441).

18. Bradley, *Slavery and Rebellion*, 61, 64, 96–97 and 107.

19. Olivier Pétré-Grenouilleau, *Les traites négrières. Essai d'histoire globale* (Paris: Gallimard, 2004), 24.
20. Neville A.T. Hall, *Slave Society in the Danish West Indies. St. Thomas, St. John and St. Croix* (Mona: The University of West Indies Press, 1994), 11; the Berbice militia before the revolt of 1763 was likewise worthless (cf. Cornelis C. Goslinga, *The Dutch in the Caribbean and the Guianas, 1680–1791* (Assen/Dover, NH: Van Gorcum, 1985), 466).
21. Craton, *Testing the Chains*, 99.
22. The uprising of 1522 in Hispaniola took place on the plantation of Diego Colombo (the son of the discoverer of America) and was defeated the following day (cf. John K. Thornton, *Warfare in Atlantic Africa, 1500–1800* (London: UCL Press, 1999), 140–141.
23. Pearson, "A Countryside Full of Flames," 41ff.
24. For the restorationist aspects of slave revolts prior to the end of the eighteenth century see Genovese, *From Rebellion to Revolution*, preface, 3 and 82ff.
25. Goslinga, *The Dutch in the Caribbean*, 461; for the enslavement of those conquered by the rebels see pp. 469, 472 and 487–88 of the same work. See also Monica Schuler, "Akan Slave rebellions in the British Caribbean," in *Caribbean Slave Society and Economy*, eds. Hilary Beckles and Verene Shepherd (Kingston and London: IRP/James Currey, 1991), 379–380; for Tack's rebellion and the revolt in St. John see Craton, *Testing the Chains*, 127 and 132, and Isaac Dookhan, *A History of the Virgin Islands, University Press of the West Indies* (Kingston, 1994), 167–168, respectively.
26. Donald Ramos, "O quilombo e o sistema escravista em Minas Gerais do século XVIII," in Reis and Gomes, *Liberdade por um Fio*, 164–192; Goslinga, *The Dutch in the Caribbean*, 376.
27. Garlan, *Les esclaves*, 181–184.
28. Love, "Negro resistance to Spanish rule," 90.
29. Goslinga, *The Dutch in the Caribbean*, 389 and 396–988.
30. Richard Price, ed., *Maroon Societies. Rebel Slave Communities in the Americas*, 3rd ed. (Baltimore: Johns Hopkins University Press, 1996), 22 and 148; and Genovese, *From Rebellion to Revolution*, 51ff. For examples of *maroon* collaboration with whites in hunting runaway slaves see, for Martinique: Gwendolyn Midlo Hall, "Saint Domingue," in Beckles and Shepherd, *Caribbean Slave Society*, 163-164, and, for Suriname: Silvia W. de Groot, "Maroons of Surinam: dependence and independence," in Rubin and Tuden, *Comparative Perspectives on Slavery*, 459.
31. Reis, "Quilombos e revoltas," 19.
32. Vainfas, "Deus contra Palmares," 165; and Schwartz, *Slaves, Peasants, and Rebels*, 124.
33. Price, *Maroon Societies*, 141; and Genovese, *From Rebellion to Revolution*, 57.
34. Price, *Maroon Societies*, 17–18.
35. Bradley, *Slavery and Rebellion*, 59 and 112; for the Iraqi revolt see Alexandre Popovic, *The Revolt of African Slaves in Iraq in the 3rd/9th Century* (Princeton: Markus Wiener, 1999), especially 129–132, and, for minor revolts involving black slaves in the same area, 22–23.

2

FOUR EXAMPLES OF A NEW EQUATION

ॐ

It is wrong to think that the peoples of the Western world were not sen- sitive to the iniquity and brutality of slavery. Despite the legal and philosophical abstractions tending to reduce the slave to a mere animated object, he was a human being, and his suffering could—and indeed did— evoke human sympathy from those who saw him arriving from Africa, wretched and naked, in a floating prison. However, for a long time, vari- ous forces, such as material interest, came together to prevent those hu- manitarian feelings from developing into serious opposition to the idea that slavery was both just and inevitable.[1] Only in the last thirty years of the eighteenth century would such opposition emerge, when new hopes for human progress helped to encourage the abolitionist approach to the problem of African slavery.

Unlike tolerationism, which was passive, that is to say, it hoped that the natural development of the world would put an end to such obvi- ously barbarous institutions, abolitionism was activist in that it wanted to change the world and had a plan of political action to do so. That plan in- volved the immediate or short-term abolition of the slave trade and, in the medium term, of slavery itself.[2] In other words, for the first time, there was a movement that sought to end slavery everywhere, and not just in the context of a small group, lineage or nation. It was that mirage, pro- pelled by an unprecedented propaganda campaign, which helped aboli- tionism to take root and flourish relatively quickly in several parts of the Protestant world, particularly in Great Britain and parts of the northern United States, whence it spread to other Western nations.

It was precisely at the time that abolitionism emerged and asserted it- self as an ideology—a time which, moreover, coincided with the so-called age of the revolutions—that slave revolts intensified, and, occasionally, changed their very nature. In fact, it was in the final quarter of the eighteenth century and the first thirty years of the nineteenth, as some American and European states began to outlaw slavery in their territories—or at least some of their territories—that frequent and at times significant uprisings of slaves began to occur throughout the colonial area. In a short period of 43 years, from 1789 to 1832, there were 20 major slave revolts, of which the insurrections in Saint-Domingue, Barbados, Demerara, and Jamaica stand out as the largest in the history of the Americas. Let us therefore begin by highlighting these four rebellions, which are key episodes for anyone wishing to investigate a possible relationship between slave rebellion and the abolition of slavery.

2.1. Saint-Domingue

The French part of the island of Hispaniola, or Santo Domingo, rightly prided itself on being the richest colony in the world. In the 1780s, it accounted for some 40 percent of French international trade and 40 to 50 percent of world coffee and sugar production. Within the colony lived 30,000 whites, together with 28,000 *gens de couleur*—that is to say, half-breeds and Negroes who were formally free but had no civil or political rights—and almost 500,000 African slaves, two-thirds of whom had been born in Africa.[3]

Despite the high number of slaves and their intensive exploitation, and despite the severe cruelty with which they were sometimes treated, society in Saint-Domingue had for a long time remained remarkably peaceful, both in the French colony and its neighboring Spanish colony, where the plantation economy was more marginal.[4] But, in the final years of the eighteenth century, the island went through an upheaval, which was so enormous in its scope and effects that from then on its name would forever be associated with the slave danger, a specter which would haunt the masters' world for decades thereafter.

The Saint-Domingue revolt was a succession of uprisings that took place in the context of the French Revolution, uprisings which strangely enough were started by the slave-owners themselves. With the convocation of the Estates-General in France in 1789, creoles and whites in the colony began to jostle to achieve their own ends. The whites, typically for a colonial population, wanted to have a free hand—or at least a freer hand—to trade and rule the colony as they saw fit (naturally excluding the half-breeds from government). Further complicating the picture of conflict, there were differences and disagreements among the whites themselves. The interests and political views of the higher stratum, the *grands blancs*, were substantially different from those of the *petits blancs*, that is to say, shopkeepers, civil servants, craftsmen or simple beggars who wandered around the towns.

It was the latter who, following the fall of the Bastille, immediately adopted the ideas and practices of the Jacobins. This led to a deepening of the split in the white population, which had divided early on into hostile factions. The situation deteriorated in 1791, when the half-breeds, who likewise sought to ensure their civic and political rights, became involved in the conflict. The mass of slaves, who, it will be recalled, outnumbered the free population by almost nine to one, then saw the colony embark on something resembling the preliminary stages of civil war.

In the late 1780s, the masses of slaves were in expectation, their attitude encouraged by a distorted understanding of what was happening in France, where they believed influential people were committed strongly to helping them. That conviction was strengthened in 1788 with the news of the founding of the *Société des Amis des Noirs*—an abolitionist organization, which counted men such as Brissot and Condorcet among its members—and was further reinforced in the following year when a false rumor began circulating in the French colonies that the king had decreed a form of half-freedom, granting slaves three days of freedom every week.[5] Then came the Revolution, far away on the other side of the Atlantic, and it found its echo almost immediately among the slaves in the colonies. The first revolt took place in the same year, 1789, in Martinique, where hundreds of slaves rose up, excited by the unfounded rumors of emancipation having allegedly been decreed in the mother country. In the following year, more conspiracies and revolts took place in Martinique, in Guiana, and in Guadalupe, and in 1791, the agitation reached Saint-Domingue. On 14 August, slave leaders in the northern plantations held a meeting to discuss recent events in France, at which partially forged documents were read out in which it was assured, amongst other things, that the king had granted the slaves partial freedom, that the masters were refusing to apply the measure, and that French troops were already on their way to impose the royal will. One week later, some two thousand slaves rose up in open rebellion. To the sound of war-like drums and chants, armed with sticks and cutlasses, they went from plantation to plantation, gathering more followers into their ranks and liberally killing, pillaging, and setting fire to the cane plantations on the way. For the first—and last—time, the world of slavery erected by the Europeans in the Americas had on its hands a revolt, on the scale of those that had taken place in the Roman empire.

In the first month of the insurrection, several hundred plantations were destroyed and almost one thousand whites were slaughtered, while those who remained took refuge in the cities or fled the island. For some of the rebels, the paramount objective was to kill all of the whites and take possession of the colony. Others, however, sought merely to achieve changes in the conditions of slavery, such as prohibiting the use of the whip and obtaining three days off every week. And Jean-François, Biassou, and other leaders—who identified themselves as defenders of the king and the church against the Jacobins—wanted only freedom for themselves and those close to them, and soon set themselves apart from the claims of the rebel mass.[6]

The fact that colonial forces were widely dispersed, and involved in continuing internal strife, made it impossible for them to suppress the revolt immediately, and the authorities were content to limit the advance of the rebels, confining them to the central region of the northern province. It is true that in late 1791 and early 1792, the rebellion tended to spread to the central and southern provinces. But in most cases, those insurrections were subdued and controlled by means of minor concessions and various ad hoc alliances according to the region involved, the correlation of forces, and the particular history of local hatreds. As Davis emphasizes, it is wrong to think that all of the slaves in the colony joined the revolt.[7]

By mid 1792, the parlous situation of the free community seemed to be on the way to resolution, the Legislative Assembly in Paris having granted civil and political equality to the half-breeds. This helped to calm them down and lowered the temperature of internal conflict. From the strictly military point of view, their prospects also improved. In August 1792, Paris decided to send an army of 6,000 men and 3 commissioners— Sonthonax, Polverel, and Ailhaud—who were imbued with the spirit of Jacobinism and had been given full powers to resolve the crisis. A small part of that army was used to counterattack the rebel slaves, and the northern plain was easily reconquered at the end of 1792. Jean-François, Toussaint, and other leaders of the revolt had to flee to the mountains, and in January of the following year, thousands of slaves surrendered. In other words, despite the political and administrative chaos caused by three years of revolutionary upheaval and civil war, the huge slave uprising that had begun in 1791 was moribund. It seemed that, at best, it was on its way to the usual dead-end of the maroon communities.[8]

In any event, in the heat of the conflict, whites and half-breeds had chosen to arm some of their slaves in order to help defeat the enemy.[9] Although this was dangerous, it was not unprecedented. The militarization of slave contingents was a more or less transitory measure adopted in cases of extreme necessity. It had been so since classical times, in Athens, Rome, and many other places.[10] However, in Saint-Domingue, that militarization proved irreversible, in that a succession of upheavals and wars encouraged and reinforced it at the same time as they destroyed the institutions of state power.

In fact, Saint-Domingue was to go through another, more violent upheaval as a result of events in the white world. Within the colony, the commissioners from Paris were unable to reconcile the discordant factions. On the contrary, they aggravated the conflict by their ideological and politically driven support for the half-breeds and free Negroes, at the same time as they marginalized or exiled realist and racist whites. In the mother country, where the Republic had meanwhile been established, the situation became far more complex; in February 1793, following the execution of Louis XVI, France went to war with Britain and Spain, who had colonies close to Saint-Domingue. In response to the appeals from the *grand blancs*, who were opposed to the libertarian and egalitarian policies of the commissioners sent by the mother country, the British effectively intervened and occupied several parts of the French colony. Earlier, the Spanish authorities on the Eastern side of the island had taken action to contain a situation that threatened the equilibrium of their own colonies. Reaffirming their counter-revolutionary rhetoric, the rebel slave leaders placed under Madrid's protection the territory they still controlled and became part of the Spanish army. It is important to emphasize that the Spanish offered these leaders weapons, land, and freedom for themselves and their families, but intended to retain slavery. The leaders of the rebellion agreed to this, and many of them became well known precisely because they favored the continuation of slavery and sold slaves to the Spanish.[11] The most conspicuous exception was Toussaint, a man who had read the *Histoire Philosophique* and who was aware of the progress of abolitionism in England and of the libertarian ideology that had triumphed in France. By mid-1793, at the latest, Toussaint had already adopted the main slogans of the French Revolution and, in his proclamations to the slaves, he invariably spoke of "Liberty" and "Equality."[12]

Faced with these internal and external threats, and with its support reduced to the half-breeds and a small armed slave militia—since the army of the mother country had mostly gone over to the *grands blancs*—commissioner Sonthonax, who governed the northern part of the colony, saw that French sovereignty could only be safeguarded with the help of the remaining slaves, who represented the bulk of the population. Clearly, these slaves would need some motivation to fight for revolutionary France, and it was this that the commissioner tried to give them: in July 1793, he proclaimed that all negroes who fought for the Republic against internal and external enemies would be given freedom, not just for themselves but for their legitimate wives and children as well. At the end of August, Sonthonax went further still and decreed general emancipation in the whole of the northern province, granting the right of citizenship to those freed. In the light of his colleague's precedent, commissioner Polverel was obliged to adopt the same principles in the western part of the colony and subsequently in the south, which he took over following the flight of his colleague Ailhaud. Paris ratified its commissioners' emancipation measure and widened its scope: on 4 February 1794, led on by the extreme left and in the midst of the revolutionary fervor then prevailing, the Assembly approved by acclamation, without even a debate, the abolition of slavery not only in Saint-Domingue, but in all France's colonies.[13]

It was in May, after learning of that law, that some of the rebel slaves in the north, led by Toussaint, went over to the French, thereby changing the balance of forces in their favor.[14] The rebellion took on a different form, or rather, it split in two as some of the rebels remained faithful to the King, to Spain, and the traditional aims of the slave revolt, while others broke away from Spanish rule and joined up to the liberating and republican principles offered to them. It should be noted that by now, Toussaint's forces were no longer the few hundred who had been with him since the beginning of 1793. Effectively, he had been joined from that time on, as a result of the tortuous progress of the revolution by white, half-breed, and even maroon troops, which considerably increased his firepower and prestige. From mid-1794 to 1798, Toussaint—now a general of the French army—fought a permanent war to drive the Spanish and the British out of Saint-Domingue and to end slavery in those provinces still under rebel slave control or under other more or less official authority. Spain withdrew from the battlefield in mid-1795, transferring many slaves and much of its equipment to its colonies, while Jean François, Biassou, and other leaders of the rebellion sought shelter in Spanish territory.[15] The British—for whom thousands of slaves had fought[16]—also withdrew, in 1798, defeated by yellow fever and by a French army predominantly made up of black rebels. In 1799 and 1800, Toussaint then subdued the half-breeds, his former allies in the south, and was appointed governor, in practice achieving full mastery of the colony. It was in that capacity, and in order to forestall any reversal of abolitionist opinion in France, that he promulgated the Constitution of 1801, which appointed him governor in perpetuity and reiterated the abolition of slavery.

This did not mean that former slaves had achieved full freedom. In 1793, Sonthonax had already introduced new labor laws to safeguard the colony's economy and under which those who had already joined the army would remain free—subject only to military discipline—but the remainder would be required to remain on the plantations, living in conditions not far removed from those they had endured until then. The demands of the war and the economy led Toussaint to continue and even enlarge the scope of the forced labor system created by Sonthonax. He accordingly encouraged the return of white planters to take charge of their property, and put the plantations and their labor force under the direct command of the generals. It is true that flogging was abolished and that the workers received a small part of their production as payment. But they could be, and often were, punished in many ways, and their fate was little different to what it had been before. Especially in the south, where the plantations were under the command of General Dessalines, the situation became unbearable at times. If productivity declined, a worker might be hanged as an example to others. Resistance and revolts against this militarized system were quickly and ruthlessly suppressed by Toussaint.[17]

Merciless actions of this type led to a great deal of discontent and would eventually facilitate the white counter-attack. France had been victorious in the struggle against colonial separatism and the threats from abroad, but former slaves had won out in the struggle for local supremacy. It was for this reason that the French, now under the consulate of Napoleon, tried to regain the island. They succeeded, in part as a result of the help they received from many half-breeds and negroes who abandoned their former leader and went over to the French side. Toussaint was captured and sent to France in June 1802, where he would eventually die in prison. But it was Napoleon's aim to reinstate the old system in its entirety, including the restoration of slavery. It is true that, as already mentioned, France had abolished it eight years earlier. It is equally true that the measure had given rise at the time to revolutionary celebrations in various French towns, to the publication of various prints and engravings, and to new songs being written to commemorate this great act of philanthropy and humanity. For the people of France, who had broken the *Ancien Regime*'s chains of bondage, words like *esclavage* and *liberté* had an almost universal meaning and made it easy for the *sans-culottes* to identify with the rebellious blacks in the colonies. But this identification was superficial and transitory: it did not have firm support in a strong and properly grounded abolitionist movement.[18]

In 1802, slavery—never abolished in Martinique, which was conquered by the British, nor in the colonies of the Indian Ocean, which refused to accept the law of 1794—was restored in Guadeloupe and in Guiana.[19] But in Saint-Domingue, the French command was unable to complete that task of restoration because the half-breed and black population, aware of what was happening in the neighboring colonies, rose up under Dessalines and other former Toussaint lieutenants. This gave rise to a new war of extermination where the methodical sadism and the horrors of the previous 12 years were surpassed, on both sides. For the leaders of the whites, the idea was to exterminate all of the negroes and import replacements uncontaminated with the ideas of freedom and equality. For the black leaders, the objective was to kill all of the whites or permanently banish them. Supplied and armed by the North Americans and the British, and under a new flag carrying the motto "Liberty or Death," Dessalines drove out the European troops who had managed to survive the fighting and the yellow fever, split permanently from France, and on 1 January 1804, founded the independent state of Haiti. In the following year, he was crowned emperor, and the whites still remaining in the colony were massacred. In 12 years of revolution and a war of devastation, some 80,000 Europeans died, in addition to an unknown number of blacks, and the former ruling class of Saint-Domingue was totally annihilated.[20]

To sum up, the revolt in Saint-Domingue was the outcome of an improbable and very specific combination of mutually reinforcing factors. In one sense, it was a sub-product of the French Revolution, and would have been inconceivable without it.[21] But the revolt succeeded because, in addition to taking place in the context of the Revolution, the struggle between local revolutionary and counter-revolutionary factions, and the war with Britain and Spain, it happened at the same time as white authority crumbled and collapsed. In that upheaval, something which began as a limited campaign for better terms of bondage progressively adjusted to events as they occurred and to the ideas of the time. It thus slid into the demand for emancipation and later into the struggle for independence. In a volatile context, some rebels ingeniously changed their aims and demands as they went along. The best example of such adaptability is Toussaint, a man who adopted the ideology and language of liberalism and the republican program itself. This was initially not properly understood or accepted by other rebels. For years, Toussaint acted as a French citizen, not as an African rebel. As he stated in a letter to the head of a maroon community, it was under the flag of the French Republic that they could be truly free and equal. While he undoubtedly had the ability to capture the spirit of each epoch, and to adjust his political behavior to that spirit, we should still not see him as an abolitionist in the strict sense of the term. It should be remembered that the Constitution of 1801 permitted the continuation of the slave trade as a means of ensuring an adequate supply of labor to the plantations.[22]

The most important point to emphasize is that in Saint-Domingue, from 1793–1794 onward, the slave revolt blended in with the body of abolitionist ideas, and that the slaves clearly and consciously fought for the end of slavery, and finally succeeded in abolishing it. For the first time, the world witnessed a slave revolt that was clearly a form of anti-slavery. But up to what point and to what extent did the example of Haiti lead to the abolition of slavery in other parts of the world?

In order to begin to clarify this issue, we have to understand the dual and contradictory nature of the Haitian example. For the slaves, the example it gave was undoubtedly encouraging. Haiti showed that blacks could overthrow slavery by taking on the strongest armies in the world. In this sense, it blazed a trail and gave other slaves the incentive to initiate rebellions, which might bring them freedom. And, in actual fact, during the time of the Saint-Domingue rebellion or its immediate aftermath, several revolts did break out, from the Caribbean to Venezuela. But they were easily suppressed, because they took place in contexts where there had been no disintegration of the slave state. In other words, Haiti continued to be unique. Its example opened up a path of insurrection leading to freedom for all, but it was a path which none were able to follow to its end. If only because, apart from the support given to Bolivar in 1815, in exchange for the promise of abolition of slavery in the lands that he liberated in South America, Haiti played no part in the emancipation of other countries of the hemisphere, not even in the neighboring colonies, where the Haitian authorities refrained from intervention for fear of retaliation.

The Haitian revolt did not lead to the abolition of slavery on the other side of the Atlantic, neither in France nor in any other Western country. On the contrary, it generally delayed it. It is true that the events in Haiti, and the examples emerging from it, lent themselves to many different readings and interpretations in Western societies. Some were burlesque, such as, for example, the satires on the way the blacks copied the European example, adapting it to their own sensibilities and circumstances. These satires persisted for a long time as the hallmark of what might be expected of future liberations and slave independence movements and, even in as distracted a country as Portugal, sixty years after the event, the

Haitian court of Christophe, with its Count Lemonade and Duke Marmalade, continued to delight racist and slave-trading parliamentarians. More frequently, however, the events in Saint-Domingue were interpreted with much greater apprehension, based on the perception that, as Haiti had shown, slaves could overthrow the slave-owning regime established by the white man.

Haiti represented a true cataclysm, engraved forever on people's memory, the outcome of which was the extermination of the white race and the ruin of the richest colony in the world. Of course, all of this also reflected fear, which may have been an incentive to abolish slavery. Contrary to what is generally argued, however, fear does not usually bring about such reactions, if only because it is unspecific. Fear was something that all slave societies had to deal with. It is true that a revolt (especially one as extensive as that which occurred in Haiti) caused enormous alarm, but that alarm was generally momentary, as the French case typically demonstrates. Not even in France did the events in Haiti contribute to the abolitionist cause; in fact, quite the opposite. Thus, in 1814, as peace was being achieved in Europe, the French even seriously considered the possibility of trying to retake Saint-Domingue in order to restore slavery. The idea was abandoned only in 1825, when Haiti agreed to pay compensation of 150 million francs, and the Paris government recognized the new Caribbean state.[23]

Fear did not therefore carry the pro-abolitionist weight with which it is generally credited, or carried it only for a short time. We need only reflect that the majority of abolitions took place 40 to 90 years after Haiti. In other words, for the West, the lesson of Haiti was precisely what should not be done. The path to abolition would have to be an alternative one, better thought out and controlled, and completely different from the path taken in Haiti.

The only country where the Haitian example had a positive impact on abolition was Britain, for three reasons:

1. A strong and militant abolitionist movement already existed there, with the ability to capitalize on events. The abolitionists insisted on the idea that the example of Haitian independence endangered the West Indies, and therefore made it imperative to end the slave trade—the primary abolitionist objective at that time—in order to prevent the arrival of more slaves from increasing the risk of an explosion in the colonies. This argument was influential in the passing of the Abolition Act, which ended the British slave trade in 1807.[24]
2. The British abolitionist movement was strong enough to absorb the negative impact of slave revolts on public opinion, without collapsing.
3. The dynamism of the British abolition movement, together with new initiatives by slaves in the colonies, helped to establish a reverse action that would turn out to be highly significant: moves towards abolition encouraged slave revolts; within certain limits, the revolts helped re-

inforce the abolitionist argument; and, reinforced abolitionist arguments helped to sharpen the movement as a whole, with further repercussions in the colonies, encouraging new revolts.

It is this process of successive chain reactions that we will examine next.

2.2. Barbados, Demerara, and Jamaica

Barbados, where there had been some abortive conspiracies and revolts in the early years of the plantation system, had been untroubled since 1702. Moreover, the preconditions for a slave rebellion in Barbados had diminished with the passing of time, as the island was almost flat and many of its forests had been cut down to make way for the plantations, thus drastically reducing the potential for possible rebels to escape by land. In addition, there were over 16,000 whites (and possibly 3,000 free blacks) to the approximately 77,000 slaves on the island at that time, in other words, 5 slaves to each white man. This ratio discouraged any uprising and was a serious obstacle to its eventual success. It should also be said that in comparative terms, the slaves in Barbados did not seem to be particularly disadvantaged, many of them owning small plots of land and domestic animals, which enabled them to supplement their daily diet and even to produce goods for local markets. In sum, given the nature of the land, given too the demographic and social conditions and the fact that there was a strong military garrison on the island, Barbados was not a good place to launch a rebellion.[25] Nonetheless, rebellion did break out on 14 April 1816, when a few hundred slaves took up arms, and many others then followed suit so that, in the space of a few hours, one third of the island was in flames. Faced with this threat, the military garrison, and notably its free black militia, quickly intervened. At the end of three days of operations, the insurrection of some 500 slaves had been put down. It is estimated that 120 negroes died on the battlefield; subsequently, a further 144 were executed and 132 deported; to these we must add the summary executions of men, women, and children carried out by the militia, in such large numbers that close to a thousand slaves may have died (as against only one death among the whites).[26]

In the eyes of the white community, the leaders of the movement were Bussa and, in the background, Francklyn, a freedman who was to have become governor if the revolt had been successful. But all of the indications are that the movement had no united leadership. There was a rebel leader on each plantation, usually someone who could read and who belonged to the so-called slave elite (coachmen, carpenters, stonemasons). Planters and colonial administrators blamed Wilberforce for the rebellion, and that charge, however simplistic in nature, reflects an undeniable relationship between abolitionism and slave uprisings. The British abolitionists had achieved a resounding victory with the outlawing of the slave trade in March 1807. Their medium-term objective was to liberate all black slaves in the British Empire, but this affected the private property of planters and other slave-owners and could not be achieved without taking into account the legal prerogatives of many of the colonies involved. We should remember that slaves were a form of property and that any change in their status required extreme caution, particularly at a time when the memory of the rebellion and subsequent independence of the North American colonies as a result of interference and unilateral policies by the mother country was still fresh. That was why even well-organized abolitionists advised against any premature government action and preferred the colonies to take on that task. It is true that in Parliament in 1796 Philip Francis put forward a plan for the gradual emancipation of slaves, just as Viefville des Essarts had done in 1791, when he put forward a draft bill in the French National Assembly to abolish slavery within sixteen years. In both cases, such initiatives were regarded as premature and did not produce any immediate result.[27]

Achieving the objective was difficult, and that is why in 1815, Wilberforce went no further than putting to the House of Commons the suggestion that a registry of slaves be maintained in all of the colonies. The registry—which was to be a record of the birth, death, and sale of each slave, drawn up by the government in London—was formally proposed as a means of preventing colonists from illegally importing more Africans in the future, and in this sense it was to be merely a complement to the anti-slave trade legislation of 1807. But the proposal had a hidden underlying purpose, since it might lead directly to the end of slavery—or so the abolitionists hoped. One of the lessons to be drawn from the Saint-Domingue Revolution was that freedom could be successful in demographic terms. The birth rate, which was traditionally low among slave populations, had risen considerably in free and independent Haiti.[28] Wilberforce's proposed registry would show the exact opposite for the majority of the British colonies, in other words, it would show up the demographic irrationality of slavery and, in the face of irrefutable statistics, arouse the still slumbering consciences of lawmakers, and possibly some planters as well. If everything went according to plan, the cut-off in the supply of African slaves to the American colonies as a result of the Abolition Act of 1807, complemented by the Registry bill of 1815, would generate a lack of manpower and this, initially, would force the West Indian planters to improve their remaining slaves' living conditions, in order to keep them alive and, subsequently, to see the financial advantages of freeing them, leading them to draw up appropriate legislation themselves.

Even though Wilberforce's proposal was a moderate one, the very idea of a compulsory register was opposed violently by colonial interest groups, who saw it from the outset as a first step toward future emancipation. The controversy produced a distorted echo amongst the negro slaves, who heard about it through rumors and information sifted through various sources. Some months before the revolt broke out, the press in Barbados had begun to highlight the discussions and decisions of the British parliament, describing the Registry bill as a plan to emancipate the slaves. Later, witness statements taken during the trial of the rebels alleged that some rebel leaders read those newspapers out loud to the masses, on occasion altering the content of news and editorial items. At the same time, those and other slaves—above all those in domestic service—spread news of the conversations taking place in their masters' houses. As Genovese reminds us, whites talked too much, and slaves heard everything.[29] From what they heard and deduced, they arrived at a conviction that they were already legally free, but that the colonial authorities were putting off applying the law; or else that they had powerful allies on the outside, but would have to act together with local whites in order to get the support of those allies and obtain their freedom. Alongside these somewhat vague and optimistic interpretations, more well-founded rumors also circulated. A few days before the uprising, slaves were telling each other that the governor, Sir James Leith—who was away—would return to the island with the liberation decree in his hand, and that the Barbados military garrison (made up of blacks and whites) would not intervene to crush any eventual revolt.

The belief in the existence of outside support, and the essential significance of that factor in the outbreak, help to explain its self-contained nature. In court, one witness told of plans to kill all of the whites and to enslave their women, but there is nothing to indicate that this was the general intention; the remaining witnesses and defendants clearly stated otherwise and, more revealingly, no white person was actually killed on the plantations. It is true that in three days of revolt, the slaves destroyed or damaged 184 properties, but, while they were setting houses, barns, and sugar-mills alight, they generally allowed whites to escape to the city or to barricade themselves in their homes. That is why the only recorded death among the free population took place in clashes between the rebels and regular soldiers.[30]

Aware of the significant part played by abolitionism in the outbreak of the revolt, Governor Leith issued a proclamation aimed at the rebels themselves, which sought to clear up misunderstandings and dispel unfounded hopes. But for the planters it was not so easy to undo those misunderstandings while Wilberforce and his peers continued to agitate on the issue of emancipation.[31]

Abolitionism was therefore a catalyst in the Barbados revolt. But the opposite is not the case, that is to say, the revolt did not contribute to the progress of emancipation in Britain; in fact, quite the contrary. Faced with colonial resistance, the accusations that rained down on the abolitionists, and the desire to accommodate colonial prerogatives, the government persuaded Wilberforce to withdraw his proposal for a slave registry, and it was decided to wait for colonial authorities themselves to produce legislation on the matter. James Stephen, the guiding light of the abolitionist strategy, was so disillusioned with this retreat that he resigned his seat in Parliament.[32]

By 1820, all of the British colonies in the Caribbean had effectively moved toward establishing registry legislation. But the laws were hollow shells that used abolitionist phraseology, but did not bring about any fundamental change in the slaveholding status quo. As often happened— and would continue to happen—opponents of abolition had adopted abolitionist positions in order better to hold their ground.[33] Faced with the ineffectiveness of the colonial authorities, the emancipation movement re-emerged, following a period after the Barbados revolt when it had been less active. The Anti-Slavery Society was founded in January 1823. Veterans like Wilberforce were members of this organization, but its new leaders, such as Thomas Fowell Buxton, belonged to a younger generation. Within two months, Buxton had submitted to the Commons a proposal for the gradual abolition of slavery, which, amongst other things, provided for the freedom of the womb—that is to say, the freeing of all slaves born after a given date—and various measures to limit masters' abuses and protect the slaves, in particular outlawing the use of the whip on female slaves.

The government, however, was able to anticipate and nullify Buxton's proposal. With the surprise approval of the planters, it suggested that the idea of freedom of the womb should be dropped, and that the law should aim merely at general emancipation in the future. In order to understand why the planters supported such a measure, we should recall that these were absentee planters, resident in the mother country. Here, far from the world of colonial brutality, and conscious of the growing strength of abolitionism, they tended to favor gradual measures, which would improve the colonies' public image. That is why, to the astonishment of their overseers and the governors back in the colonies, they themselves approved of the policy of gradual appeasement and improvement. It was based on this approach that Bathurst, the then minister at the Colonial Office, drew up a series of recommendations for improving the lives of the slaves and ensuring that they received religious instruction. These recommendations were forwarded to the colonies with a clear indication that, if they were not followed, the government itself would intervene directly.[34] Despite this, the measure was in fact a delaying tactic or, at best, yet another setback for the abolitionists.

Nevertheless, these moves toward abolition almost immediately found an echo in Demerara, the most productive of the three colonies in British Guiana—the others being Berbice and Essequibo—which had been taken from the Dutch at the beginning of the nineteenth century. In Demerara, the colonizers were heavily committed to sugar production, and conditions for the slaves were extremely hard and inhuman. Bathurst's recommendations reached the colony at the beginning of July. They were received very badly by the white community, and so much talked about that they quickly came to the attention of the slaves. Troubled by a proclamation the governor had issued restricting their access to Sunday mass, and incited by rumors that Britain had already decreed emancipation—and that, in the colony itself, the masters had covered up the existence of that decree—on 18 August 1823, some 12,000 slaves took up arms to demand what they judged to be their rights.[35]

Not all slaves subscribed to the idea that they had rights that had presumably been denied. Some thought the presumed new laws gave them three days off every week; others went further and deeper in their imaginations and believed that the new laws had freed them entirely. What was indeed universal was the refusal to accept that it was all nothing more than baseless rumor. Three weeks before the revolt broke out, some negroes had had access to Bathurst's circulars, and had been able to see that freedom was not about to be granted, contrary to prevailing rumors. But many of the rebels denied the evidence of their own eyes and remained committed to the revolt. From what we can glean of subsequent court testimonies and statements, the rebels' aims were moderate. Some of them probably did, as usual, plan to kill all of the whites and keep their women; or else they would allow white women to leave the colony but would use the men as slaves, setting them to work in the fields. But it seems that most of the leaders just wanted to hold a kind of strike. Convinced they had Britain's support, they sought to avoid unnecessary violence so as not to blow up possible bridges of understanding and conciliation with the white authorities—and with the abolitionists in the mother country. On the ground, that relatively moderate and self-contained faction prevailed. Looting was generally confined to obtaining food supplies and weapons, and the whites were not massacred. It is true that some of them were beaten, insulted, and put on the block, but only two or three were killed and, with one exception, white women were left unmolested.[36]

It is important to note that at the time of the Demerara revolt, whites made up only 4 percent of the population. Free blacks accounted for another 4 percent, and slaves made up the rest, which produces the frightening ratio of 23 slaves to each white person.[37] Even so, the authorities had no trouble taking control, particularly as many slaves opposed the rebels from the outset and took sides with their masters. A military force of 400 to 500 men confronted the thousands of slaves armed with guns, sticks, and axes, and routed them, killing about 120 rebels in this first encounter. To instill fear and crush the rebellion more speedily, 20 slaves were summarily tried on the plantations and executed by the soldiers on the spot. Once shot, they were decapitated, and their heads were put on poles at plantation entrances or along the roads. Then, as the bush was being searched for runaways, with the help of Indian natives and some faithful slaves who were rewarded by being released or paid in cash, the trials of the rebels began. There were tried 72 alleged rebel leaders, of whom 51 were condemned to death (although only 33 were effectively executed; the remainder had their sentences commuted to flogging or deportation with forced labor).[38]

The repressive terror and the ceremony that went with it were not new and were not even extreme. In former times, many rebel slaves had been executed using various sadistic refinements: some were roasted over a slow fire, others hanged on meat hooks by their ribs, yet others locked into cages where they died of starvation.[39] But in the new anti-slavery environment in the mother country, reports of the executions took on enormous significance for British public opinion. This effect was heightened to the extent that a new element—the British missionary—had come on the scene during the Demerara tragedy. In fact, setting aside sporadic missionary activity during the Dutch period, the first Protestant missionary had arrived in the colony only in 1808, sent out by the London Missionary Society, a non-sectarian organization open to missionaries of different Protestant denominations whose aim was to Christianize the pagans. That pioneer built a chapel in the same year 1808, and then started to preach the gospel to slaves on neighboring plantations. His work was subsequently continued and extended by other missionaries from the same London organization, among who was John Smith, the evangelical pastor who would take charge of the chapel from 1817 onward. Despite the fact that the missionaries had strict instructions not to get involved in the political life of the colony, and to teach the slaves that they should obey their masters, the fact is that life on the plantations was so shocking that it was practically impossible for them to avoid doing so, especially for men such as Smith, who had been brought up in a Britain which was now an anti-slavery nation. Whether deliberately or by omission, by an injudicious or relatively biased choice of excerpts from the Bible and religious teachings, Smith seems to have allowed the slaves to draw out the full revolutionary and millenarian potential of the Bible. Without his being fully aware of what was going on, the missionary's chapel seems to have become a center of political activity, and it was precisely in the area under his influence that the main pockets of rebellion were found—their leaders being, moreover, deacons in Smith's congregation. The colonial authorities had never hidden their hostility and suspicion of the evangelical missionaries' work. They blamed Smith for the revolt—and behind him Wilberforce and Buxton, whom they regarded as his mentors. Smith's demonization was not only the result of planters' paranoia, but also their desire for a scapegoat to take responsibility for what had happened and at the same time cover up the horrors of slavery. Several slaves took the same view, and one of them even asserted in court that if Smith had not been in Demerara, there would have been no revolt. Arrested in the early hours of the rebellion, the missionary was court-martialled in the autumn of 1823. Judged complicit with the rebels, he was condemned to hang, but with a recommendation for clemency. And in effect King George IV granted him a pardon, on condition that he immediately be repatriated to Britain. But when the order reached Demerara, the missionary had already died from pulmonary tuberculosis and the hardships he had suffered in jail.[40]

The revolt, and the trial of John Smith, had a major impact in Britain, flooding the newspapers and giving rise to several parliamentary inquiries. For the common man, the ordeal of an English priest—and what was more, a white man—was more important than the death of 200 slaves in a distant colony, so it was natural that attention and sentiment were focused on Smith. It was he—and not some slave—who was awarded the title "Demerara Martyr."[41] Well known abolitionists, such as Clarkson and Macaulay, became involved in the controversy, making themselves heard with articles in the press and other public venues, while Parliament received hundreds of petitions for the end of slavery. Elizabeth Heyrick, a Quaker, appealed to English women to boycott sugar produced by slaves. Heyrick, moreover, went further than this, writing a pamphlet entitled *Immediate not Gradual Abolition,* in which she argued, for the first time, for the immediate end of slavery, not its gradual abolition.[42] In Parliament, the abolitionists did not dare go so far. Even so, in June 1824, they submitted a motion to the Commons seeking to condemn the authorities in Demerara, and at the same time sought more direct mother country involvement in the government of the colony so as to ensure the immediate and humane application of legislation protecting negroes and the missionaries who educated and Christianized them. But conservative forces in Parliament were still stronger than those advocating reform in the colonies and the end of slavery, and the motion was defeated by 193 votes to 146. In this sense, as Craton emphasizes, the conjunction of Bathurst's circulars and the Demerara revolt "hindered rather than speeded the emancipation cause."[43]

Despite their defeat in 1824, the abolitionists kept up their pressure on the government. Anti-slavery petitions continued to arrive in the Lords and Commons, and new abolitionist societies sprang up all over Britain. In 1825, the Anti-Slavery Society launched its *Anti-Slavery Reporter,* a journal seeking to expose the *modus operandi* and the evildoings of colonial slavery. Even so, all of these moves were insufficient to alter the status quo. Organizations which defended planter interests also used propaganda, disseminating the idea that life for the Africans in the colonies was already improving considerably, and that the masters now treated their slaves with paternal care and moderation.[44] A large proportion of the British people were susceptible to this propaganda, and Parliament remained hesitant, continuing to compromise with colonial prerogatives and forever putting off a final decision on emancipation. It is important to note that, during the 1820s, the planters had more influence in Parliament than they had had twenty years earlier at the time of abolition of the slave trade. Between 1820 and 1830, the West Indies and their supporters had 39 to 56 representatives in the House of Commons and about 30 in the House of Lords, while the abolitionists, by contrast, had only 15 to 31 representatives in the Commons and apparently had none in the Lords.[45]

Frustrated and impatient at the lack of genuine humanitarian progress in the colonies, some younger abolitionists chose to become more radical. In 1831, a group led by Joseph Sturge and George Stephen (the son of James Stephen) formed a new anti-slavery organization, the Agency Committee, which began to campaign for the immediate abolition of slavery. To propagate its immediatist principles, the Agency Committee put in play a network of paid agents, who went from town to town organizing local committees and giving lectures. The public responded in large numbers, filling chapels, court-rooms, theaters and all of the places where abolitionists held debates and gave lectures. As a result of this propaganda campaign, the number of anti-slavery petitions submitted to Parliament increased significantly, with signatories numbering in the millions.[46]

The effects of this renewed vigor in the abolitionist camp were rapidly felt amongst slaves in the colonies: in 1831, small rebellions took place in Antigua and Tortola, followed by a much more serious uprising in Jamaica, the most important British colony in the Caribbean, where there were over 300,000 slaves to around 30,000 whites. Until that time, the planters who ruled Jamaica had resisted Bathurst's recommendations, or had implemented them only very slowly and superficially, and in response to the threat of losing the right to self-government. In November 1831, that threat became more significant when new instructions arrived from the government in London that the colony should speed up the application of anti-slavery reforms. Instructions of this sort were a major irritant to the local white community, which did not hesitate to criticize openly those who were preparing to emancipate their slaves, and also openly avowed that it would resist such a step. In this context, planters often talked of secession or of union with the United States, in order to avoid the abolitionist pressure from the mother country. In the eyes of the slaves, the planters naturally appeared to be the main obstacle to abolition. They thus helped to foster a climate of rebellion, which, as usual, was encouraged by false rumors: that half-breed slaves were already free and that blacks soon would be; that British sailors and soldiers would not fight the slaves, and that they had been sent out from London precisely in order to protect them from the planters; or that an emancipation decree would soon be arriving on the island through Burchell, a Baptist missionary who had been to England and was due to come back around Christmas time.[47]

The revolt began on 27 December 1823, with several simultaneous uprisings in plantations on the Western side of the island. The rebels' aim was freedom, or at least the right to be paid for the work that they did. In principle, according to the pre-arranged plan, the rebels were to remain on the plantations, as if on strike; they would try to ensure that no physical harm came to whites, and would retaliate only if attacked; they were also to avoid destroying the cane plantations and sugar-mills. In practice, things did not go exactly according to plan, and around 20,000 Africans set off for an armed struggle, organizing regiments to face the colony's military forces. As whites fled in the hundreds to the nearest towns, the army of rebels looted warehouses and set fire to the plantations. The first encounters were favorable to the whites, even though that did not prevent further burning of property and ambushes of military columns, without the authorities and their maroon helpers—who assisted in putting down the revolt—being able to put a stop to it. Only at the end of January 1832 did the authorities regard the revolt as having been crushed. Material and human losses of a month of upheaval were then added up: 226 properties had been destroyed or damaged, 14 whites had been killed, and 200 slaves had died in the fighting. A further 340 rebels were subsequently executed; 175 received sentences other than death (floggings, forced labor, and deportation).[48]

It was not only the slaves who felt in their very skins the anger of the white colonial community. The rebellion had started in the Baptist chapels where, in the temporary absence of white missionaries—such as Burchell, for example—the black deacons had enjoyed great freedom of action. Sam Sharpe, the main rebel leader, was one of those deacons. Indeed, most of the rebels belonged, like Sharp, to the Baptist congregation, which is why the revolt became popularly known as the Baptist War. Of course, as in Demerara previously, the missionaries did not encourage rebellion. But they did teach a doctrine of spiritual equality, which the slaves translated in political terms. Hence, this was the reason why many of them saw the missionaries as their allies. Moreover, it is significant that, later on, in the early days of emancipation, blacks joined the Baptist church in large numbers, as a way of repaying acts and support, which they judged to have been essential in helping them obtain their freedom. The white community and the colonial authorities shared that opinion, although of course in their case the feeling was anything but one of gratitude. Early in 1832, when he arrived in Jamaica from England, Burchell, the missionary, was surrounded by a baying crowd wanting to lynch him. He was only able to save himself by being immediately arrested and transferred to a ship, for his own protection. But his colleague Bleby was tarred and feathered, while Knibb and other Baptist missionaries were held for several weeks. This may, incidentally, have helped to save their lives. Many Baptist chapels were destroyed and burnt down, the authorities taking no notice whatsoever, and similar scenes took place in other parts of the Caribbean. In Barbados, for example, an angry crowd attacked and looted a Methodist church, and for a while some missionaries had to seek protection from military escorts to travel around the island.[49]

To the missionaries, it was obvious that their evangelizing mission could not continue unless there were significant changes in the colonies. And this was exactly the message they conveyed to the mother country by means of letters, or even in person. In 1832, a dozen missionaries returned to England as refugees or, as with Burchell and Knibb, as representatives of the Baptist missionaries, in order to explain what had happened and defend themselves against the charges laid against them. The testimony of these men—especially Knibb, who was given a lengthy hearing at parliamentary inquiries and gave lectures in both England and

Scotland—had a huge impact on public opinion. For the average Englishman, they were the heroes and victims of the revolt. That image bore fruit to an even greater extent than the earlier image of the "Demerara Martyr," now that there were heroes and victims in greater numbers, and who were present in person to reap the political dividend of their colonial ordeals.[50]

Persecution of the missionaries angered the British. This was the breaking point in their tolerance of colonial interests and procedures. It is true that the events in Jamaica were just one more slave revolt, and that the suppression of that revolt had not even been particularly brutal. Initially, and as usual, the revolt made for great difficulties for the abolitionists, encouraging pro-planter sentiment.[51] But things changed as soon as the missionaries' stories started to affect public opinion. Even though the attack on them was not unprecedented, it was now no longer a case of blaming a supposedly lost sheep—like John Smith. Even though the Baptist church was the main target, in one way or another, the other denominations were equally at risk. In a word, missionary activity was incompatible with maintaining slavery. This realization strongly undermined the whole propaganda edifice that the planters had built in earlier years. In the 1820s, as mentioned above, many Englishmen thought the immediatist policy too radical, and tended to accept improvement measures which, to their way of thinking, would lead to gradual abolition. But for those who thought this way, improving conditions for slaves was synonymous with Christianization. It was by learning Christian civility that the slaves might raise themselves up to become free men, useful to themselves and to the country. As soon as it became clear that it would be impossible to preach the gospel in the colonies, it became equally clear that there could be no improvement—and of course no gradual emancipation—and that the only way forward was immediatism or something very similar. In this sense, the persecution of the missionaries turned out to be decisive, that is to say, it was the strategic variable that tipped the scales in favor of emancipation. It was that persecution which showed minds already imbued with abolitionism that slavery could not be reformed. It was that persecution as well that provoked such a furious reaction against colonialism that the abolitionists themselves became alarmed. It only calmed down because Parliament itself was dissolved, in order to be reconstituted under the provisions of the recently approved Reform Bill.

The parliamentary reform helped to delay matters, calmed the public outcry, and defused the issue. Political reform and anti-slavery were in fact linked and mutually reinforcing questions, as many of those opposing a parliamentary reform, which would give the middle classes a voice—such as Wellington, for example—also supported the continuation of slavery. During the electoral campaign for the new Parliament, voters were instructed to demand that candidates give them an assurance on the slavery issue, and only to vote for those who publicly committed themselves to supporting abolition. In this connection, lists with the names of those who had committed themselves were published in the newspapers, as well as the names of those who refused to do so. In the elections of December 1832, the latter were reduced to 35 representatives in the Commons as against 104 supporters of immediate abolition.[52]

Under strong pressure from Parliament and public opinion, the British government felt obliged to proceed with radical change in this area. Thus, Edward Stanley, who was minister for the colonies at the time, introduced a bill in the Commons, which, with some amendments, was approved in August 1833. The bill stipulated that slavery would legally come to an end within a year for the approximately 800,000 slaves then in the British colonies in America and Africa, and that these men and women would for the time being be divided into two categories, according to the tasks which they had been carrying out: former domestic slaves would go through a four-year period of apprenticeship—during which they would work for nothing six days a week—and would have full freedom on 1 August 1838; former plantation slaves would be freed in 1840, after a period of apprenticeship of six years; young children would be freed immediately and be the responsibility of their mothers. To compensate the planters, an indemnity fund of 20 million pounds would be established, an enormous amount equal to *circa* 40 percent of Britain's annual budget.

The law of 1833 took into account the then prevailing balance of forces. The House of Lords—in which the Caribbean planter aristocracy was still abundantly represented—wanted to set limits to the government's proposed measures. The solutions adopted in order to soften their demands were the apprenticeship system and a lavish amount of compensation for the planters. But the immediatists disapproved strongly of the apprenticeship scheme. They saw it, understandably, as a kind of mitigated slavery. Thus, from 1834 onward, they set about attacking it, and popular opposition in Britain grew to such proportions that in 1838, in order to avoid any further and greater difficulties, the colonies themselves decided to yield and adopted full and immediate abolition.[53]

When one analyzes the whole process of emancipation in England, it becomes clear that as anti-slavery forces grew in strength, infiltrating the Colonial Office and influencing Parliament, they gave direct and indirect encouragement to slaves who fought the system. It seems obvious in the British case that abolitionism encouraged the rebellions, rather than the other way round. And it encouraged rebellions of a new kind, because rebel leaders very quickly understood what was at stake and tried to set in motion actions that would blend in with the abolitionist movement. This was suicide, but it provided the abolitionists with more arguments with which to convey the horrors of slavery to the masses. Slave resistance was, moreover, one of the themes of the anti-slavery campaign. Since the events in Saint-Domingue, abolitionists had used successive rebellions to get across the idea that while slavery existed, the colonies would be powder-kegs ready to explode at any moment. For years, they tried to show that slavery could not be maintained without high levels of repression, the corresponding outbreaks of retaliation, and barbarous executions. As that idea became embedded in the public mind, a climate of opinion developed in which colonial behavior became ever more unacceptable. The revolts of 1831 and the subsequent persecution of the missionaries were the catalysts that propelled the engine of emancipation. Of course, the self-contained nature of slave revolts greatly assisted the abolitionist cause in Britain. If the slaves in Barbados, Demerara, and Jamaica had followed the example of Saint-Domingue and massacred thousands of whites, it would have been much more difficult to get the abolitionist message across to the British people. But there had in fact been great restraint in this area. So it was possible to show that slaves had in overall terms behaved in a controlled manner, and that the colonial authorities were to blame for their excessive repression.[54] As many had foreseen, if properly exploited, the repressive behavior of the colonial authorities—especially the anger they directed at the missionaries—would affect public opinion in the mother countries and thus make it possible to end slavery sooner. And this was precisely what happened in Britain.

This interplay between abolitionism and slave rebellion could likewise have occurred in France if the ideological and political influence of the Revolution, and subsequently the war, had not derailed it from the outset. Even so, we should not forget that an outline of that interplay did nevertheless emerge, since the founding of the *Société des Amis des Noirs*, the dissemination of pro-abolitionist ideas—Toussaint read the *Histoire Philosophique*—and the rumors that circulated on emancipation stirred up great agitation among the slaves and led to an uprising in Martinique in August 1789, even before news of the taking of the Bastille had reached the island.[55]

Notes

1. João Pedro Marques, *Portugal e a Escravatura dos Africanos* (Lisboa: Imprensa de Ciências Sociais, 2004), ch. 5.
2. For the difference between tolerationism and abolitionism see João Pedro Marques, *The Sounds of Silence. Nineteenth-century Portugal and the Abolition of the Slave Trade* (New York and Oxford: Berghahn Books, 2006), 1–3.
3. Carolyn Fick, "Emancipation in Haiti: From Plantation Labour to Peasant Proprietorship," in *After Slavery. Emancipation and its Discontents*, ed. Howard Temperley (London: Frank Cass, 2000), 12. For the Haiti rebellion see Robin Blackburn, *The Overthrow of Colonial Slavery, 1776–1848* (London and New York: Verso, 1988), 163ff.; and Laurent Dubois, *Les vengeurs du Nouveau Monde. Histoire de la Révolution Haïtienne* (Rennes: Les Perséides, 2005).
4. For a case study of cruelty see David P. Geggus, "The Caradeux and Colonial Memory," in *The Impact of the Haitian Revolution in the Atlantic World*, ed. David P. Geggus (Columbia: University of South Carolina Press, 2001), 239ff.

5. Laurent Dubois, *Les esclaves de la Republique. L'histoire oubliée de la première émancipation, 1789–1794* (Paris: Calmann-Lévy, 1998), 56–57, 75, 89, and 94–95; Dubois, *Les vengeurs du Nouveau Monde*, 58ff. and 117ff.

6. Fick, "Emancipation in Haiti," 14–15n18; Cyril L.R. James, *The Black Jacobins. Toussaint L'Ouverture and the San Domingo Revolution* (London: Allison & Busby, 1980; 1st ed., 1938), 103; Dubois, *Les vengeurs du Nouveau Monde*, 174–179.

7. David B. Davis, *Inhuman Bondage: The Rise and Fall of Slavery in the New World* (New York and London: Oxford University Press, 2006), 175.

8. David B. Davis, *The Problem of Slavery in the Age of Revolution, 1770–1823* (Ithaca, NY and London: Cornell University Press, 1975), 145; Dubois, *Les vengeurs du Nouveau Monde*, 204ff.; and James, *The Black Jacobins*, 123.

9. Dubois, *Les vengeurs du Nouveau Monde*, 191ff.; David P. Geggus, "The Arming of Slaves in the Haitian Revolution," in *Arming Slaves From Classical Times to the Modern Age*, eds. Christopher Leslie Brown and Philip D. Morgan (New Haven and London: Yale University Press, 2006), 212.

10. Ver Norbert Rouland, *Les esclaves Romains en temps de guerre* (Brussels: Latomus, 1977); Peter Hunt, "Arming Slaves and Helots in Classical Greece," in Brown and Morgan, *Arming Slaves*, 14–39.

11. Dubois, *Les vengeurs du Nouveau Monde*, 212ff.; Jane Landers, "Transforming Bondsmen into Vassals: Arming Slaves in Colonial Spanish America," in Brown and Morgan, *Arming Slaves*, 130–131.

12. James, *The Black Jacobins*, 25 and 125.

13. Dubois, *Les vengeurs du Nouveau Monde*, 218ff.

14. Dubois, *Les vengeurs du Nouveau Monde*, 160.

15. Matt D. Childs, *The 1812 Aponte Rebellion in Cuba and the Struggle against Atlantic Slavery* (Chapel Hill: The University of North Carolina Press, 2006), 93.

16. Geggus, "The Arming of Slaves," 217ff.

17. Fick, "Emancipation in Haiti," 17 and 23–27; James, *The Black Jacobins*, 276–279; Dubois, *Les vengeurs du Nouveau Monde*, 240ff. The same system was used in Guadeloupe by commissioner Victor Hughes (see Dubois, *Les vengeurs du Nouveau Monde*, 176ff.).

18. Marcel Chatillon, "La diffusion de la gravure du *Brooks* par la Société des Amis des Noirs et son impact," in *De la traite à l'esclavage*, ed. Serge Daget, vol. 2 (Nantes: C.R.H.M.A./Société Française d'Histoire d'Outre-Mer, 1988), 146.

19. Olivier Pétré-Grenouilleau, *Les traites négrières. Essai d'histoire globale* (Paris: Gallimard, 2004), 233–234; Dubois, *Les vengeurs du Nouveau Monde*, 194ff.

20. For a detailed description of this period, see James, *The Black Jacobins*, 289ff.

21. Eugene D. Genovese, *From Rebellion to Revolution. Afro-American Slave Revolts in the Making of the Modern World* (Baton Rouge: Louisiana State University Press, 1992; 1st ed., 1979), 90.

22. James, *The Black Jacobins*, 150 and 265; David Geggus, "The Haitian Revolution," in *Caribbean Slave Society and Economy*, eds. Hilary McD. Beckles and Verene Shepherd (Kingston and London: James Currey Publishers, 1991), 414; and Dubois, *Les vengeurs du Nouveau Monde*, 329–330.

23. David Geggus, "Haiti and the Abolitionists: Opinion, propaganda and International Politics in Britain and France, 1804–1838," in *Abolition and its Aftermath*, ed. David Richardson (London: Frank Cass, 1985), 117–119.

24. Geggus, "Haiti and the Abolitionists," 115–116. For a different assessment of the significance of the Haitian example for the abolition of the British slave trade see Seymour Drescher, "The Limits of Example," in *The Impact of the Haitian Revolution in the Atlantic World*, ed. David P. Geggus (University of South Carolina Press, 2001), 12. For the possible impact of that example on the abolition of the North American slave trade see Drescher, "The Limits," 11 and David B. Davis, "Impact of the French and Haitian Revolutions," in Geggus, *The Impact of the Haitian Revoluion*, 6.

25. Michael Craton, *Testing the Chains: Resistance to Slavery in the British West Indies* (Ithaca,

NY and London: Cornell University Press, 1982), 114; Hilary Beckles, "Emancipation by law or War? Wilberforce and the 1816 Barbados slave rebellion," in Richardson, *Abolition and its Aftermath*, 83–85; and Genovese, *From Rebellion to Revolution*, 37.

26. Michael Craton, *Empire, Enslavement and Freedom in the Caribbean* (Kingston and Oxford: IRP/James Currey Publishers, 1997), 311–312; Beckles, "Emancipation by law," 81.
27. Davis, *Age of Revolution*, 113, 116–117, and 143.
28. Geggus, "Haiti and the Abolitionists," 132.
29. Genovese, *From Rebellion to Revolution*, 24.
30. Craton, *Testing the Chains*, 259ff.
31. Ibid., 266.
32. Davis, *Age of Revolution*, 161; and Davis, *Inhuman Bondage*, 213.
33. W.A. Green, *British Slave Emancipation. The Sugar Colonies and The Great Experiment, 1830–1865* (Oxford: Clarendon Press, 1976), 100–101; David B. Davis, *Slavery and Human Progress* (Oxford: Oxford University Press, 1984), 176–177; Roger Anstey, "Religion and British Slave Emancipation," in *The Abolition of the Atlantic Slave Trade. Origins and Effects in Europe, Africa and the Americas*, eds. David Eltis and James Walvin (Madison: University of Wisconsin Press, 1981), 38ff.
34. Roger Anstey, "The Pattern of British Abolitionism in the Eighteenth and Nineteenth Centuries," in *Anti-slavery, Religion and Reform: Essays in the Memory of Roger Anstey*, eds. Christine Bolt and Seymour Drescher (Dawson: Folkestone, 1980), 24; Green, *British Slave Emancipation*, 99–103.
35. Emília Viotti da Costa, *Crowns of Glory, Tears of Blood. The Demerara Slave Rebellion of 1823* (New York: Oxford University Press, 1994), 177 and 197ff.
36. Ibid., 184–200 and 240; and Craton, *Testing Chains*, 277–280.
37. Costa, *Crowns of Glory*, 46.
38. Ibid., 242–245; Craton, *Testing Chains*, 288.
39. See, for example, Cornelis C. Goslinga, *The Dutch in the Caribbean and the Guianas, 1680–1791* (Assen/Dover, NH: Van Gorcum, 1985), 491–492.
40. Craton, *Empire, Enslavement*, 312–313; Costa, *Crowns of Glory*, 5ff. and 239.
41. Craton, *Testing Chains*, 289.
42. David B. Davis, "The Emergence of Immediatism in British and American Anti-Slavery Thought," in *The Mississippi Valley Historical Review*, XLIX, 2 (1962): 220; Anstey, "The Pattern of British Abolitionism," 27; Clare Midgley, "Slave sugar boycotts, female activism and the domestic base of British Anti-Slavery culture," in *Slavery and Abolition*, 17, 3 (1996): 147ff.
43. Craton, *Testing Chains*, 289.
44. Davis, *Slavery and Human Progress*, 193.
45. Anstey, "The Pattern of British Abolitionism," 24–25.
46. Davis, *Slavery and Human Progress*, 186; Green, *British Slave Emancipation*, 111–112.
47. Craton, *Testing Chains*, 295; Catherine Hall, *Civilising Subjects. Metropole and Colony in the English Imagination, 1830–1867* (Cambridge: Polity Press, 2002), 105.
48. Craton, *Testing Chains*, 291 and 312ff.
49. Ibid., 317–318; Davis, *Slavery and Human Progress*, 197; Catherine Hall, *Civilising Subjects*, 11 and 105.
50. Craton, *Testing Chains*, 319.
51. Davis, *Slavery and Human Progress*, 195; Blackburn, *The Overthrow*, 451.
52. Anstey, "The Pattern of British Abolitionism," 28; Davis, *Slavery and Human Progress*, 200.
53. Green, *British Slave Emancipation*, 115–155; Davis, *Slavery and Human Progress*, 208.
54. Davis, *Inhuman Bondage*, 220.
55. David P. Geggus, *Haitian Revolutionary Studies* (Bloomington: Indiana University Press, 2002), 66; Dubois, *Les vengeurs du Nouveau Monde*, 90–91.

– 3 –

THE GENERAL RULE

❧

The analysis of the four major colonial slave revolts and their relationship to abolitionism shows that, except for Haiti, it was not those revolts that conquered freedom for Africans. Readers may nonetheless feel
that, in a context where emancipation was widespread and dozens of revolts were taking place, these four cases are not sufficiently representative, and that other revolts may show up the greater significance of the
slave threat as a factor in the Western decision to end slavery. But it is exactly the opposite. The four cases studied above are precisely those in
which it is indeed possible to establish some sort of positive causal relation between revolts and emancipation. All the others show much more
tenuous connections between those two historical facts, or none at all.

3.1. Emancipation in the American Nations

The earliest abolitions of slavery in the colonial or post-colonial world occurred in the United States and Canada, without slave revolts having
affected the context in which they took place. In 1777, Vermont had a constitutional provision allowing for a transition period that would free
new-born slaves when they reached the age of twenty-one. Three years
later, a group of Pennsylvania radicals was able to get a law passed along
the same lines, and identical measures were subsequently adopted in the
assemblies of Connecticut and Rhode Island (1784), Upper Canada
(1793), New York (1799), and New Jersey (1804). In Massachusetts, Lower
Canada and Nova Scotia, legal support for slavery ended as a result of a
number of decisions that passed into jurisprudence. Taken as a whole,
they were very cautious measures, which applied above all to slaves born
after they were ratified. Even so, and as was usual in the case of free
womb laws, the newly born would only attain full freedom as adults (be-

tween 15 and 30 years of age). In as much as the laws were long-term in their effects and affected few people, they were relatively easy to apply. In principle, the northern United States accounted for only 10 percent of slaves in the Union, and that percentage declined rapidly, because, faced with abolitionist legislation, many slave owners chose to sell them to the southern states.[1]

In the southern states the problem was much more complex, particularly because it had to do with the very roots of the Union. The South had fewer whites and, for that very reason would in principle be at a disadvantage in the legislative assemblies. Nevertheless, the demands of the war for independence from the British had had the effect that the slaves—who were a form of property—had been counted for taxation purposes. So the southerners naturally demanded that they should also be counted for the purposes of political representation. Following complex negotiations, agreement was reached on the so-called three-fifths rule, in other words, for voting purposes, three-fifths of the slave population of the South—which, of course, did not vote—would be added to the white population. This rule established a mutual commitment and equilibrium between North and South in terms of taxation and political representation. As a well known southerner said at the time, aptly summing up the matter, "The Northern States adopted us with our slaves, and we adopted them with their Quakers."[2]

However, North and South had very different expectations of that commitment. Even though they formally acknowledged slavery to be evil and a stain on their moral character, to be removed as soon as this could be done securely, the South's leaders hoped to be able to prolong slavery and also hoped that no moves would be made to question their property rights. By contrast, the aim of the northern politicians was to prevent the expansion of the slave regions and hope that they would wither away. Abolitionists, in particular, hoped that with the end of the transatlantic slave trade, which had been legally abolished in 1807, it would be possible to deal with the slavery problem in the southern states without too much disruption.

The northerners' expectations were being formed at a time when the South had some 900,000 slaves. In the years that followed, however, the problem became much more acute, and the commitment more difficult to maintain because, contrary to what the abolitionists had imagined, the South became ever more embroiled in slavery. In fact, a series of factors connected with the cotton crop had substantially changed the situation. In the late years of the eighteenth century, Eli Whitney and others invented and perfected the cotton gin, a manually-operated machine making it possible to remove the seeds and clean the raw cotton, a job which until then had been performed laboriously by hand. From that moment on, one slave could do what until then had demanded the work of many men. This, with the rapid spread of the machine, was to have profound effects on industry in the southern states. At almost the same time, in 1803, the United States government purchased French Louisiana, a territory of enormous size stretching from the gulf of Mexico to the frontiers of Canada, and which virtually doubled the area of the then United States. Add to this scenario the fact that the highly adaptable nature of the institutions of slavery enabled southerners to respond effectively to the double economic challenge of new technologies and of having more land to exploit. In fact, although the transatlantic slave trade had been prohibited since 1807, the number of slaves grew as a result of natural reproduction—an unexpected demographic anomaly in the history of colonial slavery[3]—rendering the southern states self-sufficient in terms of manpower. In 1800, there were nearly 900,000 slaves in the United States, but by 1820, their number had grown to over 1.5 million and would reach 3.2 million in 1850 and almost 4 million in 1865, making the United States the largest reservoir of slavery in the Western hemisphere.

The formation of new slave states (such as Mississippi in 1817, and Alabama in 1819) reflected economic expansion and the over-abundance of slaves, and corresponded to the formation of free states in the North. This allowed southern planters to hold on to their power. It is true that the South, despite the three-fifths rule, remained in a minority in the House of Representatives as a result of the population increase in the North, which received a large volume of white emigration from Europe. But the South was assured a majority in the Senate—which was made up of two senators from each state, regardless of population—and was able to keep it by the admission of new states to the Union, such as Arkansas and Texas.

The compromise agreement between North and South reflected a general feeling—"Americans wished a union of all fragments"[4]—but produced an imbalance, enshrined in the Constitution itself, in favor of the southern part of the country. The first political crisis arose in 1819, when Missouri applied for admission to the Union as a slave state. The House of Representatives approved the request, provided that the slaves were emancipated, but the Senate approved it without restrictions on slavery. After three years of debate and negotiation, agreement was reached that, in the future, there would be no slavery north of parallel 36° 30′—the latitude of Missouri's southern border—which was a tacit admission that it could expand south of that line. Only then did the Senate admit Maine, as a free state, into the Union.[5]

Further crises erupted in subsequent years, but, faced with the threat of secession by the South, the North—where there developed a belief that blacks were relatively well-treated on the plantations—tended to give ground and accept successive compromises. These rested as well, or above all, on a strong convergence of economic interests between the two halves of the United States. The northerners generally feared that freeing the blacks would lead to unwelcome competition in the labor market. In addition, many northerners had jobs directly or indirectly related to economic activity in the South. From the early 1820s, any well-informed person knew that cotton planted by slaves accounted for more than half of North America's exports, and that it sustained shipping, banking, insurance, and manufacturing.[6] Thus, the successive compromises in favor of the southerners dragged the problem of slavery on, like a ticking time bomb, which exploded when the South's demands reached the limits of what was acceptable to the North's notion of freedom.

Contrary to what is sometimes thought, abolitionism was not an irresistible force in the United States. Following an initial attack on slavery in the final quarter of the eighteenth century, the movement withered in the context of the political compromise, which had been reached in order to preserve the union, and also in the face of southern reaction, which made any far-reaching action against slavery in the South humanly impracticable. Either by their own volition, or because they were expelled by the authorities, the abolitionists largely disappeared from the South, and only isolated pockets remaining in North Carolina and Tennessee. It was only after it had lain dormant—or even forgotten—for a time that abolitionism reemerged at the beginning of the 1830s, driven by white enthusiasts or radicals such as Theodore Dwight Weld and William Lloyd Garrison, who were joined by several free blacks. Only from then on did a few activists start demanding the immediate end of slavery. Some fugitive slaves, such as Frederick Douglass, were hired by recently established anti-slavery organizations to publish their memoirs and give speeches to the masses, and their narratives helped greatly to undermine the belief that the South treated its slaves humanely.[7] In spite of all of this, and contrary to what happened in Britain, North American abolitionists were in a small minority, and their ability to influence and direct the mass of the people was limited, even in the northern states. Abolitionism was sometimes associated with other causes—such as the rights of women or animals, or non-violence—and it was often too radical in tone and posture for the ordinary citizen. In addition, the racist sentiments of northerners, heightened by co-existence with the free negroes who lived there, also made it difficult for the abolitionists' message to get across: when they spoke in public, they often got a hostile reception.

In mid-century, however, that hostile reaction began to diminish, largely on account of the extreme measures taken by pro-slavery political authorities. The Fugitive Slave Law, published in 1850, provided for the imprisonment of up to one year of any person who aided a slave to escape; it also permitted federal agents to recapture any fugitive slave, in any part of the national territory, and granted them the right to compel free citizens to help them in their mission (the commissioner could summon any Northerner to serve in a fugitive-hunting posse).[8] This and other similar measures produced indignation in the North. The spectacle of federal agents dragging a poor slave through the streets of Boston led to civil disobedience and an angry demonstration by many thousands of people, who were only held back when an armed force of 15,000 men intervened.[9] That feeling of indignation, together with growing pressure by southern forces such as those which produced the Dred Scott Decision in

1857—a legal decision which denied Congress any constitutional power to set limits on the expansion of slavery in the national territory—would degenerate into heightened tensions, secession, the Civil War, and the total emancipation of the slaves.

Immediate emancipation was the unforeseen outcome of a war that no-one imagined would go so far and last so long. If the North, with its vast superiority in men and material, had stopped fighting in 1862, it is very possible that emancipation would not have been decreed. President Lincoln certainly would have been content with an early southern defeat and would have backed a scheme for cautious emancipation. Lincoln was a gradualist and a prudent man. When elected president, he gave assurances that he would not interfere with the institution of slavery in the 15 states where it existed at the time, and up until 1862, the official United States government position was for gradual abolition, if any, over a period of 30 years or more. On 1 December 1862, Lincoln himself submitted an emancipation proposal to Congress, setting the distant year of 1900 as the limit for the existence of slavery in the country and giving the various states the possibility of abolishing it when they saw fit, in exchange for compensation—which would be greater or smaller according to how soon abolition came into effect.[10]

However, the military victories of Robert E. Lee dragged the conflict on until 1865. And as the escalating war brought new horrors and the numbers of the dead mounted up—in the final reckoning, some 620,000 perished—even the more cautious accepted the idea of immediate emancipation, at least as a way of weakening the southern economy. In April 1862, abolition was decreed for the over 3,000 slaves in the Washington region (with compensation for their owners). In July of the same year, a new law stipulated that southerners' property would be confiscated and their slaves—regarded as prisoners of war—would be forever free. And on 1 January 1863, a proclamation was made to the effect that all of the slaves on the plantations, in any state, would be forever free, the military authorities being ordered to acknowledge and ensure the freedom that those slaves might attain by their own efforts. This proclamation represented *de jure* release of all of the slaves of the Confederacy, and when president Lincoln entered Richmond (Virginia), he was surrounded by a multitude of slaves who glorified him as a Messiah who had come to free their children from bondage. As Freehling says, a man who had started out as "the great delayer" ended up as the "Great Emancipator."[11] It was only after Lincoln's death at the end of 1865, however, that the Constitutional amendment was ratified outlawing slavery formally and forever, thus freeing nearly 4 million Africans and Afro-Americans, with no compensation for their masters.[12]

After this brief journey through the political history of the United States, we must now examine the role of slave revolts in the compromises, crises, and ultimately explosions that would lead to general emancipation. During this period, strangely, there were only two slave revolts, both medium-sized. A rebellion led by a slave called Charles Deslondes broke out in 1811 in Louisiana; the rebels, numbering no more than 200 men, marched on New Orleans, burning plantations, and killing some whites, but they were slaughtered by an armed force. The so-called Nat Turner Rebellion took place twenty years later, in August 1831, in an isolated part of Virginia. Its objective was never entirely clear. Turner and fifty or so rebel followers started their campaign in the farms of the area, killing some 60 whites—mostly women and children. These apocalyptic events would have been much bloodier if the authorities had not succeeded in putting down the rebellion in the space of a few hours, killing and capturing all of the rebels except Turner himself, who was captured later and finally hanged in November 1831.[13]

Given the circumstances and even, at times, the incentives to revolt, these two episodes, together with two or three other abortive conspiracies, indicate that the level of rebelliousness was generally low. It is important to note that, on occasion, opinions and pamphlets circulated to the effect that it was legitimate for a slave to obtain freedom through armed struggle. Even so, positions of this sort, or even direct appeals to the slaves to rise up, such as those that occurred in the 1840s and increasingly in the 1850s, did not stir up the mass of slaves, nor did they provide a pretext for them to rebel.[14] Some agitators and militants went further than merely appealing for a general uprising. In October 1859, John Brown and a group of whites and blacks, with financial support from abolitionists, attacked and seized the arsenal at Harpers Ferry in Virginia. Their intention was to arm the slaves and set off a rebellion in the heart of the southern slave country. Arrested and condemned for treason and murder, Brown was hanged. In the North, he became a martyr who had had the courage to act according to his convictions, while in the South he was viewed as a radical who wanted to establish another Haiti. The truth is, however, that there was no slave revolt.[15]

Lincoln's laws, namely his January 1863 proclamation ordering the military authorities to recognize and safeguard the freedom that slaves might achieve through their own efforts, were an appeal—or at least a promise of support—for an eventual slave uprising. And they were so interpreted both in the South and in Europe. But that uprising never happened. It is important to emphasize that, in that time of civil war, when the South was being invaded on all sides, the approximately 4 million slaves there remained expectant and peaceful. Some may attribute that quietism to the fact that the slaves had become aware of Lincoln's emancipation proclamation and had the good sense to wait patiently for the arrival of freedom (if this was indeed the way things happened, it shows once again how slaves acted in line with outside events). Others, by contrast, might say that there was nothing abnormal in that passivity, because revolts were never frequent in the United States, the slaves being a minority of the general population. The truth is, however, that in the context of Civil War, those arguments fall down because the enlistment of white males tilted the demographic balance in favor of the blacks and, what is more, reduced southern white society to women, children, and old men. Even then, there was no revolt. Contrary to what many had forecast, the blacks did not take advantage of the absence or scarcity of white males, occupied in fighting the Yankees, to massacre their defenseless families.[16]

This does not mean that the slaves were entirely passive. Many of them risked their lives to escape and join the fighting forces, as they had done before, at the time of the war of independence. At the end of the Civil War, the number of black slaves in the Union army was huge, over double the number of active Confederate soldiers at the battle of Gettysburg.[17] But the lack of revolts during the Civil War does mean that the slaves' struggle for freedom took place in an orderly context, alongside white soldiers, and not as part of an insurrection. It also means, on the other hand, that abolitionism was not much associated with insurrection in the minds of the slaves in the South. It was not a major catalyst of insurrection, but again not entirely disassociated with it, because Nat Turner's rebellion, which took place 4 months before the Jamaica revolt, coincided with the rise of the immediatist drive in Britain and the northern United States; and earlier, in 1822, the abortive conspiracy of Denmark Vessey—a free negro from South Carolina, who worked as a slave in Santo Domingo—seems to have been based on a misunderstanding of the debate then going on about Missouri and a rumor then circulating among the slaves that Congress had already declared emancipation, but that the planters were opposed to the measure.[18]

By contrast, the—real or imagined—threat of slave revolts seems often to have been counterproductive in its effects and it set back the cause of abolitionism in the United States. It was the discovery in 1800 of an alleged conspiracy to destroy Richmond that stopped the early southern Quaker and Baptist abolitionists in their tracks. Revolts taking place elsewhere, in Barbados and Demerara, gave planters in the South a series of arguments against abolitionism, and blocked discussion of the subject in Congress, on the basis that talking about it would produce death and destruction, just as the debates in the British Parliament had stirred up the slaves in the West Indies.[19] And the facts backed up this theory when, against the backdrop of growing immediatism in England and the publication of *The Liberator*—the radical abolitionist journal of William Lloyd Garrison—Nat Turner's rebellion broke out in Virginia. That revolt was, of course, used to set up mechanisms for censoring the circulation of ideas: Congress approved a rule denying anti-slavery petitions, while in the South great crowds burned abolitionist propaganda, and mail from the North began to be meticulously inspected.[20]

The North-American model of emancipation was largely followed in the territories of Spanish America. At the beginning of the nineteenth century, the structure of the Spanish empire in the Americas was practically unchanged (with the exception of the colony of Santo Domingo, which was involved in the dramatic events in Haiti).[21] But from 1807 onward, with the mother country tied down in the Napoleonic wars, independence movements began to emerge everywhere, and the idea of emancipation soon became part of the demands and promises of such movements. It is true that at this time and in most regions, negro slavery played a relatively minor or secondary role: there were about 10,000 slaves in Mexico and Central America; in the Presidency of Charcas, in Upper Peru (equivalent to today's Bolivia), there were fewer than 5,000, mostly used in domestic service; in the Presidency of Quito (Ecuador), there were probably another 5,000; in the River Plate region, there were possibly some 30,000; and, in Chile, some 10,000 slaves existed. In mining or plantation enclaves, the number of slaves was higher: in New Granada (which corresponded roughly to modern-day Colombia), there were possibly 70,000; in the captaincy general of Venezuela, where cocoa plantations were a key element in the economy, there were 65,000 slaves; and about 40,000 slaves worked in Peru, concentrated mainly in the cities and plantations on the coast (representing 25 percent of the population). In other words, there was a total of about 240,000 slaves spread over a large area.[22] The important point to note, however, in the context which concerns us here, is that as a general rule, advances toward the abolition of slavery did not occur as a result or under the influence of slave revolts, but rather in the wake of the republican movements and wars of independence in the first quarter of the nineteenth century.

In 1810, the leaders of the Mexican independence movement proclaimed the end of slavery and the separation of castes, with the aim of increasing the numbers of their supporters and weakening those of the realists and supporters of Spain. The proclamation, reissued in 1813, was never put into practical effect, because the revolutionaries were captured and executed. Despite their defeat, however, the separatists had succeeded in putting social reform on the political agenda and the ruling powers would later implement it in an effort at reconciliation. In 1822, after the creation of the Mexican monarchy, to which Spain, powerless to intervene, had given recognition, a decree was promulgated to free slaves born on Mexican soil. Later, in 1829, at a time when Mexico had about 3,000 slaves, slavery was entirely abolished (although in Texas, North American colonists were allowed to continue to own slaves).[23]

Central America united with Mexico in 1821, but later separated and adopted the designation United Provinces of Central America (out of which would later emerge Guatemala, Nicaragua, Honduras, El Salvador, and Costa Rica). In that region, slavery was abolished in 1824, by a free womb law and the setting up of a fund for the manumission of the remaining 1,000 or so slaves.[24]

In the southern part of Spanish America, the process of emancipation was directly tied to the wars of independence. In the River Plate region, the first stirrings of independence and republican movements occurred in 1808. Two years later, a governing junta took power in Buenos Aires with

the principal aim of maintaining control, in the light of the power vac-
uum in the mother country and the disparate centripetal forces operating
locally. The inland provinces were anxious to come out from Madrid's
tutelage, but they did not want Buenos Aires taking over as the capital of
the empire. Conflict was therefore inevitable, and military necessity
meant that slaves were drafted into the army, on the assumption that they
would be free after 5 years of active service.[25] Their masters were required
to release them for that purpose and for a set price, since this was a form
of expropriation of private property. In the heat of the struggle for independence, the generals made full use of the law, which meant that the
path of recruitment into the army became for the blacks a significant way
of achieving freedom. But this was not the only path to emancipation.
Soon after, in 1813, in a bid to garner internal and external support, the
Constituent Assembly decreed freedom of the womb (with a requirement
that slaves must work up to the age of 20). It further stipulated that any
slave henceforth imported into the territory of the self-designated United
Provinces would be free. In the mid-1820s, there were probably still 6,000
slaves in Buenos Aires, but this number declined gradually up until 1853,
the year in which Argentina decreed the total abolition of slavery.[26]

The pattern of events in Uruguay was identical. There was a short period of Portuguese occupation during which slavery was temporarily restored, so that freedom of the womb would only be established again at
the end of the 1820s following the revolution that expelled the invader.
Subsequently, in the 1840s, the various regions of Uruguay gradually released the remaining slaves, with full emancipation coming in 1853.[27]

Chile followed a similar path, although progress was faster, so that it
became the first Republic in former Spanish America to end slavery completely. Steps were taken in that direction as early as 1811, with a freedom
of the womb law. Spanish reaction forced suspension of that law, but this
was only temporary. The subsequent later revolutionary and separatist
victories of 1817–18 restored the abolitionist law. A further and decisive
step was taken in 1823 in new legislation that freed all of the slaves with
no compensation for their masters (the treasury was empty as a result of
expense with the war).[28]

In the Northern half of the sub-continent, where most of the troops
loyal to Spain were quartered, emancipation proceeded according to the
same principles. Republican and separatist movements first emerged in
1810 in Venezuela. The king's local and later metropolitan armies hindered their progress, however, and they were initially unsuccessful. In the
battles, and the frequent advances and retreats that were the hallmarks of
the 1811 to 1815 period, both sides incorporated contingents of slaves into
their armies, with the promise of manumission at the end of a few years
of military service. During this turbulent time, many slaves also ran away
from the plantations, some of them acquiring weapons and joining up
with the armies of their own free will, or forming ad hoc alliances with
the parties in conflict. It is important to note that these bands of armed

runaway slaves probably took part in looting and violence, but were not active in revolts to bring slavery to an end.[29] Moreover, they were keener to join the pro-Spanish armies than the republican revolutionaries, although the latter tended to be abolitionist. They were, nevertheless, more directly associated with the planter class.[30]

The political situation changed in 1815, when Símon Bolívar was able to obtain military support from Haiti in exchange for the promise of general emancipation for the slaves—something the authorities loyal to Spain obviously could not promise. Bolívar thus held an important advantage in attracting the slave masses and increasing the support for the revolution in society as a whole. It is true that the need to respect planter property rights, so as not to alienate them, led the republicans to tread very cautiously in this respect. Initially, therefore, they continued to favor the military option, which was justified by the state of war and allowed them gradually to emancipate the slaves without necessarily being perceived as having infringed private property rights. If everyone was required to join the army, then why not the slaves as well, provided that their masters were compensated? But at the same time, Bolívar decreed emancipation of those Africans owned by people in social and political sectors opposed to him, and, in 1821, what was then known as the Confederation of Gran Colombia, made up of modern-day Venezuela, Colombia, and Ecuador, formally adopted a freedom of the womb law (with a requirement for work up to age 18), which also allowed for adult slaves to free themselves provided they compensated their owners.[31]

Around the same time, war had already broken out further south, in Peru, still under Spanish control and home to 40,000 slaves—plus 40,000 creoles and free blacks. It might appear in these circumstances, and given that the attacking armies, coming from Chile, contained a large number of recently freed blacks in their ranks, that the conditions were ripe for a Peruvian slave revolt. But that is not what happened. Some of the slaves were incorporated into the armies loyal to Spain (with the promise of freedom after 6 years of service and compensation for their masters, of course).[32] Others patiently awaited the arrival of the armies of liberation. Lima fell to the republicans in 1821; two years later, Bolívar, arriving from the North, took control of Peru and, in 1825, of Upper Peru (modern-day Bolivia). In the following year, the last troops loyal to Spain surrendered.

With the advent of peace, all of these regions would adopt freedom of the womb laws similar to the one approved in 1821, which means that Venezuela, Colombia, Ecuador, Bolivia, and Peru retained slavery, if only for a time. Bolívar sought to use his political influence to achieve freedom for all negroes as quickly as possible, in particular through manumission boards endowed with appropriate funding and working systematically for the freedom of the slaves (with compensation for their masters). These boards were effectively set up, but when Bolívar died in 1830, the task of emancipation was still far from being completed. In any event, the freedom of the womb laws and the passage of time worked away at what remained of slavery, which was finally ended for good only in the 1850s: Bolivia and Colombia abolished it in 1851, Ecuador in 1852, Venezuela in 1854, and Peru in 1855.

To sum up, the new Spanish-American powers, at the time of their independence, drafted many slaves into their armies and quickly adopted freedom of the womb legislation, with the newly-born being required to work for their mothers' masters up to the ages of 18, 21 or 25 years. As a result, the number of slaves gradually fell, making it possible to decree total abolition within three of four decades at the most. The exception to this rule was Paraguay, where there were still 25,000 slaves in the 1830s, as many as there had been in the colonial era. Paraguay only approved a free womb law in 1842, and only freed its slaves entirely in the 1860s. But whether it took place faster or slower, the whole process of emancipation generally developed without slave revolts. There was some agitation from 1824 to 1828, but this was caused mainly by demobilized black soldiers who had not been paid. Only the Peruvian emancipation in 1855 may vaguely be regarded as having been brought about by the 1851 revolts in the sugar-producing plantations of the Chicama and Cañete valleys. In the remainder of the former Spanish colonies, as Lombardi mentions in connection with Venezuela, "negro slaves were disinclined to revolt on their own."[33]

In contrast to the new Spanish-American nations, Brazil had a very large number of slaves, despite the fact that their relative size as a proportion of the total population declined over the years. At the beginning of the nineteenth century, they accounted for more than 40 percent of a total population estimated at 2.5 million people. Twenty years later, they represented only 29 percent of a population of almost 4 million, even though in certain areas, such as Maranhão, for example, they continued to be a large proportion of the local population (around 66 percent).[34]

Even so, there was no social explosion in Brazil as there had been in Haiti, although in the nineteenth century, some regions in Brazil—especially Bahia—were the scenes of successive slave uprisings. Some of them went no further than the conspiracy stage, being dismantled following denunciations by loyal slaves encouraged by the enticing prospect of a material reward or even freedom.[35] Others, however, involved fighting, death, and destruction. The most serious of these was the so-called Malês' revolt, which occurred in early 1835 in the city of Salvador itself. This was a very widespread and well-organized movement that might have had dramatic consequences for the free population if a former slave woman had not denounced the plotters, enabling the military authorities to crush the rebellion right at the start. This did not prevent some 500 Africans from creating mayhem for several hours in the streets of the town, killing nine people. The slaves were eventually defeated and dispersed, 70 of them being lost in the fray. In the repression that followed, hundreds of Africans were arrested, and many of them flogged, deported or hanged.[36]

Even though the Malês' revolt was crushed in its early stages—as were several other revolts—it sheds a great deal of light on the rebels' purposes. At times, the stereotyped rumor circulated among Brazilian slaves that the king had freed them and that the masters were refusing to obey his order. This happened, for example, in Cachoeira and Espírito Santo in 1822, in Bahia in 1823, in Campinas in 1832, and again in Espírito Santo in 1849.[37] But the rumor does not seem to have encouraged insurrection, possibly because it was so improbable. We should recall that at that time, abolitionism had no palpable influence in Brazil. For this reason, and in contrast to what happened in other places, it was not European ideologies in favor of the right to freedom and citizenship driving the rebellious Malês. The aims of their rebellion—which was inspired by Islam—was to take the city and kill all of the whites and blacks of other ethnicities who refused to join the revolt; creoles would be spared, however, so as to serve as slaves to the new masters.[38] This shows that, in the absence of a climate or context of abolitionism or revolution functioning as a framework and guidance for the rebels' demands and objectives, the latter would continue to operate in the traditional way. That is to say, they would tend to massacre the whites, seek dominion over the territory, and enslave other blacks and creoles.

The Malês' revolt terrified Brazil, more by reason of what it might have been than for what it actually was, and thereby strengthened the trend in opinion against the importation of more slaves. But as usual the alarm was transitory, and Brazilians remained deeply involved in the slave trade up until 1850.[39] And it was only in 1871 that they took any significant steps toward emancipation, by a freedom of the womb law under which newly-born slaves would be classified as *ingénuos*, their masters being free to release them at 8 years of age in return for compensation or, as an alternative, to continue to avail themselves of their labor up to the age of 21, when they would become entirely free of all obligation. In other words, the law enabled postponing the end of slavery until the 1890s.

That timescale was shortened a little because, at the beginning of the 1880s, abolitionism, inspired by Joaquim Nabuco, Ruy Barbosa, André Rebouças, and many others, developed in a truly unexpected way in Brazilian society, at the same time as slavery began to lose support. As noted by Seymour Drescher, Brazil then developed a form of activist and popular anti-slavery, with mass demonstrations and propaganda, as had occurred only in Britain and the northern United States.[40] Emancipation societies began to spring up all over the country, and in certain areas, the attitude of noncooperation with slavery spread rapidly among the population. In Fortaleza, for example, printers boycotted the publication of any article defending slavery, while at the same time, raftsmen refused to carry slaves to the ships waiting for them in port; huge crowds of people supported the boycott *in loco,* and slave manumissions—which were taking place on an individual basis—gave rise to public celebrations. In Bahia, the people refused to allow slaves to continue to be punished in the public square. In areas where the railway had already arrived, the more radical abolitionists, plotting with railway workers and others, created support networks to help slaves to flee, as had already happened in the United States with the famous Underground Railroad.[41]

The urban bourgeoisie soon joined the abolitionists, and some states and cities began to declare themselves slavery-free zones, as in Ceará initially and then in Amazonas, Rio Grande do Sul, Goiás, and Paraná. The slaves, for their part, aware of the widespread support in Brazilian society, began to agitate. In November 1882, a revolt broke out on a plantation in São Paulo province. To the sound of shouts in favor of abolitionism and the Republic, the rebels killed 5 or 6 people and then made their way to the city of Campinas, where they surrendered to the police.[42]

But violent action like this was relatively unusual. As João José Reis says, "in the final phase of slavery there were slave uprisings, and *quilombos* were established in various parts of Brazil, but these were mostly local movements, generally confined to one or two plantations."[43] By contrast, mass flight was common. From the beginning, but more frequently from 1886 on, slaves, responding to abolitionists' encouragement, abandoned the plantations *en masse,* and there were no forces available to stop the exodus. Slaves now ran away not to the hideouts in the bush, but to towns and cities like Santos and Fortaleza, where runaways knew they could count on support from abolitionists and the townspeople in general. Here and there retaliation occurred, directed mainly at overseers, but there were no revolts and none of the destruction that goes with them, although, as was common in many places, the number of slaves in proportion to the local police forces was frightening and highly unfavorable to the latter.[44]

Faced with this tide of abolitionism, the slavery sector virtually imploded. Sugar planters in the Northwest, apparently satisfied with the free labor available in their area, abandoned the cause of slavery and began to free their slaves, subsequently taking them on as salaried workers or tenants. The problem of slavery persisted only in the coffee-growing areas, that is to say, in São Paulo, Rio de Janeiro, and Minas Gerais provinces. But having no nation-wide support, the planters had to accept the spirit of the time, as well as the measures putting an end to a centuries-old method of exploitation. In 1885, the so-called law of the sexagenarians forbade the use of the whip and stipulated that all slaves who reached 60 years of age would be freed. Then, in 1888, the government decreed immediate abolition without compensation for all remaining slaves and *ingénuos.* It was Princess Isabel who signed the decree in her father's name, the Emperor D. Pedro II, at a time when the number of slaves (not counting *ingénuos*) had fallen to 5 percent of the Brazilian labor force.[45]

It is important to emphasize the fact that during the 1880s, Brazilian abolitionists and their followers incited slaves to run away from the plantations, arming many of them and helping them to confront their masters and the police.[46] It should be remembered that in the past, planters in the

British, French, and Spanish Caribbean had accused the abolitionists of being behind the slave rebellions, whether through the involvement of their agents or merely as a result of the circulation of their seditious ideas. Later on, in the mid-nineteenth century United States, abolitionists made public appeals for rebellion and were even active in the field, as we saw with John Brown. But it was in late nineteenth century Brazil that the causal relationship between abolitionism and slave resistance took on a clear, and, in a certain sense, paradigmatic form.

3.2. Emancipation in the European Colonies

Emancipation decrees in Europe were thought out, debated, and brought to fruition by parliaments and governments. Leaving aside Britain, which we have already analyzed, and passing over Sweden, which in 1847 emancipated the approximately 600 slaves it had on the island of Saint Bartholomew—its only colony in the Caribbean—let us return to France which, as already mentioned, retained slavery despite the Haiti disaster.

Once peace had been achieved, and with the memory of Saint-Domingue still very much alive, France resumed the *odious commerce* and recovered its American colonies, importing around 125,000 slaves between 1814 and 1831. The subjugation of the *gens de couleur* and the slave masses was maintained, and that subjugation gave rise to a small uprising on Martinique in 1822, which was swiftly crushed. But after those early years in which there was almost a return to the past, France once more began to wake up to the problem of abolition. The French slave trade was in fact suppressed at the beginning of the 1830s, at a time when a small group of enlightened persons was also beginning to argue the case for ending slavery. In 1834, in the wake of British emancipation, the duc de Broglie and other abolitionists founded the *Société Française pour l'Abolition de l'Esclavage,* and, in 1837, the first draft of a free womb law was submitted to the Chambers, followed two years later by Tocqueville's draft seeking to abolish slavery as the British had done, that is to say, by establishing a six-year apprenticeship period and compensating the masters. None of these ideas materialized, although they gave rise to a series of improvement measures, such as moral education for slaves and a ban on separating families or flogging women. As a general rule, the authorities were prepared to countenance the reform of slavery, provided it could be done at little expense and without putting public safety at risk. In other words, these politicians saw gradual abolition as a possibility, but there it lingered, with no concrete measures to make it real. The exception to this was the royal order of 1846, which freed all slaves belonging to the Crown. This was an undeniably modest achievement for 12 to 15 years of effort on the part of French abolitionists who, in some cases—like those of Lamartine and Victor Schöelcher—were already calling for immediate abolition (with compensation payable to owners). In the mid-1840s, with the support of the British abolitionists, the *Société Française pour l'Abolition de l'Esclavage* started publishing a journal, *l'Abolitioniste Français*, and in 1844 and 1847, two anti-slavery petitions were organized, gathering 7,000 and 11,000 signatures respectively.[47]

These numbers were not overwhelming, nor were they even representative of the extent to which anti-slavery had penetrated French society. In fact, the low level of popular support in the form of signatures on these two petitions reflected not so much a strong and widespread commitment to emancipation as social discontent and a desire for political reform, feelings which would eventually lead to the fall of the monarchy and the founding of the Republic in early 1848. It was in this context that, in an instant, abolitionism triumphed in republican France. In March, Victor Schöelcher became secretary to the Minister for the Colonies in the new provisional government, proclaiming his intention to abolish slavery. A committee was set up—with himself presiding—to study within a short time the prospects for immediate emancipation in the colonies. And, in fact, the committee reported with lightning speed: in a few weeks, a report was drawn up and a law drafted to the effect that, two months after its publication in the colonies, the slaves would be entirely free. It would be the task of the future legislative assembly to lay down the amounts of compensation to be paid to their former owners. Related legislation allocated 26 million francs to the colonies for the building of schools, hospitals, labor courts, and other institutions required in a society of free workers. The government approved the two decrees on 27 April 1848.

Prior to 1848, there had been no major revolts in the French colonies. But the rumor that the Republic was about to abolish slavery had an immediate impact in Martinique, where there were 75,000 slaves, and in Guadeloupe, where there were 88,000 slaves. Many slaves on the plantations in Martinique left their workplaces at the end of April and headed for the towns. There they anxiously awaited the arrival of the decree, and the white authorities feared that the slightest incident might lead to violence. On 22 May, there was in fact bloody fighting in which 35 slaves lost their lives. Fearing a general revolt, the municipal council appealed to the governor to decree immediate emancipation, to which he agreed. On learning of these events, the governor of Guadeloupe adopted identical measures on 27 May. In other words, freedom arrived 11 days ahead of the 27 April decrees even reaching the two islands and without the two-month transition period foreseen by the legislators. Guiana and Reunion waited for the arrival of the decrees, and the slaves were freed in accordance with their provisions.[48]

Emancipation in Denmark was unusual on several counts. Denmark possessed three islands in the Caribbean—St. Thomas, St. John, and St. Croix—but it was only in the last of these that there were large cane plantations and a sizeable sugar industry. St. Croix had been bought from France only in 1733 and it did not seem to be of particular interest to the

Danish people. Most of the white population of the island was of foreign origin—mainly Irish and Scottish—and only one of the eight members of the island's governing council was Danish. In addition, Denmark at that time was in the process of reassessing its overseas empire and seemed ready to give up any claims in this area. It therefore sold its possessions in the East to Britain in 1845, and was getting ready to do the same in regard to its African colonies—as it effectively did; the Caribbean islands remained Danish for a few decades more, but were finally sold to the United States in 1917.[49]

At the time, the Danes were in the final years of absolute monarchy, and power in the West Indian colonies rested with a governor-general, Peter von Scholten. In 1834, convinced that the days of slavery were numbered—especially after British emancipation—von Scholten drew up a plan for the future release of colonial slaves and brought about significant improvements in their lives, in order to facilitate their transition from a state of slavery to freedom. It was in this context that he allowed or encouraged evangelism; that he set legal limits on the number of hours in a slave's working day; that he limited slaveholders' discretionary powers of punishment; that he granted Saturday as a day of rest and established the rule that any work carried out in overtime should be paid for. It was also in the spirit of improvement that he set up elementary schools for slave children—the first of which opened its doors in 1841. Many people in Denmark shared this ameliorative approach. Even though there was no abolitionist movement, educated rulers had guided the kingdom toward improvement of the lives of slaves and toward abolition itself. It should be remembered that the Danes were the first Europeans to ban the slave trade, in 1792 (with a ten-year transition period). It was thus no surprise that on 28 July 1847, a royal decree established freedom of the womb for those born from then on, stipulating in addition that the year 1859 would be the time limit at which slavery would end in the Danish colonies for good. Some were prepared to accept that that timetable could be brought forward in the light of "unforeseen circumstances"; in the context of the time and place, that could only have meant a possible revolt.[50]

This was precisely what happened in St. Croix, an island having at that time some 17,000 slaves for a little over 7,000 whites and free blacks. As generally happened, rumors of imminent emancipation started circulating amongst the slaves, or even that the king had already decreed it, but that the planters were refusing to publish the decree in the colonies. On 3 July 1848, some 8,000 slaves abandoned the plantations and gathered in front of Frederikstadt, at the western end of the island, demanding full freedom. A kind of picket line prevented other slaves from working, and coercive force was employed to oblige the most reluctant among them, to support the demonstration. Opinion in the governing council, summoned to meet in Christianstadt, was divided: Irminger, the captain of a warship stationed in those waters, wanted to use force to oblige the strikers to return to work; von Scholten favored gentler methods and refused to send troops to disperse the demonstrators, although he did authorize Irminger to proceed under sail to Frederikstadt in order to keep the slaves that had gathered there in check. He himself traveled to that town over land, however, and reached it ahead of Irminger. In a speech to the massed demonstrators, he emancipated them there and then. Thus did 16 hours of disturbances come to an end, not having led to any deaths or to any significant destruction in the towns, where the demonstrators had exercised remarkable self-control. Only a few plantations were looted by the more violent or out of control groups.[51]

Irminger and the white population, however, were not happy with this solution, and on the following day, some blacks were attacked and killed near Christianstadt. This produced a reaction in the form of looting and reprisals, which lasted three days. Faced with a real crisis and the apparent loss of control of the situation, the conciliator von Scholten was forced to hand over the situation to Oxholm, the governor of St. Thomas Island, who brought in military reinforcements requested from Puerto Rico. Meanwhile, in Frederikstadt, Irminger had imposed a form of martial law, and mass detentions—over 100 people were arrested—and trials began. These took up the following weeks and led to the execution of 8 rebels.[52] The Danish government, however, did not repeal von Scholten's emancipation proclamation, confirming it on 22 September 1848, thus bringing forward by 10 years the transition period for freedom that had been stipulated. Peter von Scholten, who had meanwhile been sentenced by a court martial for failing to take adequate precautions to protect the island, was cleared by the Supreme Court in 1849.

Holland also had possessions in the islands of the Caribbean and one of them, Curaçao, was the scene of a major revolt in 1795. Thus, there was reason to fear that the slave agitation on Martinique, Guadeloupe, and St. Croix might set off a train of violence if it spread to the Dutch colonies. But there were one or two special features to these islands. The plantation economy was relatively undeveloped, and living conditions for the slaves were not particularly intolerable or harsh. Moreover, manumissions were common in the islands, where there were more free negroes than slaves. It was on the basis of this pattern of manumissions that the slaves of Saint Martin demanded freedom in 1848. The owners and local authorities had no trouble meeting the demand, if only to prevent the slaves from running away to neighboring French colonies.[53]

For the Dutch, the problem of slavery arose mainly in connection with Surinam, which had about 40,000 slaves who might rise up, given the rebellious context of the time. But this did not happen, and these slaves remained relatively calm. A few hundred succeeded in fleeing to neighboring British Guiana, but, in general, the nineteenth century was a relatively quiet period for the slaveholders. There were no uprisings of any consequence, just a few conspiracies in isolated plantations, which were quickly dismantled. Even individual violence against whites was rare in the period we are looking at here.

Even so, from the 1850s onward, the Dutch felt compelled to follow the moral example of other European nations and to move toward emancipation, despite the adverse economic consequences of prior experiences. And in the 1850s, partly due to the encouragement of the British abolitionists, abolition began to be discussed in earnest, even if with relatively little controversy.[54] Surinam and other Dutch colonies in America had a minute impact on the Dutch economy. Planters and other slaveholders seemed resigned to the inevitability of abolition. At the same time, abolitionism was not widespread in Holland itself, except among a small group within the elite. Thus, everything proceeded smoothly; the Dutch Parliament, in 1862, passed a law to end slavery and paid compensation of almost 16 million guilders to the owners. Within a year, 10,000 slaves were freed in the Dutch Caribbean—Curaçao, Aruba, Bonaire, Saint Martin, Saint Eustatius, and Saba—and the 34,000 slaves then present in Surinam started on a period of apprenticeship, which was to last ten years. When the day of emancipation arrived, on 1 July 1863, the resulting festivities produced not a single incident requiring police intervention. Only on St. Eustatius were there some violent demonstrations in 1862, when a rumor started circulating that emancipation was about to be decreed.[55]

Portugal did not face many slave revolts in its colonies, and the problem became even more remote when, with the *de facto* independence of Brazil in 1822, it ceased to have any possessions in America. But it still had its African colonies—where, according to statistics and data collected at the end of the 1840s, there were almost 120,000 slaves. Those African colonies raised the problem of emancipation. Even though there was no abolitionist organization, nor even a spirit or willingness to move in that direction, the path to emancipation was gradually followed, thanks mainly to the persistent efforts of Sá da Bandeira. It was he who, in the 1850s, promoted and had passed a series of laws seeking to fight slavery through mechanisms such as the freedom of the womb and a ban on new slaves entering the colonies. One of these laws set the year 1878 as the outer time limit for the presence of slaves on Portuguese territory. The legislation as then approved provided for a period of gradual transition towards freedom, by converting slaves into freedmen who would remain subject to periods of apprenticeship and compulsory labor lasting between 7 and 10 years. Legally, slaves ceased to exist in the Portuguese colonies in 1868, with all of those then remaining becoming freedmen. Subsequently, the end of the period of transition to full freedom, which was to have occurred by 1878 at the latest, was brought forward to 1875.[56]

No slave revolt spurred on this slow death of slavery in the Portuguese empire. On the contrary, it is even fair to say that the various forms of violence involving slaves, whether as individuals or groups, actually caused trouble for the abolitionists and may possibly have delayed the whole process.[57] After the approval of the 1875 law bringing forward the period of apprenticeship and compulsory labor, there was some agitation on the island of São Tomé. On that island—as, moreover in other Portuguese colonies—Sá da Bandeira's legislation was not fully complied with because, at the end of the apprenticeship period, the masters did not relinquish control over the freedmen, continuing to force them to work. Successive colonial governors were complacent or acquiesced in this situation. They argued that if they gave the freedmen full freedom—as provided for in Sá da Bandeira's legislation—the island would lose 50 to 60 percent of its workforce and would be unable to recover from the ensuing economic disaster. Initially, that was also the perception and practice of Governor Gregório José Ribeiro. But when the law, which finally ended the period of apprenticeship, reached the island in June 1875, the governor attempted a compromise: he would suspend the application of that law provided the masters improved working conditions for the freedmen and paid them properly. Gregório Ribeiro believed that was the best way of making a peaceful transition to a system of free labor. But the planters, convinced they could continue to rely on the weakness and complacency of the political and police authorities, did not fulfill their side of the agreement. Thus, the governor began to grant freedom to those blacks who left the plantations and came to the town to demand it, on the grounds they had already completed their period of compulsory labor.

News of these releases spread swiftly and, in October and November 1875, freedmen abandoned nearly all of the plantations and gathered in the town. The Lisbon press at the time was full of alarmist reports and of letters from planters complaining that the government had decreed freedom for the slaves "without regard for the equal freedom of the property owner" and without taking steps to guard against possible lootings and massacres.[58] But these reports and complaints were without foundation, since the freedmen who gathered in the town did not cause disturbances. The planters had no option but to seek to entice them to work by means of work contracts. On these terms, and with the prospect of receiving a salary, many of them agreed to go back to work on the plantations.[59]

Spain was the last European state to emancipate the slaves in its colonies in Puerto Rico and Cuba, two islands that had become major centers of slavery as a result of the increase in sugar production. Around 1810, Cuba already had some 210,000 slaves—40 percent of the total population—and Puerto Rico had about 18,000 slaves. And these numbers continued to rise as the century progressed, so that by the 1870s, there were perhaps 360,000 slaves in Cuba and close to 40,000 in Puerto Rico.[60] Despite these high numbers of slaves, and despite the revolutionary and abolitionist events going on in the neighboring Caribbean regions, neither Cuba nor Puerto Rico became new Haitis or new Jamaicas (even if the white population at times greatly feared that they would). This occurred, for example, in Cuba at the beginning of 1812, following a revolt on five plantations that was suppressed by the militia. A number of abortive conspiracies followed this first outbreak, and there was another revolt near the capital. This upsurge of rebellions, which led to the death of eighteen whites and was essentially planned and carried out by free negroes, became known as the Aponte rebellion. It sought to end Spanish rule and to proclaim the end of slavery.[61] There were several conspiracies and small insurrections in Cuba, but no large-scale rebellion occurred there.[62]

On the island of Puerto Rico, there was never a general slave revolt; there were just some conspiracies, denounced by loyal slaves and quickly dismantled, and isolated small-scale local revolts, which were easily put down, sometimes with the help of slaves from neighboring plantations.[63] In other words, there was nothing to hurry or force Spain down the path to abolition.

Only after the founding of the *Sociedad Abolicionista Española* (1864) did the country begin to follow that path, mainly as a result of the successful Revolution of September 1868, when the *Junta Revolucionária de Madrid* and the provisional government announced their intention of applying freedom of the womb in the American colonies. In the wake of that announcement, the so-called Moret law was drafted and approved in 1870, emancipating elderly slaves (aged 60 or over) and freeing all children born from 1868 on—albeit they were to work for their masters as apprentices up to the age of 22.

Although it was clearly very moderate, the Moret law had an impact in Puerto Rico, where 8,000 slaves were immediately released. Faced with a sudden drop in their labor force and with the prospect of losing it entirely in the medium term, local planters preferred to free all of the remaining slaves, in exchange for compensation, as was indeed laid down by law in the Spanish *Cortes* on 22 March 1873. The legislation provided for a three-year transition period, during which former slaves were required to sign work contracts with their former masters.[64]

In Cuba, progress was slower and more complex, mainly because of the outbreak of the anti-colonial rebellion in December 1868, which would lead to the so-called ten-year war. Although they were still to some extent ambivalent and hesitant, the rebels fighting for independence, who controlled the Eastern part of the island where there were fewer plantations, promised to bring freedom by the traditional military method to all slaves, maroons, and coolies—Asiatic workers imported since the 1840s—who might wish to join them.[65] Those who did—and did not die in the fighting—lived to see their status as free men recognized and ratified by the pact of Zanjón (1878), which ended the hostilities. Some slaves also obtained their freedom fighting on the government side. For the remaining 200,000, however, the war was a setback on the path to freedom, given that the forces in Cuba that had remained loyal to Spain were pro-slavery. This understandably prevented the Spanish government from moving ahead with an abolitionist policy that might antagonize them. Only in 1880, after the island had been pacified, did Madrid dare to decree the abolition of slavery, setting up a transitional arrangement—the *patronato*—which was to last 8 years. From 1884 on, the then approximately 100,000 *patrocinados* (or former slaves) were freed at a rate of 25 percent every year, starting with the oldest among them. But with slavery in its death throes, many of those former slaves reached agreement with their masters and obtained full freedom early, through compensation and other means. When, in 1886, a royal decree brought forward the end of the transitional arrangements, only some 25,000 *patrocinados* remained in Cuba.[66]

Notes

1. David B. Davis, *The Problem of Slavery in the Age of Revolution, 1770–1823* (Ithaca, NY and London: Cornell University Press, 1975), 87–89.
2. Ibid., 133.
3. Stanley L. Engerman, *Slavery, Emancipation, and Freedom: Comparative Perspectives* (Baton Rouge: Louisiana State University Press, 2007), 33–34.
4. William W. Freehling, *The Road to Disunion. Secessionists at Bay, 1776–1854* (New York and Oxford: Oxford University Press, 1990), 135.
5. Ibid., 144ff.
6. Davis, *Age of Revolution*, 83.
7. Ibid., 200ff.
8. Freehling, *The Road to Disunion*, 501.
9. Ibid., 536–537.
10. *Journal of Commerce*, 26 and 27 December 1862.
11. William W. Freehling, *The South Versus the South. How Anti-Confederate Southerners Shaped the Course of the Civil War* (Oxford and New York: Oxford University Press, 2001), xiv.
12. David B. Davis, *Inhuman Bondage: The Rise and Fall of Slavery in the New World* (New York and London: Oxford University Press, 2006), 321–322.
13. Ibid., 208; and Eugene D. Genovese, *From Rebellion to Revolution. Afro-American Slave Revolts in the Making of the Modern World* (Baton Rouge: Louisiana State University Press, 1992; 1st ed., 1979), 7–10, 44–50 and 105–116.
14. Davis, *Inhuman Bondage*, 20–21.
15. Genovese, *From Rebellion to Revolution*, 81 and 106.
16. For a forecast of this type, see Freehling, *The Road to Disunion*, 182.
17. Davis, *Inhuman Bondage*, 301. There were also some slaves in the ranks of the Confederate army, but only a few dozen, because it was only in the very last phase of the war that the southerners decided to take advantage of that resource.
18. Genovese, *From Rebellion to Revolution*, 26 and 45; Davis, *Inhuman Bondage*.
19. Davis, *Age of Revolution*, 210.
20. Ibid., 148–149. For the effects of the revolt in the narrower context of Virginia, see Freehling, *The Road to Disunion*, 181ff.
21. The Spanish part of the island of Hispaniola changed hands on a number of occasions, and this explains its erratic progress on emancipation. The colony was ceded to France in 1795, which meant that, in theory, the French abolition law of 1794 took effect there, although in practice, that probably only occurred when the colony was occupied by Toussaint's troops in 1801. But slavery was restored with the arrival of Napoleon's armies in 1802. Five years later, as a result of the Franco-Spanish war in Europe, the population of Santo Domingo rebelled, expelling the French and restoring its ties with pro-slavery Spain. In 1822, Haitian forces occupied the colony and slavery was once again abolished. Santo Domingo became independent in the 1840s. In the 1860s, there was another Spanish invasion, and there was some concern that slavery would be rein-

troduced. Finally, a victorious war of restoration solved the problem for good in 1863 (see Carlos Esteban Deive, "La abolicion de la esclavitu en Santo Domingo," and Maria Magdalena Guerrero Cano, "Incidencias esclavistas tras la emancipacion en Santo Domingo," in *Esclavitud y Derechos Humanos. La lucha por la libertad del negro en el siglo XIX*, eds. Francisco de Solano and Agustín Guimerá (Madrid: CSIC/CEH, 1986), 321–329 and 331–342, respectively).

22. Robin Blackburn, *The Overthrow of Colonial Slavery, 1776–1848* (London and New York: Verso, 1988), 334–335; Peter Blanchard, "The Slave Soldiers of Spanish South America: From Independence to Abolition," in *Arming Slaves From Classical Times to the Modern Age*, eds. Christopher Leslie Brown and Philip D. Morgan (New Haven and London: Yale University Press, 2006), 256.
23. In 1840, there were probably about 15,000 slaves in Texas, which had in the meantime become independent (Freehling, *The Road to Disunion*, 367).
24. Blackburn, *The Overthrow*, 371–372.
25. For the drafting of slaves into the armies of the Spanish regions of South America see Blanchard, "The Slave Soldiers," 258ff.
26. Blackburn, *The Overthrow*, 350–351.
27. Nelson Martinez Diaz, "La resistência a la abolicion en los países del Rio de La Plata," in Solano and Guimerá, *Esclavitud y Derechos Humanos*, 625–634.
28. Blackburn, *The Overthrow*, 358.
29. Angelina Pollak-Eltz, "Slave revolts in Venezuela," in *Comparative Perspectives on Slavery in New World Plantation Societies*, eds. Vera Rubin and Arthur Tuden (New York: The New York Academy of Sciences, 1977), 443.
30. John V. Lombardi, *The Decline and Abolition of Negro Slavery in Venezuela, 1820–1854* (Westport: Greenwood Publishing, 1971), 11, 37–46.
31. Davis, *Age of Revolution*, 90–91.
32. Blackburn, *The Overthrow*, 354ff.
33. Lombardi, *The Decline*, 131; See also Blackburn, *The Overthrow*, 363 and 368.
34. Carlos Sixirei Paredes, "Violencia blanca, rebeldia negra y abolicionismo en el Brasil del siglo XIX," in Solano and Guimerá, *Esclavitud y Derechos Humanos*, 618ff.
35. Stuart B. Schwartz, "Cantos e quilombos numa conspiração de escravos haussás. Bahia, 1814," in *Liberdade por um Fio. História dos Quilombos no Brasil*, eds. João José Reis and Flávio dos Santos Gomes (São Paulo: Companhia das Letras, 1996), 381; and João José Reis, *Rebelião escrava no Brasil. A história do Levante dos Malês em 1835* (São Paulo: Companhia das Letras, 2003), 71.
36. Reis, *Rebelião escrava*, 125–157 and 426ff.; for earlier revolts see also 78 and 90–91.
37. João José Reis, "Quilombos e revoltas escravas no Brasil," in *Revista da Universidade de São Paulo*, 14, 39 (1995–96): 28.
38. Reis, *Rebelião escrava*, 73, 95 and 268; and Pierre Verger, *Flux et reflux de la traite des nègres entre le golfe de Bénin et Bahia de Todos os Santos du XVIIe au XIXe siècles* (Paris and The Hague: Mouton, 1968), 336–337.
39. See in this connection Verger, *Flux et reflux*, 335–350 and 355ff.; and João Pedro Marques, *The Sounds of Silence. Nineteenth-century Portugal and the Abolition of the Slave Trade* (New York and Oxford: Berghahn Books, 2006), 122–123 and 164–165. As shown by Jeffrey Needell ("The Abolition of the Brazilian Slave Trade in 1850: Historiography, Slave Agency and Statesmanship," in *Journal of Latin American Studies*, 33 (2001): 681–711), there is little to support the argument put forward by those who hold that the decision to end the slave trade in 1850 had been motivated by the fear of slave revolts.
40. Seymour Drescher, "Brazilian Abolition in Comparative Perspective," in *The Abolition of Slavery and the Aftermath of Emancipation in Brazil* (Durham and London: Duke University Press, 1988), 44.
41. Robert Brent Toplin, *The Abolition of Slavery in Brazil* (New York: Atheneum, 1975), 75 and 97ff.
42. Ibid., 31.

43. Reis, "Quilombos," 30.
44. Ibid.; Drescher, "Brazilian Abolition," 47; and Robert Conrad, *The Destruction of Brazilian Slavery, 1850–1888* (Berkeley: University of California Press, 1972), 185 (for slave flight see 239ff.). For the imbalance between numbers of slaves and police forces see Toplin, *The Abolition of Slavery,* 33–34.
45. For the development of emancipation in Brazil see Conrad, *The Destruction,* 121ff. The military option was not completely unknown in Brazil. In the Farroupilha revolt, in Rio Grande do Sul, the rebels enlisted their adversaries' slaves—and those of sympathizers, once they had paid them compensation—and formed a battalion of negro lancers. Many of them were massacred by the future Count of Caxias at the battle of Porongos, in 1844. But in the peace treaty signed in the following year, former slaves who had fought in the republican armies were granted their freedom. During the Paraguay war in 1864, many slave owners enlisted slaves to fight in their place. It is estimated that of the 160,000 casualties in that war, 90,000 were negroes. In any event, an 1866 decree freed any Brazilian slave fighting in Paraguay (see Reis, "Quilombos," 29; Hendrik Kraay, "Arming Slaves in Brazil from the Seventeenth Century to the Nineteenth Century," in Brown and Morgan, *Arming Slaves,* 160ff.).
46. Toplin, *The Abolition of Slavery,* 183–187 and 204–206.
47. Blackburn, *The Overthrow,* 487 and 492ff.
48. Ibid., 496–498; Lawrence C. Jennings, *French Anti-Slavery. The Movement for the Abolition of Slavery in France, 1802–1848* (Cambridge: Cambridge University Press, 2000), 282–283.
49. Neville A. T. Hall, *Slave Society in the Danish West Indies: St. Thomas, St. John and St. Croix* (Mona, Jamaica: University Press of West Indies, 1994), 19, 31, and 209.
50. Ibid., 32.
51. Ibid., 5, 18, 208–209, and 213–218.
52. Ibid., 211–212.
53. Pieter C. Emmer, "Anti-Slavery and the Dutch: Abolition without reform," in *Abolition and Its Aftermath. The Historical Context, 1790–1916,* ed. David Richardson (London: Frank Cass, 1985), 89.
54. Ibid., 81 and 89; and J.P. Siwpersad, "Emancipation in British Guyana and its influence on Dutch policy regarding Surinam," in Richardson, *Abolition and Its Aftermath,* 169–173.
55. Emmer, "Anti-Slavery and the Dutch," 88 and 93; and Emmer, "Between Slavery and freedom: the period of apprenticeship in Suriname (Dutch Guiana), 1863–1873," in *Slavery and Abolition,* 14, 1 (1993): 89.
56. João Pedro Marques, "Uma cosmética demorada: as *Cortes* portuguesas face ao problema da escravidão (1836–1875)," in *Análise Social,* 158/159 (2001): 225n53.
57. João Pedro Marques, "Quatro assassinatos e um retrocesso: violência escrava em Angola (1860–61)," in CEAUP (Coord.), *Trabalho Forçado Africano. Articulações com o Poder Político* (Porto: Campo das Letras, 2007), 101–115.
58. Letter from Jacinto Carneiro de Sousa e Almeida, 5 January 1876, in *Jornal do Commercio,* 6 January 1876.
59. Augusto Nascimento, "A crise braçal de 1875 em São Tomé. Os comportamentos dos agentes sociais," in *Revista Crítica de Ciências Sociais,* 34 (1992): 317–329.
60. Rebecca J. Scott, *Slave Emancipation in Cuba. The Transition to Free Labor, 1860–1899* (Pittsburgh: Pittsburgh University Press, 2000), 7.
61. Matt D. Childs, *The 1812 Aponte Rebellion in Cuba and the Struggle against Atlantic Slavery* (Chapel Hill: The University of North Carolina Press, 2006), 122ff.
62. See David R. Murray, *Odious Commerce: Britain, Spain and the Abolition of the Cuban Slave Trade* (Cambridge: Cambridge University Press, 1980), 173; and Christopher Schmidt-Nowara, "The end of slavery and the end of Empire: Slave emancipation in Cuba and Puerto Rico," in *Slavery and Abolition,* 21, 2 (2000): 190–191. On the Aponte (1812) and La Escalera (1844) conspiracies, which were independence movements led by free negroes and creoles and also involved slaves, see Blackburn, *The Overthrow,* 389–390, and

especially Hubert H.S. Aimes, *A History of Slavery in Cuba, 1511 to 1868* (New York: Octagon Books, 1967), 146ff. It should be noted that of the over 4,000 involved in La Escalera's conspiracy, the slaves accounted for less than a thousand.

63. Luís M. Diaz Soler, *Historia de la Esclavitud Negra en Puerto Rico* (Barcelona: Editorial Universitaria de la Universidad de Puerto Rico, 1970), 201–224.

64. See Paloma Arroyo Jimenez, "La Sociedad Abolicionista Española (1864–1886)," in Solano and Guimerá, *Esclavitud y Derechos Humanos,* 169–176; and Schmidt-Nowara, "The end of slavery," 194.

65. Gabino La Rosa Corzo, *Runaway Slave Settlements in Cuba. Resistance and Repression* (Chapel Hill and London: The University of North Carolina Press, 1988), 207–208 and 221–222; for the abolitionist ambiguities among the rebels see Scott, *Slave Emancipation in Cuba,* 45ff., and Ada Ferrer, "Armed Slaves and Anticolonial Insurgency in Late Nineteenth-Century Cuba," in Brown and Morgan, *Arming Slaves,* 304–329.

66. Jimenez, "La Sociedad Abolicionista," 178–181; Scott, *Slave Emancipation in Cuba,* 196.

– 4 –

HISTORY OR IDEOLOGY?

ℰℐℰ

Like many educated and compassionate men of the Enlightenment, the authors of the *Histoire Philosophique*—Raynal, Diderot, and others—longed for the day when Western political rulers, finally convinced that black slavery was immoral and unjust, would decide to end it: "Kings of the Earth, … think of your duties. Refuse the seal of your authority to the infamous and criminal trade of men turned into vile herds, and this trade shall vanish" (author's translation).[1] But at the same time as it appealed to the humane instincts of those who held the reins of power, the *Histoire Philosophique* dangled the threat of a bloodbath over the heads of everyone in the colonial world. Not because black slaves were particularly aggressive or difficult to control, but because, if slaves were pushed to the limits of human resistance, they would end up adopting forms of collective reaction which would end in their own and others' destruction. For the authors of this influential work, those who ill-treated their slaves would normally be punished indirectly, because negroes, being cowards, were also extremely vindictive and would use all means at their disposal, including flight, workplace sabotage, the poisoning of domestic animals, and even suicide in order to injure their masters. Nothing would stop them on the path to vengeance:

> The fear of torture does not intimidate them. Rarely does their mind foresee the future, and they are moreover certain that they can keep the secret of their crimes despite torture. By one of those unaccountable contradictions of the human heart, but common with both the savage and the enlightened people, the negroes can join an unshakeable fortitude to their natural cowardice. The very organization that subjects them to slavery by the laziness of the mind and the softness of the fibers, grants them unheard strength and courage for an extraordinary effort: cowards all their lives, heroes for a moment (author's translation)[2]

It was precisely that capacity for momentary heroics that justified whites' fears of the large numbers of African slaves that their thoughtlessness and greed continued to accumulate on the plantations. The insults and brutalities they were normally subjected to would have only to reach a high point, coinciding with the emergence of some leader, and they would inevitably produce an eruption of apocalyptic and direct action against the white world.

> The negroes are only in need of a chief brave enough to lead them to vengeance and carnage. Where is this great man whom nature owes to their vexed, oppressed, and tormented children? Where is he? He will appear, no doubt; he will show up and lift the sacred banner of freedom. This venerable sign will gather around him the companions of his misfortune … Spaniards, Portuguese, English, French, Dutch, all the tyrants will be prey of the daggers and the flames. The American fields will gladly drink the blood they had been waiting for so long, and the bones of so many unfortunate people lying there for three centuries will tremble with joy. The Old World will join the New in applauding them. The name of the hero who will have reinstated the rights of human kind will be blessed everywhere, and trophies will be raised to his glory (author's translation)[3]

In other words, the *Histoire philosophique* carried a dual—and in some respects contradictory—message on the characteristics of the African slave and the possibility that he might obtain his freedom by taking his fate into his own hands. The most remarkable feature of the message, however, was that it was a true anti-slavery manifesto, which cried out for a black Spartacus who might stir up the mass of slaves and, in the midst of the retaliation and the slaughter, put an end to a system of exploitation that shamed the human race. It is true that only a few important figures in Europe or the United States shared the *Histoire Philosophique's* prophecy in this most radical form.[4] Even so, it is fair to say that it converged—or was compatible—with less subversive visions widely disseminated in the more learned strata of Western societies. Philosophers and reformers such as Condorcet, Adam Smith, Benjamin Franklin, and others simply did not believe that governments could be persuaded to emancipate their slaves without a war or a general uprising, even in areas where slavery was of marginal significance. And because they thought this way, they feared the inevitable consequences of non-emancipation.

The *Histoire Philosophique* was published for the first time in 1770. Twenty-one years later, the slaves of Saint-Domingue rose up in armed rebellion, and the French colony became an inferno for white planters and their families—children impaled, women raped to death over their husbands' dead bodies, people quartered—the list of horrors seemed unending, and confirmed, in the most brutal way, the darkest of the French philosophers' predictions. Nevertheless, despite the frightening specter now hanging over colonial societies—a specter which would haunt them for the next 100 years—not many more black Sparactuses would emerge.

Even when negroes embarked on large-scale open rebellions, as in Demerara and Jamaica, they were remarkably restrained. There were cases, like that of the Nat Turner rebellion in Virginia, where nearly 60 people were massacred, but these were unusual cases, and for reasons which remained obscure. Thus surprisingly, and despite the fact that the image of a black Spartacus continued to inspire prophecies, for better or worse it was the *Histoire Philosophique's* more optimistic expectations, those which appealed to the goodwill of the lords of the earth, which came to the fore. Moreover, by the time the first plantations were set on fire in Saint-Domingue, Pennsylvania and other North American states had decreed their first laws providing for gradual emancipation. That liberating tendency made slow but steady progress, so that by the end of the nineteenth century slavery had disappeared from the New World.

For the men of the nineteenth century, the disappearance of slavery was almost a miracle, if only because it had been achieved not so much through the daggers of black Spartacuses—as the *Histoire Philosophique* had anticipated—but by the enlightened will of the masters. This was so unexpected and admirable that it produced a historiographical interpretation bestowing high praise on the abolitionist policies of the Western nations.[5] It was in this self-congratulatory context that Western countries honored their humanitarian heroes—from Wilberforce to Lincoln, and Schöelcher to Sá da Bandeira—and in England, Lecky, in his treatise on European morality, publicly described the anti-slavery crusade as one of the most virtuous episodes in the history of nations.[6]

The celebrations surrounding the whites' role meant that the blacks' role was overshadowed or forgotten. Once again they were viewed as the passive beings that the *Histoire Philosophique* and many other works had been describing for centuries. That renewed belief in the docile nature and even the cowardice or listlessness of the slave provided some foundation for emerging racist theories of domination over the inhabitants of Africa— at a time when the conquest of the Dark Continent was just beginning— and over former slaves who, despite their legally free status, continued to be the target of various forms of discrimination, injustice, and violence. It is true that in overall terms, and while the memory of the terrible example of Haiti was still fresh, subsequent emancipations seemed to have taken place in a relatively controlled manner. They had been resolved in the parliaments of Europe, and blacks had often adopted an attitude of quiet expectation while they were ongoing. Nevertheless, there had been a sprinkling of unsuccessful revolts as a result of false rumors of freedom or a great desire for vengeance—or both. In other cases, emancipation had taken place against the backdrop of the drums of war, as happened in most of the American continent, where African slaves had collaborated actively with the forces of emancipation, fighting and dying alongside white and creole soldiers in the armies of Bolívar and the North American Union.

Former slaves found it difficult to foster these recollections, especially those who were uncomfortable with the memory of slavery and

preferred to sidestep a past carrying the stigma of absolute subjection—
which was humiliating to them. They were more interested in looking to
the future and building a new identity in order to prop up their still frag-
ile citizenship.[7] But this distancing from the past was not total: some believed that the new African-American identity should be based precisely
and above all on the recollection of their heroic struggle. Committed to
reacting against racism and to emphasizing the involvement of negroes in
the process of emancipation, several militant abolitionists sought to bring
that heroic struggle to the forefront of memory and, going beyond this,
started to associate emancipations—all of them—with the anti-slavery
struggle conducted in what was to become Haiti, the only place where
that struggle led to the general abolition of slavery. As previously mentioned, the Saint-Domingue rebellion was significant for the British abolitionists, who had been able to use it to campaign against any more
slaves being brought into the colonies, and later it was used against slavery itself. Now, however, some of those who had fought for abolitionism
and in the struggle for the rights of former slaves sought to put a different light on the events in Haiti. It was in this spirit that, at the end of the
nineteenth century, one of the best-known and most respected black abolitionists of his time gave a speech in Chicago in which he proclaimed
that the Saint-Domingue rebellion had been decisive in achieving universal emancipation:

> We should not forget that the freedom you and I enjoy today, that the freedom
> that 800,000 colored people enjoy in the British West Indies, the freedom that
> has come to the colored race the world over, is largely due to the brave stand
> taken by the black sons of Haiti ninety years ago. When they struck for
> freedom … they struck for the freedom of every black man in the world.

The orator clearly recognized that blacks also owed a lot to the abolitionist societies that had been set up in Britain, the United States, and
other western countries. But, as he said, they owed "incomparably more
to Haiti than to them all."[8]

The speaker was Frederick Douglass, a man who had been born a
slave in Maryland in 1818, and who was well-acquainted with the sor-
rows of slavery: the early separation from his mother, the whip, the frequent sale or rental to more or less brutal masters.[9] Douglass managed to
escape to New York in 1838, becoming an influential abolitionist and even
acting as a consul and ambassador for the United States. Understandably,
his viewpoint was one of struggle and commitment on behalf of the black
cause, a viewpoint seeking to counteract the African's reputation as a
passive and irrelevant being, as far as abolition was concerned, with the
image of a black who was fighting for freedom. In the effort to make that
contrast, Douglass reformulated or repaired the partially erroneous pre-
diction made in the *Histoire Philosophique,* by evoking a kind of worldwide
Black Spartacus whose actions, even if initially and objectively limited to
Haiti, were telescoped over time and would in the end have a decisive

bearing on the whole slave-owning world. In his interpretation, the rebellion of Saint-Domingue was not just a bloody event that frightened the colonial world for decades. It was a symbol of the anti-slavery struggle and the true well-spring of the abolition accomplished by the Western countries.

Contrary to what one might think, the image of oppressed black slaves taking up arms to break the fetters of oppression was not readily digestible in the nineteenth century, even for the romantic mind. It is true that there was a literary tradition in Western culture that celebrated and cherished the figure of the heroic slave. But it would be wrong to assume that Douglass' speeches were in line with this tradition—which dated at least from the beginning of the seventeenth century and had been enriched by some of the most celebrated names of literary romanticism, if only because the humanitarian and romantic mind, which focused on the drama of the human condition and on moral slavery, rarely addressed the problem of negro slaves who might embody the ideal of freedom through rebellion and armed struggle. I am of course not forgetting a novel like *Dred,* by Harriet Beecher Stowe, nor am I minimizing its enormous public success. Published for the first time in 1856, the work sold 165,000 copies in Great Britain in its first year and 150,000 in the United States—astonishing numbers when considered in the light of the fact that it took some ten years for Melville's *Moby Dick* to sell 2,000 copies. Over the following three years, the novel was adapted as a play and published in Austria, Bulgaria, France, Germany, Holland, Italy, Poland, and Sweden. In Stowe's narrative, Dred was the son of Denmark Vessey, the leader of the 1822 conspiracy to attack Charleston. This immediately related him to the history of black resistance in the United States. That heir to the spirit of slave rebelliousness lived as a maroon, escaping to the swamps surrounding North Carolina and Virginia and dreaming of the day when a general uprising might bring freedom to the Africans. But even if that uprising did not take place, Dred believed firmly in the liberating power of violence. As he himself said, "Nat Turner's rebellion so frightened the whites that they had come very close to decreeing emancipation."[10]

In the novel, Dred does not live to see his dream of revenge and freedom realized, because he is killed by white planters in the course of an attack on his hiding place. Even so, this work by Harriet Stowe focused more on those slaves who found a way of reacting and fighting against an oppressive system than on those who submitted to it. However, *Dred* was an unusual work in the context of the times and in relation to slave rebelliousness overall. Moreover, the novelist's previous and most famous novel, *Uncle Tom's Cabin,* extolled the virtues of the obedient, docile, and resigned slave, in the character of Uncle Tom, who would finally succumb to ill-treatment without a single gesture of revolt.[11] And even in those novels in which rebellion was an integral part of the plot and where possible options for dealing with the injustices of slavery appeared, what romanticism generally had to offer was revolts that were tangential, negative, and far removed from the individual tragedy that was the main focus of concern. *Bug-Jargal* is a good example. Published for the first time in 1826, this novel by Victor Hugo was set precisely in Saint-Domingue at the time of the 1791 revolt. But the hero, Bug-Jargal, was anything but a rebel slave. To suit contemporary standards of taste, he was portrayed as a Herculean black, the son of a king of the Congo. He spoke several languages and his gentlemanly behavior and nobility of character distanced him from the mass of rebellious slaves, bringing him closer to the standards recognized and appreciated by white morality. A love for Marie (which was not reciprocated) and a debt of gratitude to Léopold d'Auverney, meant that he gave his own life to protect the young couple caught up in the vortex of the slave revolt. Bug-Jargal was one of the leaders of that revolt, not so much because he was driven to rebel by an insatiable thirst for revenge or by the desire to be free or to invert the social hierarchy, but because leadership was inherent in his own noble origins and his prestige among the slave masses. In fact, Victor Hugo felt a constant need to emphasize the contrasts between a magnanimous, generous, almost peace-making Bug-Jargal and other rebel leaders, real people such as Jean-François, Biassou, and even Toussaint himself, who were always characterized as cruel and ignoble figures. It was those figures who appropriated the device of freedom, but did it with a cacophony of contradictory statements and such confusion of purpose that it was clear their rebel movement had no true aim. That is why Victor Hugo's novel ends up suggesting that the freeing of Haiti's slaves was due more to the hasty concessions of radical power in Paris than to the armed struggle of the slaves.[12]

Apart from the fact that Douglass' opinions were not automatically in harmony with the romantic view of slave revolts, they also lacked a historiographical foundation to bolster the mental image of a rebellious slave as the universal liberator of the black man. That historiographical foundation only began to emerge after the Second World War, thanks to the work of various Marxist-inspired historians, among whom the names of Cyril L.R. James, Herbert Aptheker, and Eric Williams stand out by virtue of the prominence they later achieved. In 1938, James, who was a native of Trinidad, published *The Black Jacobins*, a history of the revolt of Saint-Domingue, which placed black slaves at the center of the narrative as the main political actors in the anti-colonial and class struggle. James praised the courage with which the slaves had been able to take their destiny into their own hands in the face of powerful adversaries, gaining their freedom with the support of the revolutionary masses in Paris and later through their own sacrifice.[13] Herbert Aptheker did something similar for the history of the United States. In the book he published in 1943, *American Negro Slave Revolts*, he identified—apparently in very exaggerated numbers—hundreds of episodes of armed slave resistance and glorified the image of Nat Turner and other rebels. Instead of a resigned and passive negro waiting patiently for slavery to come to an end, Aptheker portrayed a permanent rebel and described the fear that rebel engendered in the white population. The whole book is based on an initial chapter entitled "The fear of rebellion," and leads to the conclusion that that fear had been significant in organizing and strengthening the abolitionist movement.[14] At approximately the same time, the idea that slave revolts had played a significant role in abolitionism extended also to Britain. Eric Williams was one of the first to highlight the role the slave threat had played in the development of British abolitionism. Through their resistance, slaves had created a pressure so strong that, at a given point, those in power in London had no other choice. In Williams' neat formula, it was either "emancipation from above, or emancipation from below. But emancipation."[15]

Initially these interpretations had a limited impact, partly because of these writers' position on the left of the political spectrum, especially Aptheker, a member of the Communist party who remained faithful to the orthodox line, supporting Stalin and suffering under McCarthyism (as would James, a self-confessed Trotskyist who was living in the United States at that time). But having remained under cover for a while, interpretations or suggestions of this sort revived strongly in the electrifying ideological climate of the 1960s. The works of James, Williams, and Aptheker were republished, and a new generation of historians began to study and celebrate the various forms of slave resistance. Thanks to their work, we now know a great deal more about the motivation of the rebels, on the ways information circulated among them, and on how conspiracies and revolts were organized. However, as has been mentioned in the introduction, some of these historians so exaggerated their thesis of slave resistance forcing open the door of abolition that they ended up relegating white politicians and abolitionists to a secondary or residual role. In 1978, Richard Hart, for example, suggested that British slaves virtually emancipated themselves by their late rebellions.[16] Hilary Beckles and others even regarded the slave revolts of Jamaica and other parts of the West Indies as the palpable manifestations of a "blacks' anti-slavery movement," which preceded by decades or centuries its European counterpart and the package of abolitionist legislation that the British Parliament approved from the end of the eighteenth century onwards. Such laws—they aver—were nothing more than a part of the final chapter of the epic struggle of slave populations down the centuries, and not even the most important part at that.[17] Evidence of the overestimation of slave resistance is likewise to be found in other historiographies. Nelly Schmidt's approach, as mentioned above, is close to that of Beckles, but even more radical. And Elikia M'Bokolo, referring to the French case, argued that the abolition of slavery had been "the triumph of a long-term struggle by the slaves," something due much more to their own efforts than to a sudden humanitarian impulse on the part of whites.[18] Moreover, M'Bokolo and other French historians interpret the Haitian Revolution as the culmination of a series of slave revolts that had troubled the slave-owning society of Saint-Domingue from the beginning.[19] Peter Blanchard considered that the end of Peruvian slavery was the result of a loss of support by its defenders and of "small victories by the antislavery forces ..., the most important of which was the resistance of the slaves." It was slave resistance—that according to Blanchard was a direct attack upon the slavery system and included actions such as running away, self-purchase, robbery, and murder, fighting other slaves or coolies, and joining a gang of highwaymen—that "stimulated white abolitionists into renewed activity."[20]

What we have here is a historiography substantially tainted by ideology. As we saw earlier, the theory that abolition was the outcome of repeated struggles by the slaves seeking freedom is a simplistic interpretation deriving from the even more simplistic paradigm of the omnipresence of slave resistance. It is true that the idea of oppression inevitably leading to rebellion has been repeated for centuries in revolutionary discourse, as has the maxim been repeated that the slaves were ever ready to overthrow the system of slavery. But these are ingenuous notions in connection with the nature of the relations of absolute power and complete domination on which slavery rested. If this were not so—as Davis pertinently asks—how could one explain the fact that two or three adult whites could keep control over a hundred or two hundred slaves in an isolated Caribbean plantation?[21]

The response of Africans—and other peoples—to slavery is very complex and is simply not compatible with schematic and simplistic perspectives. We should never underestimate the fact that, in nearly all of the revolts, many slaves preferred to remain loyal to their masters. One example will suffice, among many: in the 1733 revolt on the small island of St. John, only 14 percent of the slave population joined the rebel movement; the vast majority remained loyal and took an active part in the fight against the rebels.[22] This was common behavior, even in circumstances as extreme as those in Saint-Domingue[23]. Many rebellions were even aborted or suppressed at birth because loyal slaves exposed them. For the informers, the path to freedom involved cooperation with the white authorities, and the inevitable execution of their brothers in blood and adversity, not rebellion.

Nor should we forget that those of mixed race—like the maroons—contributed heavily to smashing rebel slave forces on the ground. In most cases, at least in the British colonies, free negro and Creole communities were generally pro-slavery: it is not realistic to expect they would take up the common cause of the rebels.[24] Nor should we forget that the vision outlined in the *Histoire Philosophique* was not necessarily that of the slaves. Life consists of resistance, resignation, and diplomacy, and the slaves, human beings that they were, were no exception to that general rule. Recent historiography has shown that the strategy usually adopted by slaves in the Caribbean and other regions was not rebellion, but continuous negotiation with the masters and overseers, and that their objectives were not always related to freedom and the rejection of slavery—as the whites saw it—but were much more comprehensible and tangible: the slaves wanted more land and more time to grow food for themselves and for selling in the local market; they wanted monetary rewards for carrying out certain services; they wanted the right to a fuller and more satisfactory family and social life (which meant being able to marry and having freedom of religious worship). All of this is possibly typical human behavior in situations of major subordination or dependency. Soldiers were often treated as slaves, often coerced or press-ganged, which in turn made them a potentially rebel mass, with the aggravating factor of being an armed mass. But most of those men were willing to obey orders and even to risk their lives fighting for some national purpose or other.[25] For thousands of years, in one way or another, the majority of human beings have been forced to work hard and to accept prevailing hierarchies of power, without that having degenerated into rebellion.

Having said this, it is also true that slave rebellions could and did take place, and there were dozens of them, especially from the end of the eighteenth century onward. But was it those rebellions that led directly or indirectly to abolition? As we have seen, the answer is generally negative. Armed revolts were always an integral part of slavery. Nevertheless, slavery persisted until the nineteenth and twentieth centuries, for two reasons: the rebels' objectives were not necessarily or generally abolitionist; and the vast majority of those revolts were defeated. The slave rebellion led by Spartacus did not end slavery; its outcome, rather, was a crushing military defeat and 6,000 slaves crucified on the Via Appia.[26] That tragic story and others like it were repeated over the centuries, in the American colonies as well where, with a few exceptions, black slave revolts were put down with enormous cruelty. Rebellion, or any other form of violent resistance, was futile and suicidal in a slave-holding society, unless, as happened in Saint-Domingue, that society was involved in a revolution and civil war dividing the slave-owners themselves. It is true that slave revolts were more frequent in colonial societies, where there was often a dangerously unfavorable imbalance of numbers in favor of blacks and usually producing great fear and apprehension. But it is also true that, as the days passed, those feelings tended to diminish, and that fear never prevented the masters from handing out weapons to some of their slaves, as it also did not prevent them from continuing to practice slavery. That is why the French remained tied to their slave-holding colonies despite the terrifying outcome of the Saint-Domingue rebellion.[27] That is why Cuba, which had the Haitian slaughter house directly in front of it, and despite the warnings of the more fearful, judged it right to import more slaves.[28]

As this analysis has shown, the vast majority of abolitions were not preceded by rebellions. On the contrary, when rebellions occurred, they generally made the path to freedom more difficult, in that they led to a hardening of masters' attitudes and to more or less bloody repression. The exceptions to this rule were the revolt of Saint-Domingue, which led to French abolition in 1794, and the revolt in Jamaica, which took place precisely during a time when British emancipationism was reaching its height. But these are special cases (and, in the French case an inconsistent one, because slavery was restored by Napoleon in 1802).

The exceptional nature of these two examples does not mean that the slaves' role was insignificant. It means merely that that role must be properly located, with due consideration of its relative importance. The theory that the slaves emancipated themselves is wholly unsustainable. As Craton says regarding Britain, "it would be perverse to claim that slaves actually achieved their own emancipation by resistance. The changes that occurred in 1808, 1834, and 1838 were decreed and enforced by the imperial parliament, after a majority of its members became convinced by arguments that slavery was at the same time, morally evil, economically inefficient, and politically unwise." Even so, Craton does attempt a compromise that attaches equal importance to emancipation by the metropolitan powers and slave agitation. His formula is as follows: "slave resistance was endemic, merely changing its forms, and in the last phase slave unrest just as much influenced metropolitan ideas and actions as vice versa."[29] But this Solomonic judgment does not completely solve the problem. The difficulty lies precisely in the combination of the word "endemic" with the quoted phrase "in the last phase." Why "in the last phase"? What was so special about that last phase, given that rebellion was known to be endemic in itself? The answer is, clearly, abolitionism (and, to a lesser extent, the spirit of independence that arose in certain American regions). Herein lay the genuinely new and specific element in an already known and long insoluble equation. And this was the element making it possible for the creole elites, who had some access to information from the newspapers or from close contact with the masters, to take on a role as leaders of the revolutionary potential of the slave masses, alongside the slaves themselves. They were thus able to lead them not towards slaughter and a new form of slavery—in the African way—but in a direction shaped by a new era, a direction compatible with what was going on in the world outside.

What was new in the context of the many revolts that took place as the eighteenth century turned into the nineteenth was that, for the first time, the slaves could count on the support of many whites who lived outside the Afro-American colonial world of slavery, of those who, like the missionaries, had ventured into that world, and also of those local inhabitants who wished to be free of metropolitan supervision and saw in the slaves valuable allies in their armed struggle for independence. The entry of these actors, and the way the slaves themselves internalized the messages received from each of these groups and adjusting them to their needs, took the urge to rebel to a higher level, which was usually less violent, and to new political objectives, exposing the barbarity with which slavery operated in the colonies or former colonies. It was that perception, of which the abolitionists clearly took advantage, that decisively changed public opinion and Western political authorities into supporters of emancipation.

It should nevertheless be emphasized that only where there was a properly established and properly grounded movement for emancipation could revolts contribute to strengthening and supporting anti-slavery arguments. We should remember that the slave insurrections that took place in 1795–96 on Granada and St. Vincent caused greater destruction and loss of life amongst the British population than the subsequent rebellions in Barbados, Demerara, and Jamaica. But in that still early phase of the emancipation movement, and because they were set in the context of the war between the French and the British, these events had little impact, and were literally wiped from the memory of metropolitan abolitionists.[30] We should also recall that the revolts that took place in the first half of the nineteenth century in Brazil found no echo, because there was little or no true abolitionism in Brazil at that time. Finally, we should underline the fact that, as far as the slaves were concerned, a sufficiently influential core of already well-educated creoles or negroes was needed in order to interpret the revolutionary or anti-slavery messages that were in circulation and to channel rebels in the direction of demanding universal freedom; if, by contrast, revolts were led by recently arrived negroes or by those who for some reason were still immune to the new Western ideologies, then they would continue to develop along the traditional lines of death to the whites and the perpetuation of the relations of slavery, with new slaves and new masters.

In sum, the role of the runaway or rebel slave in achieving his own freedom was considerable, but his role in direct action to free all slaves was limited. It was not escapes and revolts common events in the history of slavery—but other, more decisive factors, which, at a given moment, pushed the peoples of the West toward abolition. It was those factors, and especially the change of attitude regarding the just and necessary nature of slavery, which enabled a new standard of universal freedom to be developed and applied. This was very different to the individual or group freedom envisaged up to that time by slave escapes and uprisings. It is those factors—which we may label, in overall terms, as abolitionism—that constitute the strategic variable of emancipation. Those who claim otherwise are basing themselves less on profound and impartial analysis and more on a merely ideological position that seeks to restore dignity to the oppressed and their descendants by manipulating history.

Notes

1. "Rois de la terre, ...pensez à vos devoirs. Refusez le sceau de votre autorité au trafic infâme et criminel d'hommes convertis en vils troupeaux et ce commerce disparaîtra." Guillaume-Thomas Raynal, *Histoire philosophique et politique des établissements et du commerce des Européens dans les deux Indes* (Paris, 1770), Liv. XI, ch. 24, vol. III.

2. "La crainte des supplices ne les arrête point. Il entre rarement dans leur caractère de prévoir l'avenir et d'ailleurs ils sont bien assurés de tenir le secret de leur crime à l'épreuve des tortures. Par une de ces contrariétés inexplicables du coeur humain, mais communes à tous les peuples éclairés ou sauvages, on voit les nègres allier à leur poltronnerie naturelle, une fermeté inébranlable. La même organisation qui les soumet à la servitude par la paresse de l'esprit et le relâchement des fibres, leur donne une vigueur, un courage inouïs, pour un effort extraordinaire: lâches toute leur vie, héros un moment."
   Ibid., Liv. XI, ch. 22, vol. III.

3. "Il ne manque aux nègres qu'un chef assez courageux pour les conduire à la vengeance et au carnage. Où est-il, ce grand homme que la nature doit à ses enfants vexés, opprimés, tourmentés? Où est-il? Il paraîtra, n'en doutons pas; il se montrera, il lèvera l'étendard sacré de la liberté. Ce signal vénérable rassemblera autour de lui les compagnons de son infortune ... Espagnols, Portugais, Anglais, Français, Hollandais, tous leurs tyrans deviendront la proie du fer et de la flamme. Les champs américains s'enivreront avec transport d'un sang qu'ils attendaient depuis si longtemps et les ossements de tant d'infortunés entassés depuis trois siècles, tressailliront de joie. L'Ancien Monde joindra ses applaudissements au Nouveau. Partout on bénira le nom du héros qu'aura rétabli les droits de l'espèce humaine, partout on érigera des trophées à sa gloire." Ibid., Liv. XI, ch. 24, vol. III.

4. David B. Davis, *Inhuman Bondage: The Rise and Fall of Slavery in the New World* (New York and London: Oxford University Press, 2006), 159. It seems plausible to argue that the more radical tirades in the *Histoire Philosophique*, which was a collective work, were written by Pechméja. A very similar version of the bloodbath prophecy contained in the *Histoire Philosophique* also appeared in an article by Louis-Sébastien Mercier who, for some, was the true inspiration for the apocalyptic vision (see Dubois, *Les vengeurs du Nouveau Monde. Histoire de la Révolution Haïtienne* (Rennes: Les Perséides, 2005), 90–91).

5. Alexis de Tocqueville, "On the Emancipation of Slaves" (1843), in *Tocqueville and Beaumont on Social Reform*, ed. Seymour Drescher (New York: Harper & Row, 1968), 138.

6. W.E.H. Lecky, *A History of European Morals*, 6th ed., vol. 2 (London, 1884), 153.

7. David W. Blight, "If you don't tell it like it was, it can never be as it ought to be," in *Slavery and Public History. The Tough Stuff of American Memory*, eds. James Oliver Horton and Lois E. Horton (New York and London: The New Press, 2006), 27.

8. Quoted in David B. Davis, "Impact of the French and Haitian Revolutions," in *The Impact of the Haitian Revolution in the Atlantic World*, ed. David P. Geggus (University of South Carolina Press, 2001), 3.

9. In 1845, Frederick Douglass published the *Narrative of the Life of Frederick Douglass, an American Slave, written by Himself*. I used the Portuguese version translated by Luís Nogueira (*Memórias de um Escravo Africano* (Lisboa: Mareantes Editora, 2005).

10. Harriet Beecher Stowe, *Dred. A Tale of the Great Dismal Swamp* (Edinburgh: Edinburgh University Press, 1999; 1st ed., 1856), 435.

11. Harriet Beecher Stowe, *Uncle Tom's Cabin or, Life Among the Lowly* (New York: Penguin Books, 1986; 1st ed., 1852), 581–585.

12. Victor Hugo, *Romans* (Paris: L'Intégrale/Seuil, 1965).

13. Cyril L.R. James, *The Black Jacobins. Toussaint L'Ouverture and the San Domingo Revolution* (London: Allison & Busby, 1980; 1st ed., 1938).

14. Herbert Aptheker, *American Negro Slave Revolts* (New York: International Publishers, 1993; 1st ed., 1943), 18ff. and 373.

15. Eric Williams, *Capitalism and Slavery* (London: Andre Deutch, 1964; 1st ed., 1944), 208. Williams was also born in Trinidad (and was a pupil of Cyril L.R. James). He went to Oxford, where he obtained a Ph.D., and to the United States, where he lectured, before returning to the land of his birth. There he settled and formed a political party. For many years, he was prime minister of Trinidad and Tobago.

16. In the most recent edition, Hart argues for a less radical point of view, based on the belief that the actions of the slaves were decisive only in the sense that they hastened emancipation. As he says, revolts and conspiracies, in particular the 1831 rebellion in Jamaica, "made it impossible for the British government, as had been his wont, to delay indefinitely the emancipation of the slaves. The abolition of slavery was carried out from above by legislative enactment. But ... it was the rebellious slaves who re-set the time table for emancipation." Richard Hart, *Slaves Who Abolished Slavery. Blacks in Rebellion* (Mona: University of the West Indies Press, 2002), 334–335.

17. Hilary McD. Beckles, "Caribbean Anti-Slavery: The self-liberation ethos of enslaved Blacks," in *Caribbean Slave Society and Economy,* eds. Hilary McD. Beckles and Verene Shepherd (Kingston and London: James Currey Publishers, 1991), 363–364 and 371.

18. Elikia M'Bokolo, *Afrique Noire. Histoire et civilisations* (Paris: Hatier-Aupelf. Uref, 1995), Portuguese translation by Alfredo Margarido, *África negra. História e civilizações,* volume I (Lisboa: Vulgata, 2003), 342. See also the article by the same author in Le Monde Diplomatique, April 1998.

19. Cf. Giulia Bonacci, Dimitri Béchacq, and Nicolas Rey, *La Révolution haïtienne au-delà de ses frontières* (Paris: Karthala, 2006), 7 and 13.

20. Peter Blanchard, *Slavery and Abolition in Early Republican Peru* (Wilmington: Scholarly Resources Books, 1992), xiv–xv and 95ff.

21. David B. Davis, *In the Image of God. Religion, Moral Values, and Our Heritage of Slavery* (New Haven: Yale University Press, 2001), 325.

22. Isaac Dookhan, *A History of the Virgin Islands, University Press of the West Indies* (Kingston, 1994), 169.

23. Dubois, *Les vengeurs du Nouveau Monde,* 138 and 206.

24. Davis, *Inhuman Bondage,* 121; Matt D. Childs, *The 1812 Aponte Rebellion in Cuba and the Struggle against Atlantic Slavery* (Chapel Hill: The University of North Carolina Press, 2006), 68–69.

25. Davis, *Inhuman Bondage,* p. 122.

26. Keith Bradley, *Slavery and Rebellion in the Roman World, 140 B.C.–70 B.C.* (Bloomington and Indianapolis: Indiana University Press, 1998; 1st ed., 1989), 92.

27. Seymour Drescher, "The Limits of Example," in *The Impact of the Haitian Revolution in the Atlantic World,* ed. David P. Geggus (University of South Carolina Press, 2001), 11.

28. Childs, *The 1812 Aponte Rebellion,* 34–35.

29. Michael Craton, *Testing the Chains: Resistance to Slavery in the British West Indies* (Ithaca, NY and London: Cornell University Press, 1982), 242.

30. Seymour Drescher, *Capitalism and Antislavery: British Mobilization in Comparative Perspective* (New York: Oxford University Press, 1987), 105.

CONCLUSIONS

A bolitionism arose and developed in the West in the last thirty or so
years of the eighteenth century. Slavery had been rejected in both
thought and action in earlier times—in Europe and in other regions of the
world. It had been rejected at a nation, group or individual level, but
there had never been a political movement that regarded slavery as something intolerable not only endogenously but universally, as well. In this
respect, abolitionism is specific to the culture and history of the West (even
though the subsequent attitudes and actions of European and American
politicians advised it to, or imposed it on, the rest of the world).

This specific nature of abolitionism was—and continues to be—frequently underrated. From quite early on, some tried to see the abolitionist movement as the simple expression of political and material interests
connected with the West's industrialization and the development of
forms of cultural and economic imperialism. This is a narrow and cynical
view, which the historiography of the last three decades irretrievably
has—it is to be hoped—pulled apart. But there are some types of reasoning that are more difficult to dislodge, because they are often insidious or
implicit. Everyone knows that India, China, Korea, the Islamic worlds,
and sub-Saharan Africa had forms of slavery that also implied the "social
death" of the slave, in Patterson's use of the concept.[1] None of those civilizations, however, developed a *corpus* of critical assessments of slavery
like those that would arise in the West. Even so, those who rush to condemn the historical relationship of Western peoples with slavery seem
less willing to praise that critical *corpus* and the corresponding abolitionist work done by Western nations from the end of the eighteenth century
on. It seems that they do not particularly rate abolitionism perhaps because they feel that the system of negro slavery in the colonial world
was so unique in the violence it imposed that only that specific system
of slavery could have given rise to the level of total rejection inherent in
abolitionism.

I presume it will not be necessary to point out that this implication is a simple intellectual device, which hides the problem instead of solving it. In actual fact, regardless of where we may wish to place the transatlantic slave trade and the conditions of modern colonial slavery on an imaginary Richter scale of human suffering, and regardless too of our views on the ultimate nature of the abolitionist movement, it is imperative to acknowledge that there was a political, moral, and economic philosophy underlying that movement, as well as a certain sensibility, which for a time were exclusive to the Western world. Strictly speaking, this does not mean that such attributes were exclusive to western man. Millions of Africans were exported to the Americas (and, in much lower numbers, to Europe as well) and that multitude of the exploited took part in the birth and development of the Western abolitionist movement, whether directly or indirectly. In recent decades, historians have sought to examine that participation, but they have often done so in a stereotyped manner, focusing on issues relating to reactive or violent affirmation and limiting the negro slave to the role of resister or rebel.

As has already been mentioned, rebellion was not generally the path to abolitionism. Saint-Domingue was the only case where slaves who resorted to fighting were able to keep the freedom that had been given them by the French colonial authorities in 1793, a decision which Napoleonic France would later try to reverse, without success. But the events of Saint-Domingue did not start a philogenetic line tying it in to subsequent abolitionist processes. We need only think of the large chronological gap separating them from the British, French, North American, Portuguese, and Brazilian emancipations, which took place 40, 50, 70, 80, and 95 years after emancipation in Saint-Domingue. These emancipations were not offsprings of the Haitian revolt, but of a very different process. It was the decision to abolish slavery, taken in various regions of the northern United States, that started the era of emancipation, and the decisive moment of that era was the peaceful release of almost 800,000 slaves in the British colonies in the 1830s. This was always how things were understood by those who proposed and approved the abolitions. As I hope to have demonstrated, there were two pathways to abolition: the rebellious one, and the reformist and legal one. The insurrectionist pathway was successful just once. All of the other abolitions followed the path of law and reform. That is why the events following 1789 should be seen not as a continuum but as two series, each one having its own logic and tradition: there was the revolutionary method in Haiti, under which slave revolts played a key role in hastening the process; and there was the reform method (with its American variant—started in the United States—and its British variant). The two pathways and traditions rarely converged. And I use the word rarely because, in the British case, and thanks to the efforts of the rebel slaves in Barbados, Demerara, and Jamaica, the revolutionary logic sought on three or four occasions to merge with the reformist pathway.

The main contribution the slaves made to the advance of abolitionism was not therefore the direct struggle, as symbolized in the tragic events of Haiti. It was rather their relative restraint, or self-limiting struggle, in seeking harmony with the abolitionist movement, which was growing on the outside and of which the slaves soon sensed and sought to be part. As, moreover, they tried to be part of the armies fighting for the political creeds that promised them freedom. In July 1763, the 54th Massachusetts Infantry regiment—the first negro regiment formed in the northern United States—was in the front line of the attack on fort Wagner, the stronghold guarding the entrance to Charleston, South Carolina. The commander of the black troops was the young colonel Robert Gould Shaw, a member of a prominent Boston abolitionist family, who would die in the attack on the fort, in which more than 40 percent of the men in his regiment were lost. This epic story, portrayed in the excellent film *Glory* by Edward Zwick (1989), reflects the self-denial of those who gave their all to fight and die for the end of slavery. In total, 215,000 negroes (60 percent of whom were former slaves) served in the Union army during the Civil War, representing around 10 percent of the whole, a contingent that, in itself, made it difficult to retain slavery after the war—if by chance that had been the intention of the white authorities. There were 68,000 black soldiers who died or went missing in action, which represents almost 20 percent of total Union losses.[2]

But the Fort Wagner episode also reflects probably the most fruitful contribution of black slaves or former slaves to abolition, that is to say, the search for a convergence with the world of the whites, or rather, with the world of white abolitionists. What they sought was not so much radical confrontation, but proper identification of the competing forces and cooperation with those that would best defend their interests. Contrary to what slavers and racists thought, blacks were not stupid by nature, and resistance was not the only behavioral response available to them. Many slaves who rebelled or demonstrated during the nineteenth century held back their passion for revenge in the hope that their restraint and forbearance might be understood and serve the political purposes of those whites who, near or far, were fighting for their cause. Many of those rebels or demonstrators were slaughtered in Demerara, Jamaica, and other regions of America. But their exemplary sacrifice bore fruit, because it had taken place in a cultural context increasingly unfavorable to slavery, on which those who were demanding urgent change in the way Western societies integrated and exploited blacks were able to capitalize.

The search for a common voice among slaves and abolitionists brings very subtle mechanisms into play that are difficult to analyze. Nonetheless, this seems a better way of achieving an understanding of the role of slaves in abolition than the path of preconceived ideas and virtual propaganda followed by some historians.

Notes

1. Orlando Patterson, *Slavery and Social Death. A Comparative Study* (Cambridge, MA and London: Harvard University Press, 1982).
2. David B. Davis, *The Boisterous Sea of Liberty. A Documentary History of America from Discovery Through the Civil War* (New York and Oxford: Oxford University Press, 1998), 529.

BIBLIOGRAPHY

Aimes, Hubert H.S. *A History of Slavery in Cuba, 1511 to 1868*. New York: Octagon Books, 1967.

Anstey, Roger. "The Pattern of British Abolitionism in the Eighteenth and Nineteenth Centuries." In *Anti-slavery, Religion and Reform: Essays in the Memory of Roger Anstey*, edited by Christine Bolt and Seymour Drescher, 19–42. Dawson: Folkestone, 1980.

———. "Religion and British Slave Emancipation." In *The Abolition of the Atlantic Slave Trade. Origins and Effects in Europe, Africa and the Americas*, edited by David Eltis and James Walvin, 37–61. Madison: The University of Winsconsin Press, 1981.

Aptheker, Herbert. *Abolitionism. A Revolutionary Movement*. Boston: Twayne Publishers, 1992; 1st. ed., 1989.

———. *American Negro Slave Revolts*. New York: International Publishers, 1993; 1st ed., 1943.

Beckles, Hilary McD. "Caribbean Anti-Slavery: The self-liberation ethos of enslaved Blacks." In *Caribbean Slave Society and Economy*, edited by Hilary McD. Beckles and Verene Shepherd, 363–372. Kingston and London: James Currey Publishers, 1991.

———. "Emancipation by law or War? Wilberforce and the 1816 Barbados slave rebellion." In *Abolition and Its Aftermath. The Historical Context, 1790–1916*, edited by David Richardson, 80–104. London: Frank Cass, 1985.

———. "From Land to Sea: Runaway Barbados Slaves and Servants, 1630–1700." In *Slavery and Abolition*, 6, (1985): 82–83.

——— and Verene Shepherd, eds. *Caribbean Slave Society and Economy*. Kingston and London: James Currey Publishers, 1991.

Blackburn, Robin. *The Overthrow of Colonial Slavery, 1776–1848*. London and New York: Verso, 1988.

Blanchard, Peter. *Slavery and Abolition in Early Republican Peru*. Wilmington: Scholarly Resources Books, 1992.

———. "The Slave Soldiers of Spanish South America: From Independence to Abolition." In *Arming Slaves From Classical Times to the Modern Age*, edited by

Christopher Leslie Brown and Philip D. Morgan, 255–273. New Haven and London: Yale University Press, 2006.

Blight, David W. "If you don't tell it like it was, it can never be as it ought to be." In *Slavery and Public History. The Though Stuff of American Memory*, edited by James Oliver Horton and Lois E. Horton, 19–33. New York and London: The New Press, 2006.

Bonacci, Giulia, Dimitri Béchacq, and Nicolas Rey. *La Révolution haïtienne au-delà de ses frontiers*. Paris: Karthala, 2006.

Bradley, Keith. *Slavery and Rebellion in the Roman World, 140 B.C.–70 B.C.* Bloomington and Indianapolis: Indiana University Press, 1998; 1st ed., 1989.

Brown, Christopher Leslie and Philip D. Morgan, eds. *Arming Slaves From Classical Times to the Modern Age*. New Haven and London: Yale University Press, 2006.

Caldeira, Arlindo Manuel. "Rebelião e outras formas de resistência à escravatura na ilha de São Tomé." In *Africana Studia*, 7 (2004): 101–136.

Cano, Maria Magdalena Guerrero. "Incidencias esclavistas tras la emancipacion en Santo Domingo." In *Esclavitud y Derechos Humanos. La lucha por la libertad del negro en el siglo XIX*, edited by Francisco de Solano and Agustín Guimerá, 331–342. Madrid: CSIC/CEH, 1986.

Chatillon, Marcel. "La diffusion de la gravure du *Brooks* par la Société des Amis des Noirs et son impact." In *De la traite à l'esclavage*, edited by Serge Daget. Vol. II, 135–147. Nantes: C.R.H.M.A./Société Française d'Histoire d'Outre-Mer, 1988.

Childs, Matt D. *The 1812 Aponte Rebellion in Cuba and the Struggle against Atlantic Slavery*. Chapel Hill: The University of North Carolina Press, 2006.

Clarkson, Thomas. *History of the Rise, Progress, and Accomplishment of the Abolition of the African Slave Trade by the British Parliament*. London, 1839; 1st ed., 1808.

Conrad, Robert. *The Destruction of Brazilian Slavery, 1850–1888*. Berkeley: University of California Press, 1972.

Corzo, Gabino La Rosa. *Runaway Slave Settlements in Cuba. Resistance and Repression*. Chapel Hill and London: The University of North Carolina Press, 1988.

Costa, Emilia Viotti da. *Crowns of Glory, Tears of Blood. The Demerara Slave Rebellion of 1823*. New York: Oxford University Press, 1994.

Craton, Michael. *Empire, Enslavement and Freedom in the Caribbean*. Kingston and Oxford: IRP/James Currey Publishers, 1997.

———. *Testing the Chains: Resistance to Slavery in the British West Indies*. Ithaca, NY and London: Cornell University Press, 1982.

Davis, David B. *The Boisterous Sea of Liberty. A Documentary History of America from Discovery Through the Civil War*. New York and Oxford: Oxford University Press, 1998.

———. "The Emergence of Immediatism in British and American Anti-Slavery Thought." In *The Mississipi Valley Historical Review*, XLIX, 2 (1962): 209–230.

———. "Impact of the French and Haitian Revolutions." In *The Impact of the Haitian Revolution in the Atlantic World*, edited by David P. Geggus, 3–9. University of South Carolina Press, 2001.

————. *In the Image of God. Religion, Moral Values, and Our Heritage of Slavery.* New Haven: Yale University Press, 2001.

————. *Inhuman Bondage: The Rise and Fall of Slavery in the New World.* New York and London: Oxford University Press, 2006.

————. *The Problem of Slavery in the Age of Revolution, 1770–1823.* Ithaca, NY and London: Cornell University Press, 1975.

————. *Slavery and Human Progress.* Oxford and New York: Oxford University Press, 1984.

Deive, Carlos Esteban. "La abolicion de la esclavitu en Santo Domingo." In *Esclavitud y Derechos Humanos. La lucha por la librtad del negro en el siglo XIX,* edited by Francisco de Solano and Agustín Guimerá, 321–329. Madrid: CSIC/CEH, 1986.

Diaz, Nelson Martinez. "La resistência a la abolicion en los países del Rio de La Plata." In *Esclavitud y Derechos Humanos. La lucha por la librtad del negro en el siglo XIX,* edited by Francisco de Solano and Agustín Guimerá, 625–634. Madrid: CSIC/CEH, 1986.

Douglass, Frederick. *Narrative of the Life of Frederick Douglass, an American Slave, written by Himself.* Portuguese translation by Luís Nogueira, *Memórias de um Escravo Africano.* Lisbon: Mareantes Editora, 2005.

Dookhan, Isaac. *A History of the Virgin Islands, University Press of the West Indies.* Kingston, 1994.

Drescher, Seymour. "Brazilian Abolition in Comparative Perspective." In *The Abolition of Slavery and the Aftermath of Emancipation in Brazil,* 23–54. Durham and London: Duke University Press, 1988.

————. *Capitalism and Antislavery: British Mobilization in Comparative Perspective.* New York: Oxford University Press, 1987.

————. "The Limits of Example." In *The Impact of the Haitian Revolution in the Atlantic World,* edited by David P. Geggus, 10–14. University of South Carolina Press, 2001.

Dubois, Laurent. *Les esclaves de la Republique. L'histoire oubliée de la première émancipation, 1789–1794.* Paris: Calmann-Lévy, 1998.

————. *Les vengeurs du Nouveau Monde. Histoire de la Révolution Haïtienne.* Rennes: Les Perséides, 2005.

Duffy, James. *Portuguese Africa.* Cambridge, MA: Harvard University Press, 1959.

Eltis, David. *The Rise of African Slavery in the Americas.* Cambridge: Cambridge University Press, 2000.

Emmer, Pieter C. "Anti-Slavery and the Dutch: Abolition without reform." In *Abolition and Its Aftermath. The Historical Context, 1790–1916,* edited by David Richardson, 80–98. London: Frank Cass, 1985.

————. "Between Slavery and freedom: the period of apprenticeship in Suriname (Dutch Guiana), 1863–1873." In *Slavery and Abolition,* 14, 1 (1993): 87–113.

Engerman, Stanley L. *Slavery, Emancipation, and Freedom: Comparative Perspectives.* Baton Rouge: Louisiana State University Press, 2007.

Ferrer, Ada. "Armed Slaves and Anticolonial Insurgency in Late Nineteenth-Century Cuba." In *Arming Slaves From Classical Times to the Modern Age,* edited by

Christopher Leslie Brown and Philip D. Morgan, 304–329. New Haven and London: Yale University Press, 2006.

Fick, Carolyn. "Emancipation in Haiti: From Plantation Labour to Peasant Proprietorship." In *After Slavery. Emancipation and its Discontents*, edited by Howard Temperley, 11–40. London: Frank Cass, 2000.

Freehling, William W. *The Road to Disunion. Secessionists at Bay, 1776–1854.* New York and Oxford: Oxford University Press, 1990.

———. *The South Versus the South. How Anti-Confederate Southerners Shaped the Course of the Civil War.* Oxford and New York: Oxford University Press, 2001.

Freitas, Décio. *Palmares. A Guerra dos Escravos.* Rio de Janeiro: Graal, 1978.

———. *Zumbi dos Palmares.* Luanda: Museu Nacional da Escravatura, 1996.

Garlan, Yvon. *Les esclaves en Grèce ancienne.* Edited by La Découverte. Paris, 1995.

Geggus, David P. "The Arming of Slaves in the Haitian Revolution." In *Arming Slaves From Classical Times to the Modern Age*, edited by Christopher Leslie Brown and Philip D. Morgan, 209–232. New Haven and London: Yale University Press, 2006.

———. "The Caradeux and Colonial Memory." In *The Impact of the Haitian Revolution in the Atlantic World*, edited by David P. Geggus, 231–246. Columbia: University of South Carolina Press, 2001.

———. "Haiti and the Abolitionists: Opinion, propaganda and International Politics in Britain and France, 1804–1838." In *Abolition and its Aftermath*, edited by David Richardson, 113–140. London: Frank Cass, 1985.

———. "The Haitian Revolution." In *Caribbean Slave Society and Economy*, edited by Hilary McD. Beckles and Verene Shepherd, 402–418. Kingston and London: James Currey Publishers, 1991.

———. *Haitian Revolutionary Studies.* Bloomington: Indiana University Press, 2002.

Genovese, Eugene D. *From Rebellion to Revolution. Afro-American Slave Revolts in the Making of the Modern World.* Baton Rouge: Louisiana State University Press, 1992; 1st ed., 1979.

Goslinga, Cornelis C. *The Dutch in the Caribbean and the Guianas, 1680–1791.* Assen/Dover, NH: Van Gorcum, 1985.

Green, William A. *British Slave Emancipation. The Sugar Colonies and The Great Experiment, 1830–1865.* Oxford: Clarendon Press, 1976.

Groot, Sílvia W. de. "The Maroons of Surinam: agents of their own emancipation." In *Abolition and Its Aftermath. The Historical Context, 1790–1916*, edited by David Richardson, 55–79. London: Frank Cass, 1985.

———. "Maroons of Surinam: dependence and independence." In *Comparative Perspectives on Slavery in New World Plantation Societies*, edited by Vera Rubin and Arthur Tuden, 455–463. New York: The New York Academy of Sciences, 1977.

Hall, Catherine. *Civilising Subjects. Metropole and Colony in the English Imagination, 1830–1867.* Cambridge: Polity Press, 2002.

Hall, Gwendolyn Midlo. "Saint Domingue." In *Caribbean Slave Society and Economy*, edited by Hilary McD. Beckles and Verene Shepherd, 160–171. Kingston and London: IRP/James Currey, 1991.

Hall, Neville A.T. *Slave Society in the Danish West Indies: St. Thomas, St. John and St. Croix.* Mona, Jamaica: University Press of West Indies, 1994.

Hart, Richard. *Slaves Who Abolished Slavery. Blacks in Rebellion.* Mona, Jamaica: University of the West Indies Press, 2002; 1st ed., 1978.

Heintze, Beatrix. *Asilo ameaçado: oportunidades e consequências da fuga de escravos em Angola no século XVII.* Luanda: Museu Nacional da Escravatura, 1995.

Hugo, Victor. *Romans.* Paris: L'Intégrale/Seuil, 1965.

Hunt, Peter. "Arming Slaves and Helots in Classical Greece." In *Arming Slaves From Classical Times to the Modern Age,* edited by Christopher Leslie Brown and Philip D. Morgan, 14–39. New Haven and London: Yale University Press, 2006.

James, Cyril L.R. *The Black Jacobins. Toussaint L'Ouverture and the San Domingo Revolution.* London: Allison & Busby, 1980; 1st ed., 1938.

Jennings, Lawrence C. *French Anti-Slavery. The Movement for the Abolition of Slavery in France, 1802–1848.* Cambridge: Cambridge University Press, 2000.

Jimenez, Paloma Arroyo. "La Sociedad Abolicionista Española (1864–1886)." In *Esclavitud y Derechos Humanos. La lucha por la libertad del negro en el siglo XIX,* edited by Francisco de Solano and Agustín Guimerá, 169–181. Madrid: CSIC/CEH, 1986.

Jordan, Winthrop D. *Tumult and Silence at Second Creek: An Inquiry into a Civil War Slave Conspiracy.* Baton Rouge: Louisiana State University Press, 1993.

Jornal do Commercio. Lisbon, 1876.

Kraay, Hendrik. "Arming Slaves in Brazil from the Seventeenth Century to the Nineteenth Century." In *Arming Slaves From Classical Times to the Modern Age,* edited by Christopher Leslie Brown and Philip D. Morgan, 146–179. New Haven and London: Yale University Press, 2006.

Landers, Jane. "Transforming Bondsmen into Vassals: Arming Slaves in Colonial Spanish America." In *Arming Slaves From Classical Times to the Modern Age,* edited by Christopher Leslie Brown and Philip D. Morgan, 120–145. New Haven and London: Yale University Press, 2006.

Lecky, W.E.H. *A History of European Morals.* 6th ed. London, 1884.

Lombardi, John V. *The Decline and Abolition of Negro Slavery in Venezuela, 1820–1854.* Westport: Greenwood Publishing, 1971.

Love, Edgar. "Negro resistance to Spanish rule in colonial Mexico." In *Journal of Negro History,* 52, 2 (1967): 84–108.

Marques, João Pedro. "Quatro assassinatos e um retrocesso: violência escrava em Angola (1860–61)," in CEAUP (Coord.), *Trabalho Forçado Africano. Articulações com o Poder Político,* (Porto: Campo das Letras, 2007), 101–115.

———. *Portugal e a Escravatura dos Africanos.* Lisbon: Imprensa de Ciências Sociais, 2004.

———. *The Sounds of Silence. Nineteenth-century Portugal and the Abolition of the Slave Trade.* New York and Oxford: Berghahn Books, 2006.

———. "Terão os escravos abolido a escravidão? Considerações a propósito de um livro de Nelly Schmidt." In *Africana Studia,* 8 (2006): 249–273.

———. "Uma cosmética demorada: as *Cortes* portuguesas face ao problema da escravidão (1836–1875)." In *Análise Social,* 158/159 (2001): 209–247.

Mattoso, Kátia de Queirós. *Ser escravo no Brasil.* Edited by Brasiliense. São Paulo, 1988.

M'Bokolo, Elikia. *Afrique Noire. Histoire et civilizations.* Paris: Hatier-Aupelf. Uref, 1995. Portuguese translation by Alfredo Margarido, *África negra. História e civilizações,* Vol. I. Lisbon: Vulgata, 2003.

Midgley, Clare. "Slave sugar boycotts, female activism and the domestic base of British Anti-Slavery culture." In *Slavery and Abolition,* 17, 3 (1996): 137–162.

Miller, Joseph C. *Way of Death. Merchant Capitalism and the Angolan Slave Trade, 1730–1830.* Madison: The University of Wisconsin Press, 1988.

Montiel, Luz Maria Martinez. "Integration patterns and the assimilation process of negro slaves in Mexico." In *Comparative Perspectives on Slavery in New World Plantation Societies,* edited by Vera Rubin and Arthur Tuden, 455–463. New York: The New York Academy of Sciences, 1977.

Morgan, Philip D., and Christopher Leslie Brown, eds. *Arming Slaves: From Classical Times to the Modern Age.* New Haven and London: Yale University Press, 2006.

Murray, David R. *Odious Commerce: Britain, Spain and the Abolition of the Cuban Slave Trade.* Cambridge: Cambridge University Press, 1980.

Nascimento, Augusto. "A crise braçal de 1875 em São Tomé. Os comportamentos dos agentes sociais." In *Revista Crítica de Ciências Sociais,* 34 (1992): 317–329.

Needell, Jeffrey D. "The Abolition of the Brazilian Slave Trade in 1850: Historiography, Slave Agency and Statesmanship." In *Journal of Latin American Studies,* 33 (2001): 681–711.

Paredes, Carlos Sixirei. "Violência blanca, rebeldia negra y abolicionismo en el Brasil del siglo XIX." In *Esclavitud y Derechos Humanos. La lucha por la librtad del negro en el siglo XIX,* edited by Francisco de Solano and Agustín Guimerá, 607–623. Madrid: CSIC/CEI I, 1986.

Patterson, Orlando. *Slavery and Social Death. A Comparative Study.* Cambridge, MA and London: Harvard University Press, 1982.

Pearson, Edward A. "A Countryside Full of Flames: A Reconsideration of the Stono Rebellion and Slave Rebelliousness in the Early Eighteenth-Century South Carolina Lowcountry." In *Slavery and Abolition,* 17, 2 (1996): 22–50.

Pétré-Grenouilleau, Olivier. *Les traites négrières. Essai d'histoire globale.* Paris: Gallimard, 2004.

Plá, Maria del Cármen Borrego. *Palenques de negros en Cartagena de Indias a fines del siglo XVII.* Sevilla: Escuela de Estudios Hispano-Americanos de Sevilla, 1973.

Pollak-Eltz, Angelina. "Slave revolts in Venezuela." In *Comparative Perspectives on Slavery in New World Plantation Societies,* edited by Vera Rubin and Arthur Tuden, 439–445. New York: The New York Academy of Sciences, 1977.

Popovic, Alexandre. *The Revolt of African Slaves in Iraq in the 3rd/9th Century.* Princeton: Markus Wiener, 1999.

Price, Richard, ed. *Maroon Societies. Rebel Slave Communities in the Americas.* 3rd ed. Baltimore: The Johns Hopkins University Press, 1996.

Ramos, Donald. "O quilombo e o sistema escravista em Minas Gerais do século XVIII." In *Liberdade por um Fio. História dos Quilombos no Brasil,* edited by João

José Reis and Flávio dos Santos Gomes, 164–192. São Paulo: Companhia das Letras, 1996.

Raynal, Guillaume-Thomas. *Histoire philosophique et politique des établissements et du commerce des Européens dans les deux Indes*. Paris, 1770.

Reis, João José. "Quilombos e revoltas escravas no Brasil," In *Revista da Universidade de São Paulo*, 14, 39 (1995–96): 15–39.

———. *Rebelião escrava no Brasil. A história do Levante dos Malês em 1835*. São Paulo: Companhia das Letras, 2003.

——— and Flávio dos Santos Gomes, eds. *Liberdade por um Fio. História dos Quilombos no Brasil*. São Paulo: Companhia das Letras, 1996.

Richardson, David, ed. *Abolition and its Aftermath*. London: Frank Cass, 1985.

Rouland, Norbert. *Les esclaves Romains en temps de guerre*. Brussels: Latomus, 1977.

Rubin, Vera and Arthur Tuden, eds. *Comparative Perspectives on Slavery in New World Plantation Societies*. New York: The New York Academy of Sciences, 1977.

Salem, Ellen. "Slavery in Medieval Korea." Ph.D. diss., Columbia University, 1978.

Schmidt, Nelly. *L'abolition de l'esclavage. Cinq siècles de combats (XVe-XXe siècle)*. Paris: Fayard, 2005.

Schmidt-Nowara, Christopher. "The end of slavery and the end of Empire: Slave emancipation in Cuba and Puerto Rico." In *Slavery and Abolition*, 21, 2 (2000): 188–207

Schuler, Monica. "Akan Slave rebellions in the British Caribbean." In *Caribbean Slave Society and Economy*, edited by Hilary McD. Beckles and Verene Shepherd, 373–386. Kingston and London: IRP/James Currey Publishers, 1991.

Schwartz, Stuart B. "Cantos e quilombos numa conspiração de escravos haussás. Bahia, 1814." In *Liberdade por um Fio. História dos Quilombos no Brasil*, edited by João José Reis and Flávio dos Santos Gomes, 373–406. São Paulo: Companhia das Letras, 1996.

———. "Mocambos, quilombos e Palmares: a resistência escrava no Brasil colonial." In *Estudos Económicos*, 17 (1978): 21–43.

———. *Slaves, Peasants, and Rebels. Reconsidering Brazilian Slavery*. Urbana and Chicago: University of Illinois Press, 1996.

Scott, Rebecca J. *Slave Emancipation in Cuba. The Transition to Free Labor, 1860–1899*. Pittsburgh: University of Pittsburgh Press, 2000.

Siwpersad, J.P. "Emancipation in British Guyana and its influence on Dutch policy regarding Surinam." In *Abolition and Its Aftermath. The Historical Context, 1790–1916*, edited by David Richardson, 168–180. London: Frank Cass, 1985.

Solano, Fancisco de and Agustín Guimerá, eds. *Esclavitud y Derechos Humanos. La lucha por la libertad del negro en el siglo XIX*. Madrid: CSIC/CEH, 1986.

Soler, Luís M. Diaz. *Historia de la Esclavitud Negra en Puerto Rico*. Barcelona: Editorial Universitaria de la Universidad de Puerto Rico, 1970.

Stowe, Harriet Beecher. *Dred. A Tale of the Great Dismal Swamp*. Edinburgh: Edinburgh University Press, 1999; 1st ed., 1856.

———. *Uncle Tom's Cabin or, Life Among the Lowly*. New York: Penguin Books, 1986; 1st ed., 1852.

Thornton, John K. *Warfare in Atlantic Africa, 1500–1800.* London: UCL Press, 1999.

Tocqueville, Alexis de. "On the Emancipation of Slaves" (1843). In *Tocqueville and Beaumont on Social Reform,* edited by Seymour Drescher, 137–173. New York: Harper & Row, 1968.

Toplin, Robert Brent. *The Abolition of Slavery in Brazil.* New York: Atheneum, 1975.

Trevor-Roper, H.R. *Religion, the Reformation and Social Change.* London: Macmillan, 1967. Portuguese translation by Maria do Carmo Cary, *Religião, Reforma e Transformação Social.* Edited by Presença. Lisboa, 1981.

Vainfas, Ronaldo. "Deus contra Palmares. Representações senhoriais e ideias jesuíticas." In *Liberdade por um Fio. História dos Quilombos no Brasil,* edited by João José Reis and Flávio dos Santos Gomes, 60–80. São Paulo: Companhia das Letras, 1996.

Verger, Pierre. *Flux et reflux de la traite des nègres entre le golfe de Bénin et Bahia de Todos os Santos du XVIIe au XIXe siècles.* Paris and The Hague: Mouton, 1968.

Williams, Eric. *Capitalism and Slavery.* London: Andre Deutch, 1964; 1st ed., 1944.

Part II

Commentaries

1

AFRICA AND ABOLITIONISM

John Thornton

❧

One of the central issues to consider in the analysis of slavery and the reaction to slavery by its victims is that slavery is only one of a variety of systems of exploitation. Those who are exploited are likely to respond to the conditions of exploitation by trying to reduce or eliminate exploitation, and not necessarily the legal and political system that underlies it. It is for this reason helpful to think of American slavery not so much as a legal system of creating property rights of one person over another, which actually tells one very little about the lives of the slaves, but rather to look at such things as labor regimes, capacities for family life, potentials for moving from less satisfying to more satisfying work and other measures intended to gauge happiness or well being.

While recognizing the value of the concrete daily experience against the importance of larger world views is important, it is also important to consider that all of our evidence suggests that slaves disliked being slaves and sought every possible opportunity to escape it. Few refused manumission even though it often benefited them very little. Many worked very hard and struggled for years to achieve freedom for themselves, their kin or their children. Clearly, they were happy that slavery as an institution ended, but this does not mean that their actions during the time of institutional slavery were directed at ending the institution in itself rather than more limited aims.

It is possible that the resistance of the last years of the slavery period, by increasing the cost of maintaining slavery and publicizing the plight of the slaves, may have assisted in slavery's demise. Lawmakers and taxpayers, convinced by both practical and humanitarian arguments including the cumulate effect of slave resistance—especially large scale actions such as the Haitian Revolution or other movements that followed it—could well have had an impact in their time that, say, for example, the formation of Angola Janga in Palmares in Brazil did not have in its time. But it is equally true that there seems to be little evidence to suggest that slaves were seeking the end of slavery in a global or institutional sense when they took the actions they did.

The Haitian Revolution was the most dramatic slave revolt in the history of the Americas, and one might expect the fullest development of the potential of slavery to generate revolt there. We might consider Plain du Nord in Saint-Domingue, the heart of the slave revolt at the root of the Haitian Revolution, as a series of systems in which slavery played a role. There was the obviously exploitative regime at the bottom, the workers in the cane fields, with long hours in the hot sun under the lash, the wretched housing conditions, the low levels of food, and badly unbalanced sex ratios—in short, the worst that labor had to offer. To be sure, these conditions were facilitated legally by the situation of slavery, but it might be possible for similar conditions to exist without slavery as a legal system, and the workers longing to be free from it might chose several strategies. They might try low-level resistance, work stoppages, poisoning, or plotting against harsh overseers to improve their standing and conditions of life, or they might give up on such approaches and run away to the hills to join maroons. And a good number, when the situation presented itself to them, would join the Haitian Revolution.

But there was another set of conditions in Saint-Domingue, still under the legal system of slavery. This was the position of the skilled slave—sugar boiler, carpenter, domestic servant, coachman, and at the top the *commandeur d'atelier,* the slave driver. These people were more privileged within the system of slavery, their houses were better, their work more satisfying, and the food sufficient and perhaps even good. They had families and could expect their children to fall into the same class as they occupied. This is not to say that they did not see problems with slavery, as we know they did. They knew very well that managers, lawyers, and others who were neither as qualified nor as skilled as they were, were living better, and freer to move about benefiting far more than any slave from the wealth that sugar growing generated. Although the skilled slaves were the elite of the slave community in Saint-Domingue, it was they, according to most accounts, which provoked the slave revolt of August 1791. And we know that their goals were limited, for when the first commissioners arrived from Paris to look at the revolt, they presented demands, for personal freedom, and perhaps for a few more days off for the workers on the estates. The impetus to abolish slavery came as much from the outside of the revolution as from within the ranks of slaves, and as far as we can tell this came from the elite of the slaves rather than the exploited rank and file.

In fact, it is in the abolition of slavery in 1793 in Saint-Domingue that we see most clearly the reason that it was ultimately the labor regime that counted and not simply the legal position of the slaves. No sooner had slavery been outlawed than the leaders of the Revolution, or at least those leaders who had made enough of a military impact to be recognized as such by the French government, sought to reestablish the essence of slavery.[1] Toussaint Louverture, facing revolt on all sides from an attempt to recreate the plantation system, found that the end of slavery meant nothing to the former slaves if the labor system that it underwrote was not also abolished. From that point onward, in fact, the Haitian Revolution was as much about who would work, in what conditions, and for what return as about legal niceties concerning personal freedom. In the end, as history showed, the ex-slaves did manage to abolish the plantation system and created a set of peasant farming communities, which for better or worse became the future of nineteenth century Haiti.

Let us consider another interesting situation. The formation of the slave runaway community in Palmares, lying in the inland mountains of the Portuguese captaincy of Pernambuco, called Angola Janga by its residents, was the largest African-created political system outside of slavery in the New World, aside from Haiti after the Revolution. Probably as many as 30,000 people lived in the fifteen towns and dozens of villages that made up Angola Janga in 1670, and were self-governing entirely and were completely outside of the control of the colonial government.

Angola Janga came into existence thanks to the war that broke out in Pernambuco, when the Dutch West India Company captured Recife in 1630, and the subsequent indecisive fighting allowed thousands of slaves to run away and flood the existing runaway communities in the interior. In creating a system to govern their lives, the slaves of Pernambuco showed their aspirations and desires clearly. Here they formed a state, with a hierarchy of status, an army, and indeed even slavery. Angola Janga was a slave holding society, and several witnesses attest that the principal underlying its slavery was that those who fled voluntarily to the state were taken in as free citizens, while those who the Palmarinos captured were slaves. Local records reveal clearly how aggressive Angola Janga was in this regard, for a string of local complaints show dozens and sometimes more slaves being captured in raids from Palmares. But these raids were not, as one might imagine, attempts to liberate fellow slaves from their servitude, but to establish and build Angola Janga's own slave class.

There is little doubt that slavery in Angola Janga was considerably less onerous in terms of its labor regime than that of Pernambuco, and perhaps this explains why slaves there rarely if ever ran back to their former masters. But it also a fact that the society that was created in the hinterland of Pernambuco was not egalitarian or even republican as we understand it. Dissident local officials who refused to follow the orders of the king and his captains were punished, sometimes with capital punishment for their disobedience. While the ground institutions of the mocambo, Angola Janga's lowest social unit, were remarkably democratic and egalitarian, the existence of slavery and indeed, systematic cam-

paigns to capture slaves to continue their slavery in Angola Janga are jar-
ring to those who look to the runaway state as a blast against slavery. But
Angola Janga does in fact illustrate the more prosaic idea that the runaways who founded it were looking for a better life for themselves, even
if it meant creating a new system of exploitation.[2]

Of course, most runaway communities were not the size or had the
scope of Angola Janga, nor did the sometimes-violent action that created
them have the power of the Haitian Revolution. But there is much to be
learned by considering the smaller runaway communities, which dotted
virtually the entire scope of plantation America. One might start by ex-
amining Jamaican maroons in the eighteenth century. The communities
were formed in the hills of Jamaica's interior in the last quarter of the seventeenth and the first quarter of the eighteenth century from mostly Akan
runaways, and they fought British attempts to return them to slavery for
many years. When they had finally convinced the Jamaican authorities
that they would not be able to root the communities out of the hills
through military action, the British sent officials up to them to negotiate
a settlement in 1739–40. The terms of the settlement, essentially the incorporation of the maroons into the British army as a local, ad hoc militia, was celebrated by the maroons, who used the ceremonial associated
with similar commissioning practices in their African homeland to celebrate the peace treaty. They were, from all accounts, satisfied with the results, and indeed served faithfully from that point onward, including
playing a pivotal role in the suppression of Tackey's War, a major slave
insurrection in 1760–65.[3] For them, clearly, their role was in ending their
own condition of slavery, of course, but also the recognition of their community in a political system in a way that made sense to them from the
politics of their homeland.

At about the same time, and more interesting from our point of view,
an Antiguan slave named Court organized his own ceremony, very much
akin to the one used by the Jamaican maroons. His ceremony, modeled on
another Akan commissioning celebration, was held in plain sight at 2
o'clock in the afternoon before a large audience of people of all statuses
in the Antigua's main town. Although frightened officials, who saw in its
military overtones a plot to overthrow the slave regime, made it cause for
an inquest and eventually the execution of Court and a number of his as-
sociates, the trial records make it fairly clear that Court had no intention
of making a shadow government or for that matter even engaging in any
large scale seditious activity. Though still a slave, Court sought to gain
formal recognition, at least by his peers, as being the richest slave in Antigua, and one whose master had granted more or less total freedom of
property and movement than one usually considers when discussing
slavery.[4]

Though in Court's case, his attempt backfired, it was quite common
elsewhere in the Americas for slaves to stage coronations in which a for-
tunate and usually well-recognized person was elected king. In many

areas, such kings had some authority, for example, in Brazil and some parts of Spanish America, and were often recognized by colonial officials. While such customs can hardly be considered anti-slavery, they do give us an insight into ways that the slaves considered creating space in the system of slavery and, moreover, in finding mobility by both violent and nonviolent means.[5] These systems of institution building within the slave community should be considered as compromises with, and even acceptance of the condition of slavery rather than revolting against it. But the contrast with the situation of the maroons in Jamaica, or other runaway communities who sought and obtained the legal recognition of colonial authorities, places the coronations in a continuum that reveals a good deal about a range of slave ideologies and aspirations.

There were, however, some revolts that appear to have been aimed at something resembling the abolition of slavery. Tackey's War (1760–65) in Jamaica was such a revolt, for at least according to the European and settler witnesses of the time, one of Tackey's objectives was to create an African run economic order on the island and to kill all of the whites. Curiously enough, however, the same witnesses make it clear that the revolt aimed at doing so only for Coromantees, that is, slaves who originated in the Akan speaking parts of the Gold Coast, and in fact that their plan was to retain the other slaves in their servitude.[6] The evidence for the motivations of Tackey are drawn from what may well be unreliable sources: the white planters who suppressed it, and especially Edward Long, whose account is emotionally laden. But other local accounts, for example, that of Thomas Thistlewood, do suggest that the aims were rather specific to the rebels, for Thistlewood noted its strongly ethnic character, and, moreover, he felt comfortable arming the non-Coromantee slaves on his estate to fight against the rebels.[7] Like Long, he believed that the ultimate goal was simply the limited freedom that the maroons enjoyed. Clearly, they also saw Tackey's War as something less than a liberation movement, but rather as having limited objectives rooted in the community interests of the Coromantees.

The other great Akan led slave revolt, the St. John's revolt in 1736 in which most of the island was taken over by the rebels, was also led by Coromantees and revealed similar limited and group oriented objectives, though the details of their motivations are elusive, and like those of the Jamaicans who followed Tackey, given to us by those who suppressed the rebellion and feared the worst.[8]

Regarding systems of exploitation rather than legal names for such systems is also useful for looking at the African side of the Atlantic. African societies had many systems that have been described as slavery, and in fact, for Africanists, defining slavery has proven very complicated. For example, if we define as "slaves" a class of people who have been captured in war or condemned by courts, who have been placed under the jurisdiction of private people (rather than the state), and if we translate the terms in African languages for such people as "slave," then Africa had a

large number of slaves, in fact, there may well have been no African society that did not hold slaves. As I have argued elsewhere, the system of
slavery in Africa was often indistinguishable from any other member of
the lower class. In Africa, at least, it often happened that slave villages were
not exploited economically any more than the villages of their free neighbors, and only the destination of their product (dues, taxes, tributes) differ-
entiated the two, though in some cases the labor regime might be similar
to that in some plantation societies, for in the sixteenth century, slaves in
Senegal worked as much for the master as did those in São Tomé.[9] While
free people paid their dues to the state or its officials, the slaves paid
theirs to private persons, and thus helped to generate their incomes.

The African case shows us clearly that it is a labor regime that really
defines what is repugnant in American slavery more than anything else.
We know well that in Africa slaves often served as soldiers, high government officials, merchants, and indeed virtually all other roles. And while
their situation curtailed their participation in some activities, and their
status limited them in other ways, one does not find among them much
of a move to abolish slavery. It should not be surprising in this situation
to learn that slaves serving in Kongo in the eighteenth century were allowed to go and visit their families, and managed to return to their servitude without apparently any objection.[10]

Nowhere are the ambiguities of African slavery clearer than the case
of Missakoulallah, described in the seventeenth century Sudanese chronicle *Tarikh al-Fettash*, but relating to the situation in the early sixteenth
century. The emperor of Songhay owned a large number of plantations
that grew rice for his armies and navies and was located along the Niger
River. The slaves were more or less left completely on their own and required to deliver a fixed number of bags of grain at the appointed time.
When the time came for collection, an official, himself a slave, arrived at
the plantation and collected the dues, and then sailed off not to see them
again for the next tax cycle. One year, the *Tarikh* tells us, the community
informed Missakoulallah that a bad year had prevented them from de-
livering the crop, and, as a result, the slave simply forgave them their
dues. When he was later challenged for his act, he defended himself in
the name of Islamic charity and calmly paid the shortfall from his own
store of grain.[11] Clearly, this was not a system of hyper-exploitation of
slaves, and one that defies our definitions of slavery founded in the
American experience, in which constant supervision was a fundamental
characteristic, and, moreover, where even slaves in supervisory roles had
relatively little independence.

Where one can see clearcut opposition to slavery in Africa is in its
runaway communities. In some cases, these are clearly connected to resistance to export in the Atlantic slave trade, as was the case in the slave
runaway communities that grew up south of the Kwanza River in Angola, and dogged the Portuguese for virtually the whole length of their
tenure there. Likewise, the thousands of slaves who were harbored in

southern Kongo, similar runaways, were fleeing the deadly prospect of trans-Atlantic transportation and not a labor regime.[12]

Perhaps most interesting is the large scale slave revolt in Sierra Leone in around 1785, in which thousands of slaves fled their masters, built fortified towns, and then resisted persistently and valiantly the attempts of their former masters to re-enslave them. It is interesting that in this case, the revolt in Africa was led by slaves who were, in fact, concerned about punishments given by masters, and not specifically labor regimes. According to John Matthews, who was present, the cause of the revolt was the zeal of the Mandinka masters of the slaves to pursue witchcraft accusations.[13] We know the consequences of this revolt more than its causes. Was it an attempt to flee from what might have been a harsh labor regime in the rice-producing region of the coast, or was it more of a political movement, caught up in the complex maneuvering of the region following the Jihad of 1726? Alternatively, was it perhaps, like the Angola runaways, an attempt to flee Atlantic transportation?

On either side of the Atlantic, it seems that slave revolts had limited aims, at the very least to secure a better position, and perhaps freedom for the group participating in the revolt. The history of the revolts, especially the motivations of their leaders, are notoriously hard to follow. The evidence available to us normally comes from slave owners or governments that supported them, and their claims about motivations may well be imaginary. But the behavior of slave rebels and runaways suggests that, for the most part, slaves did not envision their actions in system-wide terms. They were not concerned about the legal system that made them slaves as much as the labor and living conditions in which they were held. Their goals, limited, practical, and at times attainable, were to obtain as much for themselves as they could and be content with that, even if it were not a perfect utopia. Runaway communities that could survive in the mountains or forests were sufficient; indeed, even finding subordinate positions as soldiers was acceptable as an improvement.

Those who did think system-wide appear to have been the slaves who were in a better position to see the larger world. These tended to be the privileged among the slaves, such as the *commandeurs d'atelier* who led the Haitian Revolution. For them the goal might be to make the slave system work for them in a better way and not to do away with the system itself. Certainly, the petition of Jean François and Bissau, early leaders in Haiti, to the French commissioners in 1791 pleading for personal freedom in exchange for suppressing the other slaves suggests that their goals were toward substitution, and it must be said that Toussaint Louverture's own attempts at reinstating the essence of slave labor on plantations after abolishing slavery do point to similar goals on his part. If Long's speculations about Tackey's War are true, they would only fit a mold established by other rebels and runaways.

We should not be surprised by this, in fact it is only our own romantic interpretation of slave revolts as struggles for higher causes, such as freedom and true revolution, that leads us to expect more of the would-be revolutionary leaders of such revolts or runaway movements. Modern history, especially that of the twentieth century, has confirmed it. Peasant wars in the twentieth century, as Eric Wolf called them, which were more potentially successful than those of the eighteenth century, have tended to be led by those from outside the peasant class, proclaimed high sounding goals of creation of perfect societies, and yet in many cases ended up imposing their own, sometimes harsh, labor and service regimes on the very peasants they claimed to liberate.[14]

It is probably best when thinking of the motivations of any group of people's social actions, especially those that involve substantial risk and uncertain benefits, that the tendency universally is to avoid risk and to seek limited and attainable gains. For slaves held in the Americas, the total transformation of society was probably too much of a utopian goal, and in fact, as I have argued, most sought much more limited goals. At the same time, they were probably more successful in attaining those goals, such as limiting their labor, defending small elements of independence, or seeking restricted freedom in remote areas, than they would ever have been in a more grandiose scheme of transformation. It is probably true that even in the Haitian Revolution, the participants were not thinking about overthrowing slavery as much as winning a few extra free days and a less harsh disciplinary regime.

Notes

1. Rather emphatically made in Pierre Pluchon, *Toussaint L'Overture: De L'esclavage au pouvoir* (Paris, 1979) and more guardedly also in Laurent Dubois, *Avengers of the New World: The Story of the Haitian Revolution* (Cambridge, MA, 2004).
2. John Thornton, "Les États d'Angola et la formation de Palmares," *Annales HSS* 4 (2008).
3. John Thornton, "War, the State and Religious Norms in 'Coromantee' Thought: The Ideology of an African American Nation," in *Possible Pasts: Becoming Colonial in Early America*, ed. Robert Blair St. George (Ithaca, NY and London, 2000), 181–200 (see 198–199).
4. Thornton, "War, the State and Religious Norms," 194–196.
5. Marcelo Mac Cord, *O Rosário de D. Antônio. Irmandades negras, alianças e conflitos na história social do Recife, 1848–1872* (Recife, 2005), see 62–91 for earlier manifestations. Also see Marina Mello e Sousa, *Reis negros no Brasil escravista: História da festa de coroação de Rei Congo* (Belo Horizonte, 2002).
6. Edward Long, *A History of Jamaica*, 3 vols. (London, 1774), vol. 2, book 3, ch. 3, 447–455. (see especially 447); see also Bryan Edwards, *History of the West Indies*, 2 vols. (Dublin, 1793), 2: 59–62.
7. Lincolnshire Record Office, Monson Depost 31–11, Diary of Thomas Thistlewood, entries for 1760 (my thanks to Trevor Burnard for a transcript of the diary), see especially 97 (24 May), 100 (28 May, capture of a king), 101 (29 May, arming own slaves), 102 (30 May, Coromantees raiding plantations to loot), 104 (3 June, Maroons fight on masters' side, "Col: Cudjoe's [Maroon leader] Negroes behaved with great bravery"). Excerpts

from the diary specific to these events are found in Douglas Hall, *In Miserable Slavery: Thomas Thistlewood in Jamaica, 1750–86* (London, 1989), 97–105.

8. A detailed account is found in Christian Andreas Georg Oldendorp, *Historie der Caribischen Inseln Sanct Thomas, Sanct Crux und Sanct Jan: Insbesondere der dasigen Neger und der Mission der evangelischen Brüder unter denselben*, eds. Gundrun Meier, Stephan Palmié, Peter Stein, and Horst Ulbricht, 4 vols. (Berlin, 2000–2002) 1: 597–603.

9. John Thornton, *Africa and Africans in the Making of the Atlantic World, 1400–1800*, 2nd ed. (Cambridge, 1998), 86–90 (see 88 for comparative labor regime of São Tomé and Senegal).

10. Marcellino d'Atri, "Gionate apostoliche fatte da me Fra Marcellino d'Atri...1690" [1702] in *L'anarchia congolese nel sec. XVII. La relazione inedita di Marcellino d'Atri*, ed. Carlo Toso (Genoa, 1984)(original pagination marked), 532, 537–538.

11. *Tarikh al-Fettash*, ed. O. Houdas and M. Delafosse, translated in French as *Tarikh el-Fettach ou Chronique du chercheur* (Paris, 1913–1914; reedited, 1964), 177–181 (French)/ 94–96 (Arabic).

12. Beatrix Heintze, "Gefährdetes asyl: Chancen und Konsequenzen der Flucht angolischen Sklaven im 17. Jahrhundert," *Paideuma* (1993): 321–341.

13. John Matthews, *A Voyage to the River Sierra-Leone containing an account of the trade and productions of the coutnry also of the civil and religious customs and manners of the people* (London, 1788; facsimile rep., London, 1966), Letter VII, 154–155; Thomas Winterbottom, *An Account of the Native Africans in the Neighbourhood of Sierra Leone*, 2 vols. (London, 1803; facsimile rep., ed. with new intro. John Hargreaves and E. Maurice Backett, London, 1969) 1: 154–156 (for a longer range history).

14. Eric Wolf, *Peasant Wars of the Twentieth Century* (New York, 1969).

Bibliography

Atri, Marcellino d'. "Gionate apostoliche fatte da me Fra Marcellino d'Atri... 1690" [1702] in *L'anarchia congolese nel sec. XVII. La relazione inedita di Marcellino d'Atri*, ed. Carlo Toso (Genoa: Bozzi, 1984).

Dubois, Laurent. *Avengers of the New World: The Story of the Haitian Revolution* (Cambridge, MA: Harvard University Press, 2004).

Edwards, Bryan. *History of the West Indies*, 2 vols. (Dublin: Luke White, 1793).

Hall, Douglas. *In Miserable Slavery: Thomas Thistlewood in Jamaica, 1750–86* (London: McMillian, 1989).

Heintze, Beatrix. "Gefährdetes asyl: Chancen und Konsequenzen der Flucht angolischen Sklaven im 17. Jahrhundert," *Paideuma* (1993): 321–341.

Kati, Mahmud al-. *Tarikh al-Fettash*, ed. O. Houdas and M. Delafosse, *Tarikh el-Fettach ou Chronique du chercheur* (Paris, 1913–1914; reedited, Paris: Maisonneuve, 1964).

Long, Edward. *A History of Jamaica*, 3 vols. (London: Lowndes, 1774).

Mac Cord, Marcelo. *O Rosário de D. Antônio. Irmandades negras, alianças e conflitos na história social do Recife, 1848–1872* (Recife: Editora Universitária UFPE, 2005).

Matthews, John. *A Voyage to the River Sierra-Leone containing an account of the trade and productions of the coutnry also of the civil and religious customs and manners of the people* (London, 1788; facsimile rep., London: Cass, 1966).

Mello e Sousa, Marina. *Reis negros no Brasil escravista: História da festa de coroação de Rei Congo* (Belo Horizonte: Editora UFMG, 2002).

Oldendorp, Christian Andreas Georg. *Historie der Caribischen Inseln Sanct Thomas, Sanct Crux und Sanct Jan: Insbesondere der dasigen Neger und der Mission der evan-*

gelischen Brüder unter denselben, eds. Gundrun Meier, Stephan Palmié, Peter Stein, and Horst Ulbricht, 4 vols. (Berlin: Verlag für Wissenschaft und Bildung, 2000–2002).

Pluchon, Pierre. *Toussaint L'Overture: De L'esclavage au pouvoir* (Paris: L'école, 1979).

Thornton, John. "Les États d'Angola et la formation de Palmares," *Annales HSS* 4 (2008).

Idem "War, the State and Religious Norms in 'Coromantee' Thought: The Ideology of an African American Nation," in *Possible Pasts: Becoming Colonial in Early America,* ed. Robert Blair St. George (Ithaca, NY and London: Cornell University Press, 2000), 181–200.

Idem, Africa and Africans in the Making of the Atlantic World, 1400–1800, 2nd ed. (Cambridge: Cambridge University Press, 1998).

Winterbottom, Thomas. *An Account of the Native Africans in the Neighbourhood of Sierra Leone,* 2 vols. (London, 1803; facsimile rep., ed. with new intro. John Hargreaves and E. Maurice Backett, London: Cass, 1969).

Wolf, Eric. *Peasant Wars of the Twentieth Century* (New York: Harper and Row, 1969).

2

WHO ABOLISHED SLAVERY IN THE DUTCH CARIBBEAN?

Pieter C. Emmer

ᘓᘏ

Introduction

In many ways the living and working conditions of the slaves in the Dutch Caribbean were similar to those elsewhere in the region. The Dutch Caribbean consisted of two quite distinct regions. On the one hand there were six small islands—Curaçao, Aruba, Bonaire, Saba, Saint Eustatius, and the Dutch part of Saint Martin—all heavily populated by a mixed population of slaves, free persons of color, and expatriate whites, and these rocky islands were not suited for large-scale plantation agriculture. On the other hand, there were Suriname, Berbice, Essequibo, and Demerara, all plantation colonies with a relatively small number of expatriate Europeans, a large number of slaves, large estates, and an excess of deaths over births. One feature makes the Dutch Caribbean stand out: the large number of slaves in Suriname that absconded from the plantations and lived as maroons in the interior of the colony.[1]

There are several indications that in the Dutch Caribbean the reasons and opportunities for slaves to resist and rebel were more numerous than in many of the other slave societies in the region. The ratio between whites and blacks was extremely unequal in the Dutch plantation colonies of Essequibo, Berbice, and Demerara.[2] Also, the social cohesion among the planter communities in the Dutch Caribbean was weaker than elsewhere, perhaps with the exception of the Danish islands. More than half of the whites in Suriname were of non-Dutch origin, while in the colony of Demerara, more than 80 percent of the planters were British.[3]

Religion also set the Dutch Caribbean apart from the other colonies in the region. In the Dutch Republic as well as in the Dutch colonies, only one religious denomination was officially recognized: the Dutch Reformed Church. In the Dutch Caribbean, most civil servants and some of the most influential planters were members of this church. However, there were many whites who were not, such as the large number of Sephardic and Ashkenazi Jews in Suriname, who made up about a quarter of the white population, while most of the British planters would have been Anglicans or Presbyterians. None of these religious denominations had much interest in proselytizing the slaves. It was the Roman Catholic Church that converted most of the slaves on Curaçao, while the Moravians tried to bring the slaves of Suriname in contact with the Christian faith. These religious differences contributed to deepening the rift between free and slave in the Dutch Caribbean.

Another unsettling element in the history of the Dutch islands and plantation colonies in the Caribbean were the frequent periods during which the French and the English were at war with the Dutch Republic. As the Dutch had little maritime and military power, these wars usually resulted in the occupation of the Dutch colonies in the Caribbean, with devastation and demands for ransom. In wartime, the exports to the Netherlands came to a standstill, as did the slave trade, both of which had an immediate impact on the colonial economies. Furthermore, the limited defense capacities of the Dutch weakened the dominant position of the slave owners in case of slave insurrections.

The patchwork of governmental institutions also made the Dutch West Indies stand out. The six islands as well as Essequibo and Demerara were the property of the Dutch West India Company, while two independent stockholder companies governed Suriname and Berbice. These disparate forms of ownership were not nearly as effective as a single colonial authority, particularly when it came to defending the Dutch possessions against foreign attacks and slave uprisings.[4]

Another stimulus for the slaves to run away or to resist was the geographical location of the Dutch plantations colonies. All of them were situated on the South American mainland and most of their territory consisted of unexplored hinterland, as only the narrow coastal strip and the area along the rivers had been colonized. Nowhere else in the Caribbean was it so easy to run away, as the jungle was always nearby.

Last, but not least, the unsettling effects of a wave of bankruptcies should be mentioned, which ended the single ownership of many Suriname plantations. In 1773, it became apparent that investors in the Netherlands had been far too liberal in providing the Suriname planters with mortgages and loans and that many would have difficulties in paying the yearly interest, let alone in repaying the principal. As a result, many planters had to sell their plantations; subsequently, some of these were amalgamated with other plantations, which involved the relocation of groups of slaves. During the period of 1730 to –1750, perhaps as many as a thousand slaves had to leave their plantations because of bankruptcies, and that number must have increased considerably after 1773. Going bankrupt was not uncommon elsewhere in the Caribbean, but the wave of bankruptcies after 1773 in Suriname was as unique as the result: the multiple ownership of the Suriname plantations by an assortment of metropolitan investors.[5] On these plantations, the daily management was left to hired directors and solicitors and they were more interested in short-term profits than the previous planter owners, because the director and solicitors received a percentage of the yearly profits in addition to their salary. This change in management resulted in a constant drive to increase productivity, which was highly unsettling for the slaves.

Marronage

No doubt the most prominent feature of the slave society in the Dutch colony of Suriname was marronage. Nowhere else did so many slaves run away, not even in the neighboring Dutch colonies of Berbice, Essequibo, and Demerara. It has been suggested that the larger number of Amerindians present in these smaller colonies explain the difference. Amerindians cooperated with the colonial governments and made it difficult for runaway slaves to establish themselves in the interior.

There exists no evidence that the slaves became maroons in order to undermine the system of slavery, let alone to abolish it. In fact, their attacks against the plantations had no effect on the metropolitan agenda for slave emancipation.[6] That the maroons had no objection to slavery—with the exception of themselves—is confirmed by the terms of the peace treaties that, over time, were concluded between the principle maroon communities and the colonial government. All of these treaties stipulated that the maroons no longer would accept additional runaway slaves into their communities, but, instead, they would return them to their owners.[7] Also, in exchange for the promise not to attack any more plantations, the colonial government provided them with gunpowder, bullets, and the household necessities. That seems to underline the assumption that the attacks on the plantations by the maroons had a practical objective and not an ideological one. It would be wrong to assume that the runaway slaves were forced to accept these peace treaties by a dominant colonial government. On the contrary, it was the colonial government that asked for peace as it realized that a war against the runaway slaves could not be won and would never end. The maroons accepted the terms of the peace treaties in spite of the fact that they were aware that the colonial government could not defeat them by military means. In addition, during the nineteenth century, when the maroons no longer posed a threat to the plantations, several maroon communities established commercial relations with the plantations for the sale of bananas and firewood.[8]

The maroons might not actively have supported slave emancipation in Suriname or influenced the abolition debate in the Netherlands, but their actions did affect negatively the plantation economy. They might not have realized it themselves, but the maroons made plantation agriculture in Suriname less profitable and some plantations could have postponed or even avoided bankruptcy had there been no marronage.[9] However, there is no evidence that the maroons consciously supported abolitionism.

Yet, we should not exaggerate the maroon threat. During the second half of the eighteenth century, the maroons in Suriname made up about 10 percent of the total slave population. This would have crippled Suriname's position as a cash crop producer if it had not been for the fact that in compensation, large-scale slave rebellions in Suriname were relatively scarce because of the "maroon escape hatch."[10]

Second, the chance of being attacked by the maroons seemed small, albeit these chances increased for those plantations situated in the interior of the colony. Various calculations indicate that the chance of a maroon attack affected only one percent of the plantations in Suriname and a maximum of 250 slaves per year. However, when we calculate the chance of an attack on the plantations that were situated at the frontier of the plantation belt, the chances of an attack increased dramatically, and especially during the period between 1750 and 1759, on average such plantations were attacked once every three years.[11]

All told, with a slave population of 40,000 during the eighteenth century, the average number of runaway slaves per year amounted to 300, of whom 200 for various reasons returned to their owners out of their own initiative.[12] The number of runaway slaves remains the same in the nineteenth century, which suggests that the various peace treaties had little effect.[13]

The low number of slaves who fled to colonies neighboring Suriname, once slavery had been abolished there, also demonstrates that running away had no connection to the fight against the *system* of slavery. At no stage did the maroons in Suriname try to escape to British Guiana after 1833 or to French Guiana after 1848, in spite of the fact that the French and British colonial governments would not return runaway slaves to the Dutch authorities, and in spite of the fact that the rivers separating the three colonies were hardly patrolled. The colonial secretary in the Netherlands reported to the King in 1839 that the slave emancipation in British Guiana of 1833 posed no threat to slavery in Suriname.[14] And he was right. In the years 1844 to 1854, on average only 14 slaves per year fled to British Guiana.[15] It was with some satisfaction that the colonial administration reported to The Hague that several of these runaway slaves had returned, once they had discovered that even freedmen in British Guiana worked on the plantations.[16] The same occurred on Saint Martin, where planters from British Guiana had offered to buy the freedom of a substantial number of slaves in the hope that they would come to British Guiana as indentured laborers. However, the slaves on Saint Martin were not interested in obtaining their freedom this way and stayed put.[17] Had marronage been linked to an anti-slavery ideology, the incidence of running away should have increased during the nineteenth century and the slaves no longer would have absconded to the interior, but to the neighboring colonies, where slavery had been abolished.

Slave Rebellions in the Dutch Caribbean

No doubt, the most important slave rebellion in the Dutch Caribbean occurred in 1763 in Berbice, where the slaves almost succeeded in bringing the colony under their exclusive control. Several elements contributed to this rebellion. First of all, Berbice was a relatively small plantation colony with an extremely small white population. The number of whites at the time of the rebellion came to around 350, while there were about 95 plantations with 4,000 slaves. There was hardly any other colony in the Caribbean where the ratio between free and slave was so unequal.[18] Second, the military forces were virtually nonexistent. In February 1763, only 10 (!) soldiers manned the main fort of the colony, and the militia composed of the adult whites in the colony was not effective. Furthermore, contagious diseases had reduced the number of whites even further. Three ships at anchor in the river could not sail home, because too many of the crew had died and no additional sailors could be hired.

No wonder the rebels were able to conquer most of the colony very quickly, and during this time their leaders, a slave named Coffy, corresponded with Governor Van Hoogenheim about a possible negotiated peace settlement. Coffy had captured a mulatto boy as well as a white girl, both of whom could write. In one of the letters to the governor, Coffy explained that he did not want to continue the rebellion, and that the colony should be divided into two halves, one for the rebels and one for the whites. In case the whites wanted slaves, they should not try and recapture the rebels, but import additional slaves from Africa.[19] That seems to suggest that the insurgents were not interested in abolishing the institution of slavery.

In addition to the marronage in Suriname and the slave uprising in Berbice, the Dutch slave colonies experienced other forms of slave resistance in ways that were similar to those elsewhere in the region. The closest the slaves in the Dutch Caribbean came to promoting abolitionism was on the island of Curaçao. At the end of the eighteenth century, the population of that island counted about 12,000 persons, of whom 5,000 were slaves, 4,000 whites, and 3,000 free persons of color. There were no large plantations on Curaçao as the climate and particularly the long droughts made it impossible to cultivate sugarcane, coffee or tobacco. Slaves were used in all kinds of jobs and only a few slave owners possessed more than 10 slaves. Time and again, travelers remarked that slavery on Curaçao was far "milder" than in the Dutch plantation colonies.[20]

It was the position of Curaçao as a free port and as a center of information in the region that sparked the slave insurrection in 1795, headed by a slave named Tula. Tula and his fellow rebels asked for the abolition of slavery as all men were created equal. Yet, that demand did not originate on the island, but the rebels must have learned about the French occupation of the Netherlands and heard rumors that the abolition of slavery by the National Convention in Paris should also be implemented on Curaçao. "Undoubtedly the slaves were aware of the revolutionary principles of the French Revolution spread by free coloreds from the French islands."[21] There is no indication that the Curaçao slaves did anything else but follow ideas originating in Europe.

During the nineteenth century, Suriname also witnessed several slave conspiracies, some of which would be suppressed in their infancy. In 1836, on the plantation Leasowes in the district of Coronie, a slave called Colin acted as the leader of a slave conspiracy. Colin explained to his fellow slaves on the plantation that his spirit had moved to other parts of the world, where he had liberated slaves. Now he wanted to liberate his fellow slaves of Suriname, as the configuration of some stars seemed to indicate that the moment had come in which the blacks would turn into whites and the whites into blacks and that the whites would work for the blacks as slaves.[22] This idea certainly can be classified as an "ideology of liberation," but not as an ideology striving to abolish slavery.

Similarly, the self-liberation of the slaves on the Dutch section of the island of Saint Martin had its origin in Europe and in the French emancipation law of 1848. That law gave the slaves on the Dutch part of Saint Martin the opportunity to liberate themselves by absconding to the French section of the island. That happened so frequently that the slave owners of Dutch Saint Martin petitioned the Dutch government rapidly to emancipate their slaves and not to wait for a general emancipation law. Most slaves, however, remained in the Dutch section of Saint Martin in spite of the fact that they would have been free on the other side of the island. In this situation, the slave owners on Saint Martin could do little else but relinquish their ownership. The slaves remained the property of their masters on paper, but in actual practice had become free workers. They found their own jobs and kept their own pay. The slave owners no longer could rely on the fact that their slaves would work for them.[23] A committee advising the Dutch government on slave emancipation and compensation concluded that, on Saint Martin, slaves had no longer any value. Some planters on the island tried to introduce a system of contract labor, hoping that the slaves would agree to work if they were offered to keep half of what they had produced, but the owners discovered that the slaves had no inclination to honor such contracts.[24] In the end, the slaves on Saint Martin were emancipated on 1 July 1863, as were all other slaves in the Dutch Caribbean. The slave owners on Dutch Saint Martin, however, received only 30 guilders in compensation per slave, while the slave owners of the other Dutch islands in the Caribbean received 200 guilders.[25]

Conclusion

There is no indication that the slaves in the Dutch Caribbean abolished slavery or even ever questioned the principles of unfree labor. And why should they? Except for the few slaves who accompanied their masters to Europe, no African or Caribbean slave had any experience of what a society without slaves looked like. That explains why the runaway slaves in Dutch Guiana wanted to escape the conditions of slavery, but were not opposed to others remaining slaves. It also explains why the leaders of the Berbice slave rebellion of 1763 proposed to divide the colony into two parts, suggesting that in one of these, the slave trade and slavery should continue to exist. None of the acts of slave resistance were started in order to get rid of the *system* of slavery, but in order to put pressure on the slave owners and plantation management to force them to make changes *within* that system.

The fact that the slaves did not strive to abolish slavery does not indicate that the slaves in the Dutch Caribbean were indifferent toward influencing the conditions of slavery. They constantly strove to obtain more free time in order to manage their own lives. They wanted time for themselves so that they could tend to their own gardens, sell their produce at other plantations or at slave markets, go fishing and hunting and to own guns, visit relations at other plantations, and stay away from their plantation from time to time. And over time, the slaves had their way. During the last decades of slavery, the institution went through a series of important changes as no new slaves arrived from Africa, as the slave population was ageing, as the metropolitan government was under international moral pressure to abolish slavery and wanted to preempt such criticism by constantly improving the living and working conditions of the slaves. These changes gave the slaves much more leverage than before in realizing their own preferences, as the Suriname slaves could threaten to run away to the neighboring colonies where they would be free.

However, creating more freedom within the system of slavery and abolishing slavery require two opposite agendas. The process of amelioration reduced the resistance against slavery in a similar way as the improvements in wages, housing, health care, and in working and living conditions reduced the hostility of the European proletariat toward capitalism. If left to the slaves, slavery in the Dutch Caribbean could have continued for several decades—as it did in Cuba and Brazil. Abolitionism in the Dutch Caribbean arrived from Europe. In 1860, slavery in the Dutch colonies was abolished as of 1 July 1863 by the Dutch legislature in The Hague. Yet, that decision cannot be seen as the triumph of the free labor ideology in The Netherlands. There might have been a few believers in that maxim of Adam Smith, but in general the Dutch remained skeptical about free labor in view of the rapid decline of the post-emancipation economies of the British and French Caribbean. That is why the

Dutch parliament instituted a period of apprenticeship of ten years, longer than anywhere else had instituted it.

Notes

I would like to thank some of the participants of the annual meeting of the Association of Caribbean Historians in Paramaribo (May 2008), and particularly Gert Oostindie, for their critical commentary and suggestions.

1. On the Suriname maroons see Wim Hoogbergen, 'De Bosnegers zijn gekomen' Slavernij en rebellie in Suriname (Amsterdam: Prometheus, 1992).
2. Franklin W. Knight, The Caribbean. The Genesis of a Fragmented Nationalism (New York: Oxford University Press, 1990), 366, 367 (table 4).
3. Cornelis Ch. Goslinga, The Dutch in the Caribbean and in the Guianas, 1680–1791 (Assen: Van Gorcum, 1985), 353 (Suriname), 454 (Demerara).
4. Henk den Heijer, De geschiedenis van de WIC (Zutphen: De Walburg Pers, 1994), 187; and G.W. van der Meiden, Betwist bestuur. De eerste eeuw bestuurlijke ruzies in Suriname, 1651–1753, 2nd ed. (Amsterdam: Bataafse Leeuw, 2008), 36–46.
5. Ruud Beeldsnijder, 'Om werk van jullie te hebben'. Plantageslaven in Suriname, 1730–1750 (Utrecht: Vakgroep Culturele Antropologie, [Bronnen voor de Studie van Afro-Suri-naamse Samenlevingen, 16], 1994), 219.
6. Seymour Drescher, "The Long Goodbye. Dutch Capitalism and Antislavery in Comparative Perspective," in Fifty Years Later, Antislavery, Capitalism and Modernity in the Dutch Orbit, ed. Gert Oostindie (Pittsburgh: the University of Pittsburgh Press, 1995), 50.
7. Hoogbergen, 'De Bosnegers zijn gekomen,' 46.
8. A. Kappler, Zes jaren in Suriname, 1836–1842. Schetsen en taferelen (Zutphen: De Walburg Pers, 1983), 136.
9. Pieter Emmer, The Dutch in the Atlantic Economy, 1580–1880. Trade, Slavery and Emancipation (Aldershot: Ashgate/Variorum, 1998), 28, 29.
10. Wim S.M. Hoogbergen, "Het verband tussen marronage en slavenopstanden in Suriname," SWI Forum, vol 7 (1990): 28–60.
11. Beeldsnijder, 'Om werk van jullie te hebben,' 223, 224.
12. Beeldsnijder, 'Om werk van jullie te hebben,' 221.
13. J.P. Siwpersad, De Nederlandse regering en de afschaffing van de Surinaamse slavernij (1833–1863) (Groningen: Bouma/Castricum: Hagen, 1979), 23.
14. Siwpersad, De Nederlandse regering, 17,18.
15. Siwpersad, De Nederlandse regering, 23.
16. A.F. Paula, 'Vrije'slaven. Een sociaal-historische Studie over de dualistische slavenemancipatie op Nederlands Sint Maarten, 1816–1863 (Zutphen: De Walburg pers, 1993), 68.
17. Paula, 'Vrije' slaven, 68.
18. Stanley L. Engerman and Barry W. Higman, "The Demographic Structure of the Caribbean Slave Societies in the Eighteenth and Nineteenth Centuries," in General History of the Caribbean, vol. III, The Slave Societies of the Caribbean, ed. Franklin W. Knight (London and Basingstoke: UNESCO Publishing/MacMillan Education, 1997), 48, 49 (table 2.1).
19. Goslinga, The Dutch in the Caribbean, 461.
20. W.E. Renekema, "De export van Curaçaose slaven 1819–1847," in Exercities in ons verleden. Twaalf opstellen over de economische en sociale geschiedenis van Nederland en koloniën 1800–1950, eds. P. Boomgaard, L. Noordegraaf, H.de Vries, and W.M. Zappey (Assen: Van Gorcum, 1981), 204, 205.
21. Cornelis Ch. Goslinga, The Dutch in the Caribbean and in Surinam 1791/5–1942 (Assen/Maastricht: Van Gorcum, 1990), 5.

22. Sendew Hira, *Van Priary tot en met De Kom. De geschiedenis van het verzet in Suriname, 1630–1940* (Rotterdam: Futile, 1982), 164–166.
23. Paula, *'Vrije'slaven,* 131.
24. Paula, *'Vrije'slaven,* 131–135.
25. Paula, *'Vrije'slaven,* 145.

Bibliography

Beeldsnijder, R., *'Om werk van jullie te hebben'. Plantageslaven in Suriname, 1730–1750* (Utrecht: Vakgroep Culturele Antropologie, [Bronnen voor de Studie van Afro-Surinaamse Samenlevingen, 16], 1994).

Boomgaard, P., L. Noordegraaf, H.de Vries, and W.M. Zappey (eds), *Exercities in ons verleden. Twaalf opstellen over de economische en sociale geschiedenis van Nederland en koloniën 1800–1950* (Assen: Van Gorcum, 1981).

Emmer, Pieter, *The Dutch in the Atlantic Economy, 1580–1880. Trade, Slavery and Emancipation* (Aldershot: Ashgate/Variorum, 1998).

Goslinga, Cornelis Ch., *The Dutch in the Caribbean and in the Guianas, 1680–1791* (Assen: Van Gorcum, 1985).

Goslinga, Cornelis Ch., *The Dutch in the Caribbean and in Surinam 1791/5–1942* (Assen/Maastricht: Van Gorcum, 1990).

Heijer, Henk den, *De geschiedenis van de WIC* (Zutphen: De Walburg Pers, 1994).

Hira, Sendew, *Van Priary tot en met De Kom. De geschiedenis van het verzet in Suriname, 1630–1940* (Rotterdam: Futile, 1982).

Hoogbergen, Wim, *'De Bosnegers zijn gekomen'Slavernij en rebellie in Suriname* (Amsterdam: Prometheus, 1992).

Kappler, A., *Zes jaren in Suriname, 1836–1842. Schetsen en taferelen* (Zutphen: De Walburg Pers, 1983).

Knight, Franklin W., *The Caribbean. The Genesis of a Fragmented Nationalism* (New York: Oxford University Press, 1990).

Knight, Franklin W. (ed.), *General History of the Caribbean*, vol. III, *The Slave Societies of the Caribbean* (London and Basingstoke: UNESCO Publishing/MacMillan Education, 1997).

Meiden, G.W. van der, *Betwist bestuur. De eerste eeuw bestuurlijke ruzies in Suriname, 1651–1753*, 2nd ed. (Amsterdam: Bataafse Leeuw, 2008).

Oostindie, Gert, *Fifty Years Later, Antislavery, Capitalism and Modernity in the Dutch Orbit* (Pittsburgh: the University of Pittsburgh Press, 1995).

Paula, A.F., *'Vrije'slaven. Een sociaal-historische Studie over de dualistische slavene-mancipatie op Nederlands Sint Maarten, 1816–1863* (Zutphen: De Walburg pers, 1993).

Siwpersad, J.P., *De Nederlandse regering en de afschaffing van de Surinaamse slavernij (1833–1863)* (Groningen: Bouma/Castricum, Hagen, 1979).

3

SLAVE RESISTANCE AND EMANCIPATION: THE CASE OF SAINT-DOMINGUE

David Geggus

☙❧

The ending of slavery and the slave trade in the Americas emerged out of a matrix of factors of which slave resistance was one among many. From Massachusetts in 1780 to Brazil in 1888, it seems to have played an essential or preponderant role, without which abolition would not have ensued for some time, in only two cases. One of these was the Danish West Indies in 1848, where a slave uprising led to immediate abolition. Even here, it should be noted, a gradual emancipation program had been instituted the previous year, and the rebellion was touched off by news of slave emancipation in the French colonies. The other case was the French Caribbean in the 1790s, where the French government's first, and short-lived, abolition of slavery is impossible to imagine without the 1791 uprising in Saint-Domingue.

The importance of the Saint-Domingue slave revolt in bringing about the local emancipation proclamations of 1793 and the decree of 4 February 1794 for the whole French empire seems to me difficult to dispute. The time lag between the uprising and the proclamations tells us that it was not a sufficient cause, but it was nonetheless a necessary cause. France's colonial policy throughout the French Revolution was usually made in reaction to events in the West Indies; at least until Napoleon Bonaparte's rise to power, the initiative tended to lie with Caribbean actors. Although the scholarship of the last twenty years has given novel emphasis to the colonial question's importance in Revolutionary France, no one could argue that either metropolitan revolutionary idealism or the salon-based anti-slavery of the Amis des Noirs would have ended colonial slavery had not thousands of slaves in northern Saint-Domingue taken matters into their own hands.

João Marques is nonetheless right, I think, to stress that the 1791 insurrection did not by itself lead to the abolition in 1793. From its first few days, it was by far the largest and most destructive slave rebellion in the Americas. And it clearly provoked, during the following year, a new and more widespread concern in France with abolishing slavery.[1] However, this new concern remained confined to a handful of revolutionaries, and it is difficult to see how it would have ended colonial slavery if France had not gone to war with Spain and Britain at the beginning of 1793.[2] War radically shifted the balance of power between the French and the insurgent slaves. The Spanish in Santo Domingo successfully recruited the main insurgent leaders in May with offers of freedom for themselves and their families, and they began seizing parts of Saint-Domingue in late June. War with England meant that France could no longer safely send troops across the Atlantic, and that the colony's fate would be decided locally. The prospect of foreign intervention also encouraged white colonists to rebel against the authoritarian civil commissioner Sonthonax. This led to the destruction of the colony's main city and to Sonthonax's first, limited, abolition proclamation of June 21, which was applied only in the North Province and only to men who would fight for the Republic. Because of its failure to win over many black insurgents, and the mounting threat of foreign intervention, the proclamation was progressively extended down to October to embrace complete emancipation for all of the colony's slaves.[3]

Historians who have written that Sonthonax's proclamations did no more than recognize an emancipation that the slaves had already seized are incorrect. The 1791 uprising was massive, but, as Marques states, it remained generally confined to the central and eastern parts of Saint-Domingue's north province. The civil war between whites and free coloreds through the early months of 1792 and slave rebellions that were usually brief and local intermittently interrupted production in many other parts of the colony. Yet, the plantation regime was still largely intact in August 1793.[4]

Marques, however, tends to understate the scope and strength of the black revolution. Although in some details he exaggerates its impact— probably only a few hundred whites, not a thousand, were killed in its opening month—it is risky to claim it was "moribund" at the beginning of 1793. There is no doubt that the insurgents were then in full retreat before a long-delayed military offensive. In the north, they suffered heavy casualties, were driven from the plains and most of their mountain camps, and many surrendered. In the south, the stronghold of Les Platons was captured. However, the white troops' casualties (chiefly from disease) seem to have brought the offensive to a standstill, and we simply do not know how events would have turned out if Sonthonax had not halted the campaign in early February 1793. By April, the insurgents regained most of the ground they had lost.[5]

Marques notes the variety of demands put forward by or attributed to the rebel slaves during the first year of the insurrection. Yet he concludes and emphasizes that the revolt was essentially "a limited campaign for better terms of bondage." Although for some insurgents the "paramount objective was to kill all of the whites and take possession of the colony," the majority, he claims, had only reformist goals. This question of the slave insurgents' aims is a difficult matter of interpretation; the evidence is contradictory and questionable, and after thirty years of researching the issue, I cannot claim to have a clear picture myself. Marques' formulation, however, as to what the majority and a minority wanted, reverses the view of most modern historians, who tend to contrast the self-interested and limited aims of the slaves' leaders with the more radical ambitions of the masses they led.[6]

Marques is absolutely correct to underline the limited objectives of the main leaders Jean-François and Biassou. More than once they sought to negotiate a secret settlement that would have returned most of their followers to slavery. They rounded up women and children on the plantations and sold them to their Spanish neighbors. And the one piece of documentary evidence that purports to show them demanding liberty for all is fairly certainly a forgery.[7] Even so, there is no reason to suppose that the aspirations of the majority of insurgent slaves went no further than those of their leaders, especially as the leaders' negotiations with the whites appear to have failed partly because of their followers' resistance. Expectations no doubt fluctuated with military fortunes, but it seems unlikely that the insurgents would have killed and destroyed on such a massive scale unless they were expecting to live afterwards free from the possibility of French revenge. Moreover, since the best evidence we have of the rebels' expecting to drive out the French dates from the very beginning of the uprising, one cannot characterize their aims as progressing from reformist to revolutionary, as several scholars have done.[8]

While it is reasonable to suppose that the Saint-Domingue insurgents hoped to win freedom for themselves, rather than just a reform of slavery, there is little to suggest that they sought to emancipate all of the colony's slaves, that is, the majority who were not participants in the insurrection. The insurgents' correspondence that survives in French and Spanish archives has far more to say about their supposed royalism than about libertarian ideology, and it scarcely invokes the pursuit of freedom as a reason for their revolt until after slavery was abolished in Saint-Domingue in the late summer of 1793.

I agree, therefore, with João Marques's central thesis that "from 1793–94 onward, the slave revolt blended" or became increasingly identified with the abolitionist cause. This was the view of Haiti's first historian, Thomas Madiou, and Eugene Genovese evoked a similar idea in his *From*

Rebellion to Revolution.[9] Strangely, however, Marques weakens his own argument at this point. Rather than making *commissaire* Sonthonax the prime mover in the pursuit of emancipation for all, he seems to regard Toussaint Louverture as the key figure. For him, Sonthonax was a pragmatic politician desperately maneuvering through a dire political crisis, whereas Toussaint had read Raynal and was inspired by British abolitionism and the French Revolution. It may well be that Toussaint was an idealist who hoped to end slavery, but the only documentary evidence we have on this question prior to mid 1793 shows him twice attempting to negotiate a peace treaty (in December 1791 and September 1792) that would have left almost all of the insurgents enslaved. Most historians have depicted him as seeking "la liberté générale" by mid June 1793, but they unwittingly relied on a nineteenth century fraud. When, in late August 1793, Toussaint first associated himself with liberty and equality, he was clearly following in the footsteps of Sonthonax, who for several weeks had been signaling his intention to free all slaves.[10] During the period after August 1793, when black insurgents gradually rallied to the French Republic and, in Marques's words, "consciously fought for the end of slavery," they were technically no longer slaves.

Most surprising of all, Marques is unaware of Sonthonax's abolitionist credentials. In the 1980s, Robert Stein and Yves Benot brought to light a newspaper article Sonthonax had anonymously written in September 1790 that advocated abolishing slavery and giving political rights to former slaves.[11] This discovery gives new weight to metropolitan and idealist factors in interpretations of the Haitian Revolution as opposed to local and materialist ones. It should force historians to reevaluate many of Sonthonax's actions in Saint-Domingue. Above all, it makes his emancipation proclamation seem somewhat less of a desperate act of *Realpolitik*.

In treating the international impact of the revolution, Marques's analysis resembles his treatment of the revolution itself: he understates the case for Haitian influence, but does not push his own counterargument far enough. There also seems some contradiction in claiming that Haiti's example had a positive impact on British abolition but "did not lead to the abolition of slavery ... in any Western country."

I agree that Haiti's value for abolitionists in the propaganda war over slavery has generally been exaggerated. It is by no means clear whether the revolution and the new state it created enhanced whites' opinions of blacks or merely hardened existing prejudices.[12] Nor do contemporaries seem to have been convinced by the argument that abolition was needed to defuse the threat of rebellion.[13] Conversely, the revolution was probably not very important in delaying abolition either. The 1791 slave revolt did not prevent the British anti-slavery movement from achieving its first major success in April 1792, whereas the failures of the following decade can be attributed to the republican revolution in France, the fear of which was sufficient to doom all reforming efforts in Britain. In the nineteenth century, pro-slavery spokesmen held up Haiti as a warning, but by the late 1820s, many were acknowledging that, born of revolution, it was not a reliable guide as to how other societies might develop after slavery.[14]

Nevertheless, I would argue that the Haitian Revolution had a positive influence on anti-slavery in a few ways. One was in relaunching the British anti-slavery campaign in early 1804 in the wake of Haitian independence. Disingenuously or sincerely, the argument of imminent danger was foregrounded by the abolitionists and apparently accepted by Prime Minister Pitt. It was no more than a contributory factor in anti-slavery's revival, but it was important enough to convert the pro-slavery newspaper *The Times* to supporting an end to the slave trade.[15]

The most compelling argument in favor of Haiti's influence, however, (apart from the assistance given to Simón Bolívar, which Marques very briefly acknowledges) concerns Anglo-French rivalry. The Haitian Revolution enabled British politicians to vote their consciences in 1807 and 1833, without the fear that it would significantly advantage their traditional enemy, France, which the revolution had removed as a serious competitor in the tropical produce market.[16] It is difficult to imagine Parliament ending the slave trade, or slavery, if France had remained a commercial as well as a political rival. Although France's status as Britain's traditional enemy was fading fast by 1833, British legislators surely would have been much less likely to risk disrupting colonial production to their competitors' advantage, if Saint-Domingue had still been a French colony.

In view of the fact that Marques does not address this point, I am surprised that, at the end of an analysis that minimizes the Haitian role and the imminent threat argument, he abruptly concludes that they were, nonetheless, influential in passing the 1807 abolition act. However useful the case of Haiti proved in relaunching the anti-slavery movement in 1804, it seems to me that the work of Roger Anstey and Seymour Drescher demonstrates that the Haitian Revolution was not a significant issue in the parliamentary debates.[17]

* * *

I agree with João Marques that eagerness to redress the distorted interpretations of previous generations has often caused contemporary historians to inflate the incidence and importance of slaves' resistance to slavery. This has taken a variety of forms. Sometimes conspiracies that never reached fruition are called revolts. Sometimes the dimensions or frequency of maroonage or revolts is exaggerated. Acts of revenge or self-aggrandizement are claimed, without evidence, as politically motivated, and the fear inspired in slave owners is overstated. Although the inflation of slave resistance's role in ending slavery has not been confined to the Americas, it seems likely that the racial nature of American slavery has made such distortions more likely.[18] The influence of the Haitian Revolution, easily the most important instance of slave resistance, went for a long time largely unrecognized, but in recent years historians have tended to go too far in emphasizing its impact, for example, on the Louisiana Purchase or the development of democracy, as well as in inspiring rebellion and propelling abolition elsewhere.[19]

It seems to me that both of these distortions are present in Marques's treatment of the Haitian case. While I think the general thrust of his argument is both sound and salutary, he does not give the revolution and its repercussions their full due, but, at the same time, does not go far enough in his revisionism.

Notes

1. Yves Benot (*La Révolution française et la fin des colonies* (Paris, 1987)) showed that Chaumette, Marat, and Claude Milscent were the first Jacobins to, belatedly, write in favor of abolition in the wake of the slave uprising. The first abolition proposal put to the French legislature came in February 1792 in a report by the Girondin deputy Guadet that was delivered in his absence by Jean-Philippe Garran Coulon. It was very tentative but was followed by other proposals from Ducos and Armand Kersaint. See *Archives parlementaires de 1787 à 1860 (première série)* (Paris, 1867–1913), 39: 209–220; 40: 584–598.

2. One needs to specify "colonial slavery," because it is usually forgotten that slavery in France was abolished—and blacks were enfranchised—by the National Assembly in September 1791. This had nothing to do with the Saint-Domingue slave uprising, news of which reached France only in late October.

3. On the Spanish intervention, see David Geggus, "The Exile of the 1791 Slave Leaders: Spain's Resettlement of Its Black Auxiliary Troops," *Journal of Haitian Studies* 8:2 (2002): 52–67; on the emancipation decrees, Robert Stein, "The Abolition of Slavery in the North, West, and South of Saint Domingue," *The Americas* 41 (1985): 47–55.

4. See David Geggus, *Slavery, War, and Revolution: The British Occupation of Saint Domingue, 1793–1798* (Oxford, 1982), 42–43, 100–105.

5. For a representative account, see *Histoire des désastres de Saint-Domingue* (Paris, 1795), 256–279.

6. For example, Laurent Dubois, *Avengers of the New World: The Story of the Haitian Revolution* (Cambridge, MA, 2004), 124–128; Carolyn Fick, *The Making of Haiti: The Saint Domingue Revolution from Below* (Knoxville, 1990), 114–117; Geggus, *Slavery, War, and Revolution*, 43.

7. David Geggus, "Print Culture and the Haitian Revolution: the Written and the Spoken Word," *Proceedings of the American Antiquarian Society* 116, part 2 (October 2006): 308–311; Geggus, "The Caribbean in the Age of Revolution," in *Age of Revolutions or World Crisis? Global Causation, Connection, and Comparison, c. 1760–1840*, ed. David Armitage and Sanjay Subrahmanyam (forthcoming).

8. E.g., Michel-Rolph Trouillot, *Silencing the Past* (Boston, MA, 1995), 89; Laurent Dubois, "An Enslaved Enlightenment: Rethinking the Intellectual History of the French Atlantic," *Social History* 31 (2006): 12. For the evidence, see Geggus, "Print Culture," 308–309; Geggus, *Slavery, War, and Revolution*, 302.

9. Thomas Madiou, *Histoire d'Haïti* (1847–48; Port-au-Prince, 1922), 1: 490; Eugene Genovese, *From Rebellion to Revolution: Afro-American Slave Revolts in the Making of the Modern World* (Baton Rouge, 1979).

10. David Geggus, "Toussaint Louverture et l'abolition de l'esclavage à Saint-Domingue," in *Les abolitions dans les Amériques*, ed. Liliane Chauleau (Fort de France, 2001), 112–113; Geggus, "Toussaint Louverture and the Haitian Revolution," in *Profiles of Revolutionaries in Atlantic History, 1750–1850*, ed. R. William Weisberger (New York, 2007), 120–122.

11. Robert L. Stein, *Léger Félicité Sonthonax: the Lost Sentinel of the Republic* (Rutherford, 1985), 21; Benot, *La Révolution française*, 125–126.
12. David Geggus, "The Influence of the Haitian Revolution on Blacks in Latin America and the Caribbean," in *Blacks, Coloureds and National Identity in Nineteenth-Century Latin America*, ed. Nancy Naro (London, 2003), 47.
13. Seymour Drescher, "The Limits of Example," in *The Impact of the Haitian Revolution in the Atlantic World*, ed. David Geggus (Columbia, SC, 2001), 11–12.
14. David Geggus, "Haiti and the Abolitionists: Opinion, Propaganda and International Politics in Britain and France, 1804–1838," in *Abolition and its Aftermath: The Historical Context, 1790–1916*, ed. David Richardson (London, 1985).
15. Geggus, "Haiti and the Abolitionists," 115–116.
16. David Brion Davis, *Problem of Slavery in the Age of Revolution, 1770–1823* (Ithaca, NY, 1975), 117, 440; Robin Blackburn, *The Overthrow of Colonial Slavery* (London, 1988), 145.
17. Roger Anstey, *The Atlantic Slave Trade and British Abolition, 1769–1810* (London, 1975), 321–402; Seymour Drescher, *Capitalism and Antislavery: British Mobilization in Comparative Perspective* (New York, 1986), 96–99, 105–106.
18. Pierre Dockès, *Medieval Slavery and Liberation* (Chicago, 1979), was widely criticized for exaggerating the significance of resistance in the ancient world.
19. David Geggus, "French Imperialism and the Louisiana Purchase," in *The Louisiana Purchase and its Peoples: Perspectives from the New Orleans Conference*, ed. Paul Hoffman (Lafayette, 2004), 25–34; Geggus, "The Caribbean in the Age of Revolution"; Geggus, "The French and Haitian Revolutions and Resistance to Slavery in the Americas: an Overview," *Revue française d'histoire d'Outre-Mer* 282-3 (1989): 107–124.

Bibliography

Anstey, Roger. *The Atlantic Slave Trade and British Abolition, 1769–1810* (London: Macmillan, 1975).

Benot, Yves. *La Révolution française et la fin des colonies* (Paris, 1987).

Blackburn, Robin. *The Overthrow of Colonial Slavery* (London: Verso, 1988).

Davis, David Brion. *Problem of Slavery in the Age of Revolution, 1770–1823* (Ithaca, NY: Cornell University Press, 1975).

Dockès, Pierre. *Medieval Slavery and Liberation* (Chicago: Chicago University Press, 1979).

Drescher, Seymour. "The Limits of Example," in *The Impact of the Haitian Revolution in the Atlantic World*, ed. David Geggus (Columbia, SC: University of South Carolina Press, 2001).

Drescher, Seymour. *Capitalism and Antislavery: British Mobilization in Comparative Perspective* (New York: Macmillan, 1986).

Dubois, Laurent. "An Enslaved Enlightenment: Rethinking the Intellectual History of the French Atlantic," *Social History* 31 (2006): 1–14.

Dubois, Laurent. *Avengers of the New World: The Story of the Haitian Revolution* (Cambridge, MA: Harvard University Press, 2004).

Fick, Carolyn. *The Making of Haiti: The Saint Domingue Revolution from Below* (Knoxville: University of Tennessee, 1990).

Geggus, David, "Toussaint Louverture et l'abolition de l'esclavage à Saint-Domingue," in *Les abolitions dans les Amériques*, ed. Liliane Chauleau (Fort de France, 2001).

Geggus, David. "French Imperialism and the Louisiana Purchase," in *The Louisiana Purchase and its Peoples: Perspectives from the New Orleans Conference*, ed. Paul Hoffman (Lafayette, 2004).

Geggus, David. "Haiti and the Abolitionists: Opinion, Propaganda and International Politics in Britain and France, 1804–1838," in *Abolition and its Aftermath: The Historical Context, 1790–1916*, ed. David Richardson (London: Frank Cass, 1985).

Geggus, David. "Print Culture and the Haitian Revolution: the Written and the Spoken Word," *Proceedings of the American Antiquarian Society*, 116, part 2 (October 2006): 308–311.

Geggus, David. "The Caribbean in the Age of Revolution," in *Age of Revolutions in Global Context, c. 1760–1840*, ed. David Armitage and Sanjay Subrahmanyam (Basingstoke: Palgrave Macmillan, 2009).

Geggus, David. "The Exile of the 1791 Slave Leaders: Spain's Resettlement of Its Black Auxiliary Troops," *Journal of Haitian Studies* 8:2 (2002): 52–67.

Geggus, David. "The French and Haitian Revolutions and Resistance to Slavery in the Americas: an Overview," *Revue française d'histoire d'Outre-Mer* 282–3 (1989): 107–124.

Geggus, David. "The Influence of the Haitian Revolution on Blacks in Latin America and the Caribbean," in *Blacks, Coloureds and National Identity in Nineteenth-Century Latin America*, ed. Nancy Naro (London: Institute of Latin American Studies, 2003).

Geggus, David. "Toussaint Louverture and the Haitian Revolution," in *Profiles of Revolutionaries in Atlantic History, 1750–1850*, ed. R. William Weisberger (New York, 2007).

Geggus, David. *Slavery, War, and Revolution: The British Occupation of Saint Domingue, 1793–1798* (Oxford: Oxford University Press, 1982).

Histoire des désastres de Saint-Domingue (Paris, 1795).

Madiou, Thomas. *Histoire d'Haiti* (Port-au-Prince, 1922).

Eugene Genovese, *From Rebellion to Revolution: Afro-American Slave Revolts in the Making of the Modern World* (Baton Rouge, Louisiana State University Press, 1979).

Stein, Robert L. *Léger Félicité Sonthonax: the Lost Sentinel of the Republic* (Rutherford, 1985).

Stein, Robert. "The Abolition of Slavery in the North, West, and South of Saint Domingue," *The Americas* 41 (1985): 47–55.

Trouillot, Michel-Rolph. *Silencing the Past* (Boston, MA: Beacon Press, 1995).

4

CIVILIZING INSURGENCY:
TWO VARIANTS OF SLAVE REVOLTS
IN THE AGE OF REVOLUTION

Seymour Drescher

ᏟᎧ

Give me a lever long enough and a fulcrum on which to place it and I shall move the world.
—Archimedes

How was slavery abolished? João Pedro Marques sets his sights on deflating a new master narrative that places insurgent slave revolts at the center of the story. Both the traditional and new narratives agree that the successful and climactic assaults on this perennial institution began at the end of the eighteenth century. However, in the new narrative, African slave resistance long preceded Euro-American abolitionism. Slaves themselves instigated incessant and often massive revolts for centuries before the emergence of political abolitionism. They were also the primary and principal catalysts in the two major stages in the emancipation process: ending the intercontinental slave trade and the dismantling of the institution itself.

The temporal extension of the new approach is clear. The process began long before the pivotal "age of abolition," in the 1770s. Various forms of slave resistance must be re-imagined as one long uninterrupted struggle against the institution. One should include in the process all flights from enslavement and all autonomous communities formed by ex-slaves beyond the zone of slavery.[1] The final stage of the emancipation process was introduced by a series of massive collective uprisings, forcing the closure of the institution. All forms of collective resistance, before and after the age of revolution (c. 1775–1830), thus eroded the institution and portended its destruction. The great slave uprisings in Saint-Domingue in 1791 and Jamaica in 1831 were only the climactic and decisive moments in the process.

Marques challenges this narrative both logically and empirically. You cannot explain a variable by a constant. Slavery was a millennial institution that produced millennial resistance of every type catalogued in its later New World embodiments. The level of revolts in both ancient Roman and Medieval Muslim slavery produced uprisings of scale and durability that matched or exceeded similar conflicts in the Americas. Against the catalogue of day-to-day resistance, flight, and marronage must be set the robustness of the institution over centuries and its flexibility in using manumission and maroon communities to stabilize the institution. Three centuries after the founding of the Atlantic system, the cumulative effect of slave revolts on both sides of the Atlantic had neither eroded the imperial commitment to the institution nor halted its expansion. On the contrary, as Marques concludes, for three centuries Western colonial slaves struggled for individual or group freedom, just as Old World slaves had done before them. But they neither sought nor succeeded in eliminating the institution. Nor did they formulate "an anti-slavery conception of human relations." Slave rebellion was not synonymous with anti-slavery, either in intention or impact.[2]

I. The Impact of the Haitian Revolution

I will concentrate on two events Marques designates as examples of *his* "new equation," the slave revolts that broke out in the critical four decades between 1791 and 1832: in Saint-Domingue (1791–1804); in Barbados (1816); in Demerara (1823); and in Jamaica (1831–32). Marques emphasizes that these four uprisings occurred within the context of a quantitative surge in major uprisings throughout the colonial world, of which these were only "key" episodes.

In terms of its impact upon the institution of slavery, the Saint-Domingue/Haitian uprising was notable for its shifting combination of traditional and novel elements. The rebels' appealed to both African ceremonies and royalist symbolism as powerful sources of solidarity. The pattern of insurgent slave behavior and ideological options in the colony lurched as military fortunes shifted both within and beyond Saint-Domingue. Various groups of slaves adhered to or withdrew allegiances from the French, British, and Spanish monarchies before coalescing under Toussaint Louverture in favor of France and general emancipation. Then, under Dessalines, they coalesced against France and re-enslavement. In dramatic contrast with the insurgents in Dutch Berbice three decades earlier, the rebels were aware of the new possibilities opened up by a divided France and a divided and embattled Europe. Within this context, slaves had opportunities to maneuver first for their personal freedom, then for the freedom of all of the colony's slaves, and, finally, for independence from European domination.

In terms of impact, Haiti transmitted news of its radical revolution to slave populations throughout the Atlantic world. To slaves and non-slaves alike, it demonstrated the possibilities and dangers entailed in the dramatic and violent destruction of the relationship into which they were bound. Two major messages were sent out and variously interpreted by this international audience. The first was the possibility that ex-slave communities might establish an independent polity based upon European models of republics or monarchies and create new societies and economies based upon free or coerced labor. The second message was the potential of such a revolution to intensify brutalization and exterminatory violence. For most articulate Frenchmen and many other Europeans the message of Saint-Domingue's revolutionary years were framed by the twin images of the initial uprising in the summer of 1791, with its destruction of life and property, and the massacre of the remaining French population in 1804 in the wake of Haiti's independence.

A glance at the sites of both rebellion and repression beyond Haiti indicates the impact of this long revolution on the greater Caribbean.[3] As Marques notes, the revolt did not dampen imperial ambitions during their struggles in the 1790s. Nor did it halt the appetites of Europeans for more slaves. Between 1791 and 1804, the slave trades of every imperial power not aligned with France (and thus exposed to British naval predation) thrived. The British, the Spanish, and the Portuguese trades' all expanded. Even the Danish colonies, which officially terminated the importation of Africans in 1802, experienced the biggest trade in their entire existence during the period of the Haitian revolution. As for the new United States of America, more enslaved Africans were unloaded in its ports after 1791 than in any previous equivalent period in its colonial history. On the eve of the abolition of the US transatlantic trade, America's imports actually reached their all time peak. More Africans landed there in 1806–1807 than during the entire period between the end of the Seven Years War and the Saint-Domingue Revolution.[4] Nowhere did the revolutionary threat deter slavers or their governments from filling their slave ships with what abolitionists already called the "seeds of destruction."

This leads me to what is an overstatement in Marques' evaluation of the impact of the Haitian revolution. In Britain, he maintains, revolution had a positive impact in the acceleration of the abolition of the slave trade in 1807. Of course, between 1789 and 1804, abolitionists did succeed in constricting some new potential frontiers of British slave expansion. One regulatory restriction, in 1799, probably did diminish Britain's competitive edge in the trade, but Saint-Domingue played no part in the discussions of either slave frontier restrictions or shipboard regulations. Between the outbreak of the Saint-Domingue slave revolution and the final assault on the British slave trade in 1806–1807, British slavers remained the premier transporters of Africans to the New World.

Did the "fear factor" at least deflect the pattern of the trade away from the neighborhood of the slave revolution? No. The pattern of slave imports into the Caribbean indicates that the Saint-Domingue revolution seems, instead, to have stimulated planters' appetites for slaves in direct proportion to a colony's proximity to Hispãnola, i.e., to Jamaica, Cuba, and Puerto Rico. Of the three, Jamaica was first off the mark in 1791 and remained the principal British colonial beneficiary of the Haitian revolution. Jamaica's exports of sugar increased by 35,000 tons from the export period of 1786–1790 to 1801–1805. That quantity was more than three and a half times greater than Cuba's increase. The result was that in the first decade of the nineteenth century, Jamaica led the world in exports of both sugar and coffee.

Rather than fearing the "seeds of destruction," Jamaica led the West Indian attack on abolition as being ruinous to its own future growth and competitiveness.[5] We may therefore surmise that the "fear factor" in the British empire, as elsewhere, was inversely proportional to the distance of the Britons from the epicenter of the revolution. David Geggus has drawn attention to Jamaica's enigmatic status as an island of stability in the revolutionary Caribbean of the 1790s. How much more enigmatic then was its relative freedom from slave uprisings throughout the entire "Age of Revolution." One of the most turbulent British colonies before the last quarter of the eighteenth century, Jamaica experienced no major uprising between Tacky's revolt in 1760 and the great "Baptist War" in 1831.[6]

What then, of the "fear factor" in the British metropole itself? Marques makes claims for Haiti's significant contribution to the ending of the British slave trade in 1807. This assessment does not rely upon any empirical analysis of British governmental policy, public discussion, or even abolitionist positions in the period just preceding British abolition. Begin with governmental policy: did the British government, in any of its activities before 1807, act on the premise that the danger of accumulating slaves outweighed the risks of expansion? In 1806, the most pro-abolitionist ministry to come into office during the twenty year struggle over the slave trade made a firm decision to retain that portion of Dutch Guiana (Demerara) that had the highest percentage of newly imported Africans in Guiana. This percentage was higher than those in any of Britain's long-established colonies. So Britain was determined to acquire slave colonies brimming with freshly imported Africans on the very eve of abolition.

Moreover, the government also decided that, if they restored the rest of Guiana (Suriname) to its former Dutch rulers, the British government was prepared to ask for nothing less than Cuba in compensation. Cuba had just become the largest single importer of slaves in the Caribbean. Beyond the Caribbean, in Africa in 1806, the British navy had just added the slave-importing Dutch Cape Colony to its roster of conquests. In South America, a British expeditionary force captured Buenos Aires, the slave-importing capital of Rio de la Plata.[7] The British empire had thus increased its potential as a slave empire more than ten-fold.

Let us turn to parliament. In February 1805, during the last debate on abolition of the British slave trade before 1807, anti-abolitionist MPs noted, with some sarcasm, that the government was itself purchasing and arming African slaves for defense and expansion in the West Indies. This was no hyperbole. During 1806, British government purchases of African slaves for West Indian regiments reached their all-time peak.[8] For a government with deep concern about the risk of slave revolts, especially in colonies worked by newly landed Africans, multiplying such risks in three separate areas of the globe would have been a policy bordering on insanity. The British Ministers, however, were far from acting irrationally. They, like the British planters, made the identical assessment of the high value of the slave trade to *foreign* colonies. In fact, so did the abolitionists. In 1805 and 1806, it was the abolitionists who led the charge in demanding that British slave traders be prohibited from carrying Africans to foreign or conquered colonies. To bring slaves to foreigners, they insisted, was to advance foreign colonial development while retarding Britain's development. Interdicting the slave trade would hobble the economy of the enemy. Note well that the rationale for passing foreign trade prohibition a few months before the Act of 1807 was that fresh slaves were "seeds of production," not "seeds of destruction." It was no accident that an abolitionist, James Stephen, was the author of Britain's most important polemic in favor of interdiction and was the drafter of the 1806 Bill for the government.[9]

What then of the role of the Haitian revolution as a decisive factor in the enactment of total abolition in1807? Begin by looking at the public sphere: abolition was discussed in some constituencies during the general election of 1806. Saint-Domingue was not part of the discussion. What about abolitionist propaganda? At the beginning of 1807, William Wilberforce published a *Letter on the Abolition of the Slave Trade*. It was by far the longest abolitionist tract ever to appear against the slave trade. For the first 320 pages of its 350 pages of text, Africans were unrelentingly portrayed as helpless enslaved victims of brutality, racism, degradation, and neglect. Finally, on page 320, Wilberforce announced that he had to "mention two or three additional considerations"—but he promised that he would "not dwell long on them." Among them was the "danger of insurrections." Why the understatement? For Wilberforce in 1807, Haiti still represented "the wild licentiousness of a neighboring kingdom," enjoying none of the blessings of "true liberty" under the British Constitution.[10] The danger arising from slave imports might ultimately be inevitable. At the moment, however, Britain enjoyed "a happy interval" in which she might "providentially" "avert the gathering storm."

How long was this "happy interval"? Lord Howick, the Cabinet member who introduced the crucial second reading of the Bill in the House of

Commons in 1807, was more precise than Wilberforce. He preempted the pro-trader assertion that even a discussion of abolition would arouse the revolutionary passions among the British slaves. Nonsense, replied Lord Howick. For 20 years, he declared, the question had been continually debated, and declared contrary to humanity: "Look at the state of [our] islands for the last 20 years," he countered, "and say, is it not notorious, that there never were so few insurrections amongst the negroes, as at the very time they knew that such an abolition of this infamous traffic was under discussion?"[11]

One other major anti-abolitionist argument had to be parried. The Bill's opponents denounced the abolitionists as hypocrites. If slavery violated humanity and justice as much as the Atlantic slave trade, why did abolitionists actively oppose any motion for even free-birth emancipation in 1807? The abolitionist response was: look at Saint-Domingue. Immediate emancipation, warned Howick, would only produce "horrors similar to those at St. Domingo." If colonial slaves were human and brethren they were still largely African and savage: "It must be remembered," noted another abolitionist, that "Dessalines himself was an imported African."[12] Both pre- and post-revolutionary Haiti were models to be avoided, not emulated.

II. Civilizing Insurgency: Demerara

After Haiti, Marques aptly shifts his attention to the large-scale British slave uprisings that erupted between the ending of the Napoleonic wars and British slave emancipation. Three successive revolts shook the British West Indies: Barbados in 1816; Demerara in 1823; and Jamaica in 1831. All were stimulated by increasingly intrusive metropolitan interventions into the relationship between masters and slaves. I focus on Demerara, whose uprising I consider to be the most revealing and transformative event in the shift toward slave emancipation. Although the insurgents in Barbados revealed important new facets of slave behavior, the revolt's immediate impact on the metropolitan political scene still closely resembled the impact of the Saint-Domingue revolution. Both uprisings contributed to a hiatus in major abolitionist initiatives. The negative impact of Saint-Domingue lasted for about a decade after 1791. That of Barbados lasted for nearly seven years.

In the wake of Barbados, British abolitionists skillfully developed arguments to mitigate and even defend the slaves' resistance, but their posture remained largely defensive. It probably reflected the largely negative metropolitan public opinion.[13] When Thomas Fowell Buxton took over parliamentary leadership of abolitionism in the early 1820s, his chief concern in taking the first step toward emancipation remained the fear that further discussion of emancipation in Britain "might lead to servile insurrection in the West Indies." His very use of the term "servile insurrections" evoked the atrocities of slave revolts in classical antiquity and Saint-Domingue.

It was the Demerara insurrection that shifted the balance of opinion in favor of sympathy toward the slaves and antipathy toward the planters. The Demerara uprising deserves careful scrutiny because the comparative behaviors of the slaves and masters contributed crucially to that shift. The outbreak itself was not based, as were so many prior events, on rumors of a nonexistent document or a decree in favor of liberation. The slaves' conspiracy was a direct result of the failure of Demerara's governor, under planter pressure, to publicize a very modest metropolitan list of amelioration measures. After the revolt's suppression, abolitionists were able to demonstrate that the immediate publication of the same document in neighboring Berbice had resulted in no disturbances whatsoever.

Concealment from above fueled conspiracy from below. The range of rebel demands reflected both their aspirations for full freedom and their wish to get whatever advantages might be hidden in the document. The post-rebellion investigations revealed that the insurgents had devoted an enormous amount of time and energy into trying to learn the actual contents of the reforms contained in the government's document. For weeks, they hesitated to turn to action. Both in planning and in action the rebels talked of presenting their grievances to the governor.

The second novel aspect of the revolt was its organizational reliance upon a recently developed institution in Demerara. A missionary chapel became the site of the discussion of plans for collective action. Denied other autonomous space outside the plantation, the leaders used their minimal allotment of religious freedom and their status as deacons within the chapel to communicate more freely with each other.[14] The missionary presence that had thrived after slave trade abolition was crucial to the new pattern of action.

The uprising itself clearly revealed that its leaders did not intend to overthrow British authority. Plantations were seized; masters and their families incarcerated. Humiliation was sometimes inflicted. There was no repetition of the atrocities of the Berbice revolt in 1763 or of those in Saint-Domingue between 1791 and 1804. In Demerara, where 77,000 slaves and 10,000–12,000 insurgents vastly outnumbered the 5,000 whites and free blacks, only two or three whites died in hostile action. Above all, the leaders attempted to impose self-discipline among the insurgents and to negotiate with the British governor. Demerara's rebel leaders attempted to rewrite the rules of slave contention.

The exemplary moment was most evident at the "crisis" point of confrontation—500 advancing British troops and mobilized auxiliaries came face to face with, and were surrounded by, 3,000 to 4,000 slaves. They were asked by the commanding officer about their grievances. The responses ranged from demands for time off to attend Sunday services to demands for clarification about the rumors that they had been freed. Jack

Gladstone, one of the slave organizers, handed the British colonel a document signed by captured managers and masters, testifying to their good treatment. Colonel Leahy responded by reading the governor's formal declaration of martial law. He ordered the rebels to lay down their arms and return to work. After a long silent standoff, the troops opened fire. Their disciplined barrage broke the deadlock. Then began the process of suppression. On-site round ups and summary executions were followed up by formal but equally summary trials and, in later stages, by more formal trials of the leadership.

The outstanding result of the revolt was its transformation into a quasi-metropolitan popular contention. This process was certainly accelerated by the colonial government's indictment of the missionary whose chapel had been the major site of the conspiracy. Reverend John Smith was indicted, convicted, and condemned to death on the basis of slave testimony obtained under duress and later recanted. The dramatic impact of the Demerara cycle of insurgency was quickly registered in the metropolis. When news of the uprising first reached Britain, Thomas Clarkson had to interrupt his organizing tour because abolitionists were widely targeted as "traitors of our country."[15] By the time the account of the repression circulated through the press, it was the planters who were depicted as the vengeful and uncivilized agents in the confrontation.

Smith's death in prison and colonial attacks on other missionaries aroused an enormous backlash in Britain. Some historians are inclined to emphasize the fact that the one casualty of the Demerara uprising who was selected as its iconic martyr was a white missionary rather than any of the hundreds of executed black workers. In other words, the missionary "stole the martyr's crown." This overlooks the fact that the death of this freeborn native Englishman was converted into decisive evidence that the brutal suppression of the rebellion had been an assault on native-born Christian Britons as well as overseas Christian West Indians. Missionary Smith was the abolitionists' Archimedian fulcrum. It enabled them to raise popular contention in the New World to the level of the Old. His death allowed the rebels to be identified not just as fellow men and brothers, but also as fellow freedom-loving Christians. The Demerarans had reacted to their unnatural deprivation as would any freeborn Briton.

In response to Smith's death, hundreds of petitions were sent to parliament by dissenting congregations. No previous suppression had ever induced such a mass metropolitan mobilization. British non-conformist chapels became a mainstay of future anti-slavery petition campaigns. They also were the driving organizational force in the radicalization of abolitionist demands for emancipation. The parliamentary general election of 1826 became the first, since 1806, in which slavery was an electoral campaign issue.

Thus, the most important step in the "Anglicization" of the slaves and the detoxification of slave insurgencies occurred within the cycle of the Demerara revolt. The leaders membership in chapels linked their enslavement to their Christianization. Their actions were reconfigured on the emerging English class-relations model as a "general strike" against intolerable working conditions. Colonel Leahy, the commanding officer in the climactic confrontation, inadvertently emphasized that he had been dealing with men who knew how to participate in an orderly negotiation. He acknowledged that he had made a list of the insurgents' demands, but had destroyed it as useless. "For abolitionists, the dialogue between slaves and authorities justified their comparison of the conduct of the rebels in Demerara and that of workers at home."[16]

The rebel leaders did not, I must emphasize, undertake their action in the belief that a measured challenge to imperial authority was tantamount to suicidal martyrdom.[17] They gambled on reconfiguring the rules of contention and aimed at aligning their situations as closely as possible with those of Britons. They were fully aware that the language of contention they articulated was framed within the religious, moral, and legal constructs of powerful agents of change in the metropolis.

Nine years later, on the eve of emancipation, the injustice of colonial slavery had been so deeply domesticated that abolition, in its own turn, became fused with a campaign to limit child labor in factories. By 1832, it was almost impossible to find a meeting, petition or tract in favor of protecting British children, which did not demand "the immediate abolition of slavery both at home and abroad."[18] By becoming fellow Christians and fellow workers, slaves were already perceived as individuals who loved and yearned for freedom in its civilized (and British) sense.

One must remain wary, however, of overevaluating the power of either revolts or threatened revolts to determine the actual terms of entry into full legal freedom. Many historians have echoed Eric Williams's succinct manifesto on the impact of the great Jamaican uprising of 1831–32. It was, he wrote, an overpowering ultimatum to parliament and people: "Emancipation from above or emancipation from below. But EMANCIPATION." When Parliament did pass the emancipation act in 1833, it also determined that full freedom would come only after a transition period of "apprenticeship" lasting up to eight years. Buxton vehemently objected to this "slavery-by-another-name." He invoked Jamaica and grimly warned MPs of another dreaded and inevitable "servile Insurrection."[19] On 1 August 1834, however, the Emancipation Law duly came into operation with apprenticeship and without bloody insurrections. Abolitionists around the Atlantic hailed this peaceful transition as one of the most extraordinary events of their century.

III. Conclusion

Marques' final chapter opens with a pre-revolutionary dream of liberation. French philosophers saw only two sorts of actors who might fulfill that dream—a philosopher king from among the lords of the earth or a black Spartacus arising from the wretched of the earth. His chapter then reviews the heroes who did emerge—statesmen like Wilberforce, Lincoln, and Schoelcher, and insurgent slave leaders like Gladstone of Demarara and Sharpe of Jamaica.

In most processes of emancipation, however, neither philosopher kings nor slave generals played the principal roles. Rulers vied with each other to expand and defend their systems. Slaves and non-slaves alike participated in such schemes. When slave systems ended through violent conflicts among the free and powerful, slaves often attached themselves to and fought alongside those who could best promise them the greatest opportunity or security. This held true for both the Western hemisphere, which attracts Marques' attention, and the Eastern hemisphere. Most slave systems ended without the decisive intervention of single "heroes," who, in any event, were mightily constrained by circumstance.

Ironically, the empire in which slave insurgents acting on their own had the greatest impact was the one in which ordinary free men and women were also the most influential. The British economy was more prosperous than its more slave-dependent competitors. It civil society allowed more leeway for continuous political action. Its state was for a brief but crucial period the nation with the longest reach on earth. Able to stand on the fulcrum of British "free soil," abolitionists also moved the great lever of their empire, by fits and starts, toward the termination of the institution of slavery and the oceanic slave trades. The abolitionists, in turn, were soon joined by unfree abolitionists on the slave soil of their own empire. Not always and forever, but on occasion, rebels with narrow room for action generated enough support to accelerate the dismantling of a millennial institution. In global terms, the most significant turning point may not have been from servile insurrection to revolution in Saint-Domingue, but to self-disciplined insurgency in Demerara.

Notes

I would like to thank Stanley Engerman, and David Geggus for reviewing and discussing this chapter with me.

1. Marques, *Slave Revolts and the Abolition of Slavery,* part 1, ch. 1.
2. David Patrick Geggus, *Haitian Revolutionary Studies* (Bloomington: Indiana University Press, 2002), ch. 1. During the very year that the largest slave system in the New World was abolished by constitutional amendment, a Sudanese slave revolt broke out in the Egyptian army. It was abolitionist neither in intention nor outcome. See Ahmad Alawad Sikainga, "Comrades in Arms or Captives in bondage: Sudanese Slaves in the Turco-Egyptian Army, 1821–1865," in *Slave Elites in the Middle East and Africa: A Comparative Study,* eds. Miura Toru and John Edward Philips (London: Keegan Paul International, 2000), 197–214.
3. See David Barry Gaspar and David Patrick Geggus, eds., *A Turbulent Time: The French Revolution and the Greater Caribbean* (Bloomington: Indiana University Press, 2007); and

Geggus, ed., *The Impact of the Haitian Revolution in the Atlantic World* (Columbia, SC: University of South Carolina Press, 2001).

4. David Eltis et al., eds., Slave Trade Database, http://www.slavevoyages.org.

5. Seymour Drescher, "Econocide, Capitalism and Slavery: A Commentary," *Boletin de estudios Latinoamericanos y del Caribe* 36 (June 1984): 49–65, esp. 57, Table 5. Using slave prices as an indicator of planters' willingness to invest in the future of slavery, one might note that Cuban planters were willing to pay more for both African males and females in 1806 than in 1790. The increase for prime age females, however, had risen more steeply than for males. See Laird W. Bergad et al, *The Cuban Slave Market, 1790–1880* (New York: Cambridge University Press, 1995), 174, Table B.2. On the simultaneous surge of African slaves into neighboring Louisiana, see Paul F. LaChance, "The Politics of Fear: French Louisianans and the Slave Trade, 1786–1809," *Plantation Society* 1 (1979): 164–170. Louisiana and Mississippi received nearly 20 percent of the Africans who reached North America between 1790 and 1810. See Allan Kulikoff "Uprooted Peoples: Black Migrants in the Age of American Revolution 1790–1820," in *Slavery and Freedom in the Age of the American Revolution,* eds. Ira Berlin and Ronald Hoffman (Charlottesville: University Press of Virginia, 1983), 143–171, Table 1, 149.

6. See Davis Geggus, "The Enigma of Jamaica in the 1790s: New Light on the Causes of Slave Rebellions," *William and Mary Quarterly* 44: 2 (1987): 274–299.

7. Seymour Drescher, *Econocide: British Slavery in the Era of Abolition* (Pittsburgh: University of Pittsburgh Press, 1977), 102–103.

8. Roger Norman Buckley, *Slaves in Red Coats: The British West India Regiments, 1795–1815* (New Haven: Yale University Press, 1979), 55, Table 1. Even the rate of resistance aboard slave ships appears to have dropped during the decade before 1807. The 19 recorded incidents during the decade 1797–1806 were little more than one-third of the 53 recorded in 1783–1792. This earlier decade was the last one of peace before abolition as well as the apogée of the entire transatlantic trade. My thanks to David Eltis for his help in searching the database.

9. Roger Anstey, *The Atlantic Slave Trade and British Abolition 1760–1810* (Atlantic Highlands, NJ: Humanities Press, 1975), 368.

10. William Wilberforce, *A Letter on the Abolition of the Slave Trade* (London: T. Cadell and W. Davis, 1807), 258–259. Still more pointedly, James Stephen, the principal abolitionist advisor to the Prime Minister, explicitly avoided invoking the Haitian Revolution in his long public appeal for the passage of the abolition Bill. See Stephen, *Dangers of the Country* (London: J. Butterworth, 1807).

11. *Hansards Parliamentary Debates* (Hereafter, *P.D.*) ser. 1, vol. 8 (1806–1807), col. 952.

12. Ibid., cols. 955, 970, 975._

13. Gelien Matthews, *Caribbean Slave Revolts and the British Abolitionist Movement* (Baton Rouge: Louisiana State University Press, 2006), 36, 64.

14. Emilia Viotti da Costa, *Crowns of Glory, Tears of Blood: The Demerara Slave Rebellion of 1823* (New York: Oxford University Press, 1994), 145. For much of the account of the revolt, I rely upon *Crowns of Glory,* as well as on Michael Craton, *Testing the Chains: Resistance to Slavery in the British West Indies* (Ithaca, NY: Cornell University Press, 1982), ch. 16. For a comparative perspective on slave rebellions in British and other political orbits, see David Brion Davis, *Inhuman Bondage: The Rise and Fall of Slavery in the New World* (New York: Oxford University Press, 2006), ch. 10. For the revolt's impact upon US opinion, see Edward Bartlett Rugemer, *The Problem of Emancipation: The Caribbean Roots of the American Civil War* (Baton Rouge: Louisiana State University Press, 2008).

15. Matthews, *Caribbean Slave Revolts,* 49.

16. Ibid., 76.

17. In fact, Gladstone was reprieved at the request of the governor himself. The Governor praised Gladstone's "good behavior, intelligence, and usefulness," and "humanity to whites," "even during the insurrection," see Viotti da Costa, *Crowns of Glory,* 244, 367n97.

18. Seymour Drescher, "Cart Whip and Billy Roller: Anti-Slavery and Reform Symbolism in Industrializing Britain," *Journal of Social History,* 15:1 (1981): 1–24, 12.

19. Eric Williams, *Capitalism and Slavery* (Chapel Hill: University of North Carolina Press, 1944/1994), 208; and, for Buxton's threat, see *P.D.*, ser. 3, vol. 19 (24 July 1833), col. 1190. In the wake of the Jamaica slave insurrection at the end of 1831 and the passage of the Reform Bill in 1832, the Jamaican Assembly claimed that West Indians were no longer represented in Parliament. They refused to cooperate in the further operation of ameliorative Orders-in-Council on colonial slavery. The British Cabinet now feared both further slave and planter unrest. In voting for emancipation in the next year, the imperial parliament agreed to a huge compensation package and an apprenticeship system in order to assure the peaceful acceptance of emancipation. (See Miles Taylor, "Empire and parliamentary reform: The 1832 Reform Act revisited," in *Rethinking the Age of Reform: Britain 1780–1850,* eds. Arthur Burns and Joanna Innes (Cambridge: Cambridge University Press, 2003), 295–311.

Bibliography

Anstey, Roger. *The Atlantic Slave Trade and British Abolition.* Atlantic Highlands, NJ: Humanities Press, 1975.

Baird, Laird W. et al. *The Cuban Slave Market, 1790–1880.* New York: Cambridge University Press, 1995.

Buckley, Roger Norman. *Slaves in Red Coats: The British West India Regiments, 1795–1815.* New Haven: Yale University Press, 1979.

Craton, Michael. *Testing the Chains: Resistance to Slavery in the British West Indies.* Ithaca: Cornell University Press, 1982.

Davis, David Brion. *Inhuman Bondage: The Rise and Fall of Slavery in the New World.* New York: Oxford University Press, 2006.

Drescher, Seymour. "Cart Whip and Billy Roller: Anti-Slavery and Reform Symbolism in Industrializing Britain," *Journal of Social History.* 15:1 (1981), 1–24.

Drescher, Seymour. "Econocide, Capitalism and Slavery: A Commentary, "*Boletin de studios Latinoamericanos y del Caribe.* 36 (June 1984), 49–65.

Drescher, Seymour. *Econocide: British Slavery in the Era of Abolition.* Pittsburgh: University of Pittsburgh Press, 1977; rept. Chapel Hill: University of North Carolina Press, 2010.

Eltis, David, et al. Transatlantic Slave Trade Database http//www.slavervoyages .org/tast/index.faces.

Gaspar, David Barry and David Patrick Geggus eds. *A Turbulent Time: The French Revolution and the Greater Caribbean.* Columbia, SC: University of South Carolina Press, 2001.

Geggus, David Patrick. *Haitian Revolutionary Studies.* Bloomington: Indiana University Press, 2002.

Geggus, David. "The Enigma of Jamaica in the 1790s: New Light on the Causes of Slave Rebellions," *William and Mary Quarterly,* 44:2 (1987), 274–299.

Hansards Parliamentary Debates, ser. 1, vol. 8, 1806–07; ser. 3, vol. 19, 1833.

Kulikoff, Alan. "Uprooted Peoples: Black Migrants in the Age of the American Revolution," in Ira Berlin and Ronald Hoffman eds. *Slavery and Freedom in the Age of the American Revolution.* Charlottesville: University Press of Virginia, 1983, 143–171.

La Chance, Paul F., "The Politics of Fear: French Louisianans and the Slave Trade, 1786–1809," *Plantation Society,* 1 (1979), 164–170.

Matthews, Gelien. *Caribbean Slave Revolts and the British Abolitionist Movement.* Baton Rouge: Louisiana State University Press, 2006.

Rugemer, Edward Bartlett. *The Problem of Emancipation: The Caribbean Roots of the American Civil War.* Baton Rouge: Louisiana State University Press, 2008.

Stephen, James. *Dangers of the Country.* London: J. Butterworth, 1807.

Taylor, Miles. "Empire and Parliamentary Reform," in *Rethinking the Age of Reform.* eds. Arthur Burns and Joanna Innes, Cambridge: Cambridge University Press, 2003.

Toru, Muira and John Edward Philips eds. *Slave Elites in the Middle East and Africa: A Comparative Study.* London: Keegan Paul International, 2000.

Viotti da Costa, Emilia. *Crowns of Glory, Tears of Blood: The Demerara Slave Rebellion of 1823.* New York: Oxford University Press, 1994.

Wilberforce, William. *A Letter on the Abolition of the Slave Trade.* London: T. Cadell et al, 1807.

Williams, Eric. *Capitalism and Slavery.* Chapel Hill: University of North Carolina, 1944–1994.

5

THE WARS OF INDEPENDENCE, SLAVE SOLDIERS, AND THE ISSUE OF ABOLITION IN SPANISH SOUTH AMERICA

Peter Blanchard

A bolition in the Americas was, as João Pedro Marques has argued, a much more complex process than simply the result of slave rebellion. Yet, the role of slave activism, at least in the case of Spanish South America, was a vital factor in ending slavery, even if that activism rarely reached the level of rebellion and the resulting abolition laws were not always immediate. This is evident from an examination of the independence era (1808 to 1826), which marked a defining stage in the region's movement toward abolition. Only Chile abolished slavery during these years, and the influence of its rather small slave population on the process seems to have been marginal, supporting Professor Marques' argument; elsewhere, a generation passed before other nations began to follow Chile's lead. Nevertheless, the wars had a profound impact by creating unprecedented opportunities for the slave population to act, and their resulting initiatives seriously undermined slavery in the new states. In the case of Venezuela, slave activism included a rebellion that was of sufficient scope to arouse fears of Haitian-style racial warfare. More commonly, however, slaves reacted in ways that were less threatening, yet they still managed to raise serious questions about slavery. Their actions were largely tied to the length and the demands of the wars and, in particular, the insatiable demand for soldiers. As the fighting spread, royalist and patriot recruiters began targeting slaves, resulting in the largest mobilization of this sector of the population for military purposes during the history of slavery in Spanish America. With freedom being granted in return for military service, thousands of male slaves became freedmen. The military recruiting also had an impact on slave women, as many of them were left to care for their families in the absence of their soldier-husbands. They, too, became active, seeking improvements for themselves and for their families. Occurring simultaneously with this activism—and responding in part to it—was the issuance of anti-slavery laws that, along with the disruptions of the wars, further challenged the institution. These developments may not have compelled the new governments to issue abolition legislation in the first years after independence, but they seriously weakened the commitment to slavery and helped set in motion the various measures that would eventually achieve the end of this long-standing pillar of colonial social and economic life.[1]

Since the wars were struggles for independence and not for abolition, the abolitionist gestures must be seen as by-products of the events—and not always anticipated or desired by-products. The slaves seemed cognizant of this, as their principal objective during this period—in keeping with Professor Marques' views—was not to end slavery, but rather to secure their personal freedom. Their ultimate hope may have been that their actions would bring about the destruction of slavery in their respective areas, as many of them—perhaps the majority—had family members who were still in bondage, but there is little to suggest that the wars caused slaves to press for abolition decrees. This should not be surprising, for at the time the international crusade to abolish slavery was still gaining traction and the aim of most abolitionists was the termination of the African slave trade and not slavery itself. Yet, slave hopes were aroused as slavery came under attack and prominent figures began calling for its end. Indeed, many people seemed to believe that abolition had been achieved as a result of wartime actions.

The slave agitation marking the war years was not a new phenomenon in the region. Resistance of various sorts had been a part of local realities since the introduction of the first black slaves in the sixteenth century. But it seemed to intensify in response to the late colonial developments that are associated with the reigns of Carlos III (1759–88) and his son, Carlos IV (1788–1808). These included the administrative and economic reforms that antagonized many sectors of the population and provoked outbursts of violent opposition and even rebellion; the expulsion of the Jesuits in 1767, resulting in the sale of their extensive holdings, including their slaves; the opening up of the slave trade that saw the importation of thousands of new slaves, largely young men who remembered what it was like to be free; the spread of French revolutionary ideas; the aborted attempt at introducing a slave code in the late 1790s; and, of course, the slave revolt on the neighboring island of Saint-Domingue. These developments had little impact on some of Spain's American colonies, but in many parts of Spanish South America, they were followed by outbursts of slave agitation, as slaves ran away, joined some of the late colonial risings, participated in risings of their own, and engaged in various sorts of criminal activity. A less violent but common form of resistance at the time was to turn to the courts, where they could air their grievances and seek redress. In this regard, Renée Soulodre-La France has noted a shift in the focus of Colombian slave resistance from owners to the state, marking in her view the beginning of pressure for abolition. Slaves may have accepted their status and the right of enslavement, but in seeking improvements they charged that owners were not complying with the King's rules, a reference to the still languishing slave code.[2] Thus, the activism of the independence period built upon both a long history of resistance as well as more recent disruptive elements that produced an atmosphere of uncertainty just as the independence struggles erupted.

While the attempts by creoles to establish a greater degree of self-rule over their respective regions following the Napoleonic invasion of Spain and the abdication of Ferdinand VII in 1808 did not provoke an immediate response among the slave community, nevertheless their lives, like those of other sectors of the population, were soon affected, especially with the outbreak of fighting. As the opposing sides mobilized troops, a few royalist and patriot owners began donating their slaves to the military and even arming slaves, helping to pave the way for more extensive slave recruitment. In Buenos Aires, one of the first donors was Father José Zambrana, whose gesture in July 1810 was of sufficient note to merit a story in the local newspaper. Four months later, the royalist governor of Popayán in Colombia armed slaves who worked in the area's mines for use against creoles who were demanding self-rule.[3] Other slaves took advantage of the disruptions and the mobilizations to run away, claim to be freedmen, and then join one of the armies in a pattern that would prove to be increasingly common.

The creoles' call for self-rule and its accompanying discussions of the concepts of liberty seemed to create the basis for a close relationship between themselves and the slaves. Their condemnation of the colonial period as a period of slavery provided further rhetorical grounds to draw slaves to support their cause.[4] A few anti-slavery initiatives by patriot governments also created a possible framework for establishing close relations. Among these was the Chilean congress' approval in October 1811 of proposals that included a free womb law, a law prohibiting the introduction of new slaves into Chile, and a law freeing recently arrived slaves after six months' residence. The initiative had wider repercussions than Chile, for three years later, representatives of the government of Antioquia in Colombia referred to it as they debated similar measures before passing a manumission decree in July 1814.[5] In both cases, the legislation was of short duration, ending when royalist forces crushed the two creole governments. Yet despite the creoles' rhetoric and initiatives, slaves were not sufficiently swayed to lend their unquestioning support to the patriot cause, at least in the early years of the struggles. Rather, they tended to weigh their options, basing their actions on a careful consideration of which side was more likely to deliver the personal freedom that they craved. For a long time, and in many areas, they preferred the royalists. In Venezuela, their rejection of the creoles developed into a bloody rebellion, which followed the establishment of the First Republic in 1811 and the failure of the new creole rulers to address slavery. Stimulated by royalist agitators, the rebellion of slaves and free *pardos* initially focused on the patriots and helped the royalists to defeat the republican government. However, it soon broadened to become less politically and more socially motivated, resulting in royalist complaints about its anarchic nature and calls for its suppression. This would not be achieved for several years because of the divisions and sanguinary warfare in Venezuela, and order was not entirely restored until after independence was won. The rising remained a warning to slave owners and officials both here and elsewhere, and certainly had an impact on patriot leaders from the region, notably Simón Bolívar.[6]

The slave revolt was a factor in Venezuela becoming the bloodiest theater of the independence struggles, but it was an exceptional form of slave activism during this period. While lesser risings occurred in other areas, a more common response was for slaves to take advantage of offers that seemed to promise them their personal freedom. As Professor Marques notes, military service for a defined period of time became the preferred route for many. In Argentina, a series of recruiting laws between 1812 and 1816 resulted in the recruitment of over 2,000 slaves, who fought throughout the viceroyalty as well as in the invasions of Chile in 1817 and Peru in 1820.[7] In the northern part of the continent, Bolívar began turning to them in 1816 following his promise to the president of Haiti to free all slaves in lands that he liberated in return for supplies. But that freedom was conditional on military service. Following the battle of Boyacá in Colombia in 1819, he began recruiting local slaves in large numbers, as his victory gave him access to the supplies of that region, including its abundant slave population. He issued requests for 1,000, and then for 2,000, and eventually for "all useful slaves" who would be freed after they completed three years of service.[8] The royalist forces, too, turned to slaves in various areas to meet their growing military needs, offering freedom in return for their service and attracting significant numbers, especially in Venezuela. Over time, however, as royalist fortunes declined along with the area under their control, slaves preferred the patriot cause. Nevertheless, both armies came to be composed largely of free blacks and slaves, as the comments of observers and officials indicated.[9] But this also meant that slaves were killing slaves, a factor that prevented them from developing a united, racially motivated movement at a time when the elites were bitterly divided and also killing one another.

Aroused by the offer of personal freedom, slaves demonstrated a definite wish to join the military in some fashion. Although most were compelled to serve, being legally conscripted or donated by their owners, or accompanying their owner when the latter enlisted, others sought an opportunity to join. In Buenos Aires, a number indicated to their owners their wishes in this regard; one even offered to pay to be permitted to enlist.[10] Many volunteered, as the disruptions of the wars left slaves without owners or overseers to control their movements. The armies also welcomed those slaves who belonged to owners considered enemy supporters. Further indicators of the slaves' desire to obtain their freedom, even if it meant risking their lives, were the untold numbers who ran away and signed up as freedmen as well as those who deserted and then joined the enemy side because it seemed militarily superior and more likely to provide the desired reward. In sum, military recruiting gave freedom to thousands of male slaves, most of whom were in their prime. It reduced the numbers left in bondage, which had serious short- and long-term implications with regard to the labor system, prompted many to flee their owners, and aroused the hopes of countless others.

And it was not just male slaves whose hopes were aroused, as the war years were marked also by female slaves becoming actively involved and making their own demands on owners and officials. Female activism began at an early stage in places such as Buenos Aires, as royalist supporters abandoned the area and left their property to be sold. Many more female slaves were affected by the outbreak of warfare. Few actually fought, but several accompanied the armies as servants and camp followers. Some served as spies and others as nurses. They then sought and in some cases were granted their freedom on the basis of their contributions. Large numbers became active after male family members were recruited, as they now found themselves the head of the household. In this role, they were determined to protect the family unit, appealing for financial assistance and charity, especially as loved ones were killed or returned home badly wounded. In the process, they became aware of their rights and in some cases displayed a profound sense of self-confidence in making demands. Angela Batallas, an Ecuadorian slave who appealed directly to Bolívar for her freedom and equated her personal freedom with that of her new nation, was exceptional in some respects, but she was not alone in her willingness to voice her concerns and appeal to the new authorities.[11] Other slaves were challenging their owners and approaching officials in similar fashion, indicating once again how slavery was being undermined.

Adding to the pressures on the system and further stimulating slave activism was the anti-slavery legislation that accompanied the recruiting. Particularly important were laws abolishing the African slave trade and declaring all children born in the new states to be free, thereby ending both the importation as well as the internal reproduction of slaves. The reasons behind the legislation were usually mixed. On the one hand, legislators were trying to win slave support, which in some cases was a reaction to the slaves' obvious willingness to agitate and take up arms. On the other, they were responding to the enlightened and humanitarian ideas of the time. For example, the Argentine commander, José de San

Martín, wrote in the preamble to the free womb law that he introduced in Peru in August 1821: "When humanity has been greatly abused and their rights violated for a long time, a singular act of justice is ... to take the first steps in complying with the holiest of all obligations. ... I shall not try to attack this ancient abuse with a single blow: it is necessary that time itself which has sanctioned it will destroy it, but I would not be responsible to my public conscience and to my private feelings were I not to prepare for the future with this merciful reform." His subsequent law ending the African slave trade was described as "in keeping with the philanthropic principles that all the governments of the civilized world have now adopted."[12] Similar laws were introduced elsewhere, and while they may have been imperfectly applied, they nevertheless opened the way for further legislation and were an essential step in the movement toward total abolition.

The passage of these laws and the language surrounding them attest to the growth of abolitionist feelings in the region. Abolitionist movements per se may not have existed in Spanish America during these years, but individuals were pressing the issue or at least indicating sympathy for the slave population and a desire to alter the situation. Prominent among them were judicial officials who challenged the system in the courts by freeing slaves who had served in the military, even those who had not fulfilled the mandated length of time. Many army officers were similarly inclined, describing the attempts by owners to regain control of their slaves as iniquitous and unjustified.[13] In both cases, they already may have had anti-slavery feelings, but their words indicate that they were also responding to the slaves' recent actions. They frequently drew attention to the sacrifices that the slave recruits had made for king or *patria* and expressed their desire to reward it. As an Argentine court noted in one case: "[B]ecause he has passed to the worthy class of freeman by dedicating his energies to the defense of the nation, to reduce him to the painful slavery which he has left would be tyrannical and monstrous."[14]

Discerning what lay behind statements such as these is equally difficult when evaluating the actions and words of the most prominent abolitionist figure of this period, Simón Bolívar. His motivations will always remain a subject of controversy.[15] Was his adoption of abolitionism an opportunistic and calculating move, a recognition of his need to win over the black population who had been opposing his political objectives? Or was he responding to the enlightened ideas of the time and the realization that liberating a nation while leaving some of its population in chains was irrational, as he claimed in an oft-cited statement?[16] That he was responding to black activism is without question. Their hostility to the patriot cause aroused his ire on numerous occasions. An "inhuman and atrocious people, feeding on the blood and property of the patriots, committing ... the most horrible assassinations, robberies, violence, and destruction," was his evaluation in one instance.[17] There is also clear evidence that he feared the black population, and his recruitment of blacks, including slaves, was in part designed to reduce their numbers and thereby prevent black rule or "pardocracy." But at the same time, he became committed to end what he called in 1819 "the dark mantle of barbarous and profane slavery."[18] Consequently, in 1820 at the congress of Angostura, he issued a call for abolition. Frustrated by the delegates, he tried again at the congress of Cúcuta in July 1821, the congress that created the nation of Gran Colombia, encompassing today's Colombia, Panama, Venezuela, and Ecuador. The congress was prepared to issue a manumission law, declaring that "a truly just and philanthropic republican government cannot exist without trying to lighten the load of all the classes of degraded and afflicted humanity," but it refused to abolish slavery completely and immediately.[19] Bolívar tried once more in Bolivia in 1826, as his constitution for that country included an abolition clause, but once more it languished unrealized.

The abolitionist cause was, thus, weak, helping to explain why slavery survived the wars. One also has to take into account the fact that slavery remained too important and the slaveholders too influential for it to be introduced at this time. Haiti may have remained a constant warning of potential slave unrest, but the desire to restore damaged economies was now paramount in the new leaders' minds. In other words, just as abolition had been of secondary importance during the wars, far behind the desire for independence among all of the patriot leaders, including Bolívar, at wars' end economic imperatives prevailed over humanitarian concerns and racial fears. Hesitation about challenging slavery had already been evident in many of the anti-slavery actions during the wars. The recruiting laws, for example, always included compensation for owners, as officials sought to protect property rights. The various anti-slavery laws may have seemed like a commitment to abolition, but their passage had been predicated on the fact that they ensured a controlled and gradual process that would occur over what proved to be decades. Gran Colombia's manumission law, for example, was typical in this regard. It was designed to achieve the extinction of slavery "without compromising public tranquility or violating the rights enjoyed by the owners." It declared free all children born in Gran Colombia, although those born of slaves had to serve their mother's owner until the age of eighteen. Bolívar noted that with regard to freeing the newborn, "in this manner property rights, political rights, and natural rights will be brought into harmony."[20] Adults were supposed to be freed through the creation of a manumission fund administered by local juntas and financed by a variety of taxes and duties, but money in the new states was scarce so that the funds available for manumission were extremely limited and only a handful of slaves were freed under the law.

Nonetheless, the extensive legislation and the apparently declining power of the slaveholders left many convinced that slavery had ended. As early as 1815, a Venezuelan estate slave named Juan Izaguirre informed fellow slaves that they were as free as anyone else.[21] In Colombia, following the issuance of the manumission law in 1821, a common belief was that with the passage of this law, "there was no longer slavery in Co-lombia."[22] A female slave in Peru in asking for her own freedom and that of her two children in 1822 claimed their freed status on the basis of some undefined decree. Another in 1823 referred to the "superior decrees is-sued in favor of freedom promulgated by edict in this capital" and criti-cized "those laws contrary to freedom" that were still being applied in Lima. Her owner responded that slaves did not understand that the laws were permitting slaves merely to change owners.[23] He may have been correct, but possibly the slaves did understand and were attempting to expand their rights as much as possible at a time when "freedom" was on everyone's lips. The frequent complaints at wars' end that slaves were acting as if they were free give further evidence of the wartime empow-erment that had occurred.

The developments of the wars had, thus, seriously weakened slavery almost everywhere. It had not been destroyed, yet the wars had made many aware that Spanish American slaves were an effective and even threatening mass, rekindling the fears aroused by the Haitian revolution. Elites tried to ignore or downplay the threat, contrasting their situation with what they saw elsewhere and concluding that the conditions that had existed in Saint-Domingue before its slave rebellion were far removed from the local reality. In this regard, claims were made almost every-where about the "gentleness" of the local slavery system.[24] The assertion was largely unjustified, but the institution of the late 1820s was signifi-cantly different from its pre-war entity. It had been so seriously under-mined that various attempts to challenge the anti-slavery legislation and even to re-establish the slave trade had delaying effects, but could not stop the abolitionist momentum. Indeed, one effect of these reactionary efforts was to provoke further slave agitation over the post-war decades, as various writers have shown.[25] Simultaneously, other anti-slavery fac-tors now came into play, such as the rise of the international crusade against slavery, the spread of modernizing trends, and the securing of al-ternative workers. The declining size and aging profile of the remaining slaves also worked against its survival. And eventually a few abolitionist figures would even appear. But to all intents and purposes, the institution was moribund and the reasons for that can be found in the developments of the war years. Slave activism had seriously challenged the institution and undermined the willingness of slaveholders and those committed to slavery to defend it.

In the end, however, none of this refutes Professor Marques' basic point. In the case of Spanish South America, slave rebellion did not pre-cede and ensure abolition. Even asserting that slave resistance was the crucial factor in emancipating slaves throughout the region is problem-atic because of the lack of studies of the abolition processes in many of the countries. Yet, slave agitation occurred. It aroused the concerns of gov-ernment officials and slaveholders, and remained a warning of what could happen. This was true even in those two countries, Cuba and Brazil, which had not been torn by independence struggles and had remained even more heavily reliant on and tied to slavery. The centrality of slavery to their economic systems explains the commitment and the consequent survival of slavery late into the century. But even here slave agitation occurred and served as an accelerator of the abolition process.[26] So, while Professor Marques may be strictly correct, we cannot adequately understand the ending of slavery in Latin America if we fail to address and acknowledge the significant role of the region's slaves. The eventual abolition decrees may not have been preceded by slave rebellion, but equally effective actions had taken place, which both directly and indirectly paved the way for slavery's demise.

Notes

1. The arguments of this chapter, along with the illustrative evidence, can be found in greater detail in Peter Blanchard, *Under the Flags of Freedom: Slave Soldiers and the Wars of Independence in Spanish South America* (Pittsburgh, 2008).
2. Renée Soulodre-La France, "Socially not so dead! Slave identities in Bourbon Nueva Granada," *Colonial Latin American Review* 10, no. 1 (2001): 87–103. For other indications of slave agitation in the late colonial period, see Sherwin K. Bryant, "Enslaved rebels, fugitives, and litigants: the resistance continuum in colonial Quito," *Colonial Latin American Review* 13, no. 1 (2004): 7–46; Jeanette C. de la Cerda Donoso de Moreschi and Luis J. Villarroel, *Los negros esclavos de Alta Gracia: Caso testigo de población de origin africano en la Argentina y América* (Córdoba, 1999); Florencia Guzmán, "El destino de los esclavos de la Compañía: el caso riojano," in *El negro en la Argentina: Presencia y negación,* ed. Dina V. Picotti (Buenos Aires, 2001), 87–108; Lyman L. Johnson, "'A lack of legitimate obedience and respect': slaves and their masters in the courts in late colonial Buenos Aires," *Hispanic American Historical Review* 87, no. 4 (2007): 631–657; Carlos Lazo García and Javier Tord Nicolini, *Del negro señorial al negro bandolero: cimarronaje y palenques en Lima, siglo XVIII* (Lima, 1977); Wilfredo Kapsoli Escudero, *Sublevaciones de esclavos en el Perú. s. XVIII* (Lima, 1975); Anthony McFarlane, "*Cimarrones* and *palenques*: runaways and resistance in colonial Colombia," *Slavery & Abolition* 6, no. 3 (1985): 131–151; José Marcial Ramos Guédez, "La insurrección de los esclavos negros de Coro en 1795: algunas ideas en torno a posibles influencias de la revolución francesa," *Revista Universitaria de Ciencias del Hombre … Universidad José María Vargas* 2, no. 2 (1989): 103–116; Renée Soulodre-La France, "Los esclavos de su Magestad: slave protest and politics in late colonial New Granada," in *Slaves, Subjects, and Subversives: Blacks in Colonial Latin America,* eds. Jane G. Landers and Barry M. Robinson (Albuquerque, 2006), 175–208; Pierre Tardieu, *Noirs et nouveaux maîtres dans les «vallées sanglantes» de l'Équateur 1778–1820* (Paris, 1997).
3. *Gaceta de Buenos Aires,* 19 July 1810; Fernando Jurado Noboa, *Esclavitud en la costa pacífica: Iscuandé, Tumaco, Barbacoas y Esmeraldas, siglos xvi al xix* (Quito, 1990), 379.
4. Peter Blanchard, "The language of liberation: slave voices in the wars of independence," *Hispanic American Historical Review* 82:3 (1993): 499–523.
5. Guillermo Feliú Cruz, *La abolición de la esclavitud en Chile: estudio histórico y social,* 2nd ed. (Santiago, 1973), 38–50; Brian R. Hamnett, "Popular insurrection and royalist reaction: Colombian regions, 1810–1823," in *Reform and Insurrection in Bourbon New Granada and Peru,* eds. John R. Fisher, Allan J. Kuethe, and Anthony McFarlane (Baton Rouge,

1990), 309–310; Relación de Juan del Corral, Archivo General de la Nación, Bogotá, Colombia, Archivo Restrepo, Caja 4, Fondo I, vol. 7: ff. 368–371, 377–425, 430–431.

6. John Lynch, *The Spanish American Revolutions 1808–1826*, 2nd ed. (New York, 1986), ch. 6.

7. Archivo General de la Nación, Buenos Aires, Argentina, Guerra, Rescate de esclavos, 1813–1817, Sala X-43-6-7; Rafael M. Castellano Sáenz Cavia, "La abolición de la esclavitud en las Provincias Unidas del Río de la Plata (1810–1860)," *Revista de Historia del Derecho* (Buenos Aires) No. 9 (1981): 90–108.

8. *Cartas Santander-Bolívar*, 6 vols. (Bogotá, 1988–1990), vol. 2: 1–2, 50, 153–154, 183.

9. Timothy E. Anna, *The Fall of the Royal Government in Peru* (Lincoln, 1979), 202; Núria Sales de Bohigas, *Sobre esclavos, reclutas y mercaderes de quintos* (Barcelona, 1974), 64; Del Pino to Señor Ministro de la Guerra, 1 January 1821, Archivo General de Indias, Seville, Spain, Caracas 55.

10. Archivo General de la Nación, Buenos Aires, Guerra, Rescate de esclavos, 1813–1817, Sala X-43-6-7; Solicitudes Militares, 1815, Sala X-8-7-6.

11. Camilla Townsend, "'Half my body free, the other half enslaved': the politics of the slaves of Guayas at the end of the colonial era," *Colonial Latin American Review* 7, no. 1 (1998): 105–128.

12. "Colección de los bandos publicados por el gobierno de Lima independiente," (Lima: Imprenta de Rio, 1821), found in Archivo General de Indias, Lima 800; Perú, *Colección de leyes, decretos y ordenes desde su independencia en el año de 1821, hasta 31 de diciembre de 1830*, 7 vols. (Lima, 1831), 1: 16, 83.

13. See, for example, *Gaceta de Buenos Aires*, 14 February 1821; Archivo General de la Nación, Bogotá, Archivo Anexo, Solicitudes, 12: 133–144.

14. "Doña Manuela Tadea Pinazo solicitando la entrega de los esclavos europeos," 1816–1817, Archivo General de la Nación, Buenos Aires, Argentina, Administrativos, legajo 32, expediente 1123, Sala IX-23-8-6.

15. For an in-depth discussion of Bolívar's motivations, see John Lynch, *Simón Bolívar: A Life* (New Haven, 2006).

16. *Cartas*, 2: 137.

17. Quoted in Lynch, *Spanish American Revolutions*, 198.

18. Lynch, *Spanish American Revolutions*, 213, 215.

19. *Correo del Orinoco* (Angostura, Venezuela), 5 February 1820; Vicente Lecuna, comp. and Harold A. Bierck, Jr., ed., *Selected Writings of Bolívar*, 2 vols., translated by Lewis Bertrand (New York, 1951), 1: 274.

20. Lecuna and Bierck, *Selected Writings*, 1: 274.

21. "Sumaria información promovida contra Juan Izaguirre por propagar ideas de rebeldía entre los esclavos," Maracay, 19 April 1815, Archivo General de la Nación, Caracas, Venezuela, Archivo de Aragua, tomo LXXV, 1815, f. 78.

22. Hamilton to Canning, No. 7, 8 February 1825, Foreign Office files 18/12, National Archives, London, England.

23. "Los que sigue María Anselma Vellodas con su ama, Da Mariana Melendez, sobre su libertad y la de dos hijos suyos," Archivo General de la Nación, Lima, Peru, Expedientes Judiciales, Causas Civiles, 7 December 1822, legajo 14, cuaderno 3; "Autos que sigue Clara LaValle con Doña Mercedes Palacios," 20 September 1823, legajo 17, cuaderno 7.

24. See, for example, Norman A. Meiklejohn, "The implementation of slave legislation in eighteenth-century New Granada," in *Slavery and Race Relations in Latin America*, ed. Robert Brent Toplin (Westport, 1974), 197–198; Josefina Plá, *Hermano negro: La esclavitud en el Paraguay,* (Madrid, 1972), 74, 77, 147; Elena F.S. de Studer, *La trata de negros en el Rio de la Plata durante el siglo XVIII* (Buenos Aires, 1958), 331–332.

25. Carlos Aguirre, *Agentes de su propia libertad: Los esclavos de Lima y la desintegración de la esclavitud, 1821–1854,* (Lima, 1993); Peter Blanchard, *Slavery & Abolition in Early Republican Peru* (Wilmington, 1992); Christine Hünefeldt, *Paying the Price of Freedom: Family and Labor Among Lima's Slaves, 1800–1854* (Berkeley, 1994); Russell Lohse, "Reconciling

freedom with the rights of property: slave emancipation in Colombia, 1821–1852, with special reference to La Plata," *Journal of Negro History* 86, no. 3 (2001): 203–227.

26. A full explanation of the abolitionist pressures in Cuba and Brazil where developments were sharply different from those in Spanish South America is beyond the scope of this article. Fortunately, the literature on their respective abolition processes is extensive. Two works that consider the role of slave activism are Ada Ferrer, *Insurgent Cuba: Race, Nation, and Revolution, 1868–1898* (Chapel Hill, 1991), and Robert Brent Toplin, "Upheaval, violence, and the abolition of slavery in Brazil: the case of São Paulo," *Hispanic American Historical Review* 49, no. 4 (1969): 639–655.

Bibliography

Aguirre, Carlos, *Agentes de su propia libertad: Los esclavos de Lima y la desintegración de la esclavitud, 1821–1854,* (Lima: Pontificia Universidad Católica del Perú Fonda Editorial, 1993).

Anna, Timothy E., *The Fall of the Royal Government in Peru* (Lincoln: University of Nebraska Press, 1979).

Blanchard, Peter, "The language of liberation: slave voices in the wars of independence," *Hispanic American Historical Review* 82:3 (1993): 499–523.

Blanchard, Peter, *Slavery & Abolition in Early Republican Peru* (Wilmington: Scholarly Resources Inc., 1992).

Blanchard, Peter, *Under the Flags of Freedom: Slave Soldiers and the Wars of Independence in Spanish South America* (Pittsburgh: University of Pittsburgh Press, 2008).

Bryant, Sherwin K., "Enslaved rebels, fugitives, and litigants: the resistance continuum in colonial Quito," *Colonial Latin American Review* 13, no. 1 (2004): 7–46.

Cartas Santander-Bolívar, 6 vols. (Bogotá: Biblioteca de la Presidencia de la República, 1988–1990).

Castellano Sáenz Cavia, Rafael M., "La abolición de la esclavitud en las Provincias Unidas del Río de la Plata (1810–1860)," *Revista de Historia del Derecho* (Buenos Aires) No. 9 (1981): 90–108.

de la Cerda Donoso de Moreschi, Jeanette C., and Luis J. Villarroel, *Los negros esclavos de Alta Gracia: Caso testigo de población de origin africano en la Argentina y América* (Córdoba: Ediciones del Copista, 1999).

Feliú Cruz, Guillermo, *La abolición de la esclavitud en Chile: estudio histórico y social,* 2nd ed. (Santiago: Editorial Universitaria, 1973).

Ferrer, Ada, *Insurgent Cuba: Race, Nation, and Revolution, 1868–1898* (Chapel Hill: University of North Carolina Press, 1991).

Guzmán, Florencia, "El destino de los esclavos de la Compañía: el caso riojano," in *El negro en la Argentina: Presencia y negación,* ed. Dina V. Picotti (Buenos Aires: Editores de América Latina, 2001), 87–108.

Hamnett, Brian R., "Popular insurrection and royalist reaction: Colombian regions, 1810–1823," in *Reform and Insurrection in Bourbon New Granada and Peru,* eds. John R. Fisher, Allan J. Kuethe, and Anthony McFarlane (Baton Rouge: Louisiana State University Press, 1990), 292-326.

Hünefeldt, Christine, *Paying the Price of Freedom: Family and Labor Among Lima's Slaves, 1800–1854* (Berkeley: University of California Press, 1994).

Johnson, Lyman L., "'A lack of legitimate obedience and respect': slaves and their masters in the courts in late colonial Buenos Aires," *Hispanic American Historical Review* 87, no. 4 (2007): 631–657.

Jurado Noboa, Fernando, *Esclavitud en la costa pacífica: Iscuandé, Tumaco, Barbacoas y Esmeraldas, siglos xvi al xix* (Quito: Ediciones ABYA-YALA, 1990).

Kapsoli Escudero, Wilfredo, *Sublevaciones de esclavos en el Perú. s. xviii* (Lima: Universidad Ricardo Palma, 1975).

Lazo García, Carlos, and Javier Tord Nicolini, *Del negro señorial al negro bandolero: cimarronaje y palenques en Lima, siglo xviii* (Lima: Biblioteca Peruana de Historia Economía y Sociedad, 1977).

Lecuna, Vicente, comp. and Harold A. Bierck, Jr., ed., *Selected Writings of Bolívar,* 2 vols., translated by Lewis Bertrand (New York: The Colonial Press Inc., 1951).

Lohse, Russell, "Reconciling freedom with the rights of property: slave emancipation in Colombia, 1821–1852, with special reference to La Plata," *Journal of Negro History* 86, no. 3 (2001): 203–227.

Lynch, John, *The Spanish American Revolutions 1808–1826,* 2nd ed. (New York: W.W. Norton & Company, 1986).

McFarlane, Anthony, "*Cimarrones* and *palenques*: runaways and resistance in colonial Colombia," *Slavery & Abolition* 6, no. 3 (1985): 131–151.

Meiklejohn, Norman A., "The implementation of slave legislation in eighteenth-century New Granada," in *Slavery and Race Relations in Latin America,* ed. Robert Brent Toplin (Westport: Greenwood Press, 1974), 176-203.

Perú, *Colección de leyes, decretos y ordenes desde su independencia en el año de 1821, hasta 31 de diciembre de 1830,* 7 vols. (Lima: Imprenta de José Masias, 1831).

Plá, Josefina, *Hermano negro: La esclavitud en el Paraguay,* (Madrid: Paraninfo, 1972).

Ramos Guédez, José Marcial, "La insurección de los esclavos negros de Coro en 1795: algunas ideas en torno a posibles influencias de la revolución francesa," *Revista Universitaria de Ciencias del Hombre ... Universidad José María Vargas* 2, no. 2 (1989): 103–116.

Sales de Bohigas, Núria, *Sobre esclavos, reclutas y mercaderes de quintos* (Barcelona: Editorial Ariel, 1974).

Soulodre-La France, Renée, "Los esclavos de su Magestad: slave protest and politics in late colonial New Granada," in *Slaves, Subjects, and Subversives: Blacks in Colonial Latin America,* eds. Jane G. Landers and Barry M. Robinson (Albuquerque: University of New Mexico Press, 2006), 175–208.

Soulodre-La France, Renée, "Socially not so dead! Slave identities in Bourbon Nueva Granada," *Colonial Latin American Review* 10, no. 1 (2001): 87–103.

de Studer, Elena F.S., *La trata de negros en el Rio de la Plata durante el siglo XVIII* (Buenos Aires: Universidad de Buenos Aires, 1958).

Tardieu, Pierre, *Noirs et nouveaux maîtres dans les «vallées sanglantes» de l'Équateur 1778–1820* (Paris: L'Harmattan, 1997).

Toplin, Robert Brent, "Upheaval, violence, and the abolition of slavery in Brazil: the case of São Paulo," *Hispanic American Historical Review* 49, no. 4 (1969): 639–655.

Townsend, Camilla, "'Half my body free, the other half enslaved': the politics of the slaves of Guayas at the end of the colonial era," *Colonial Latin American Review* 7, no. 1 (1998): 105–128.

6

SHIPBOARD SLAVE REVOLTS
AND ABOLITION

David Eltis and Stanley L. Engerman

ॐ

João Marques makes three key propositions in his extended essay on the impact of abolition. First, the idea that no one individual should be a slave as opposed to the natural desire for people not to be themselves enslaved is a concept that emerged only in the western world. Second, slaves generally did not bring about the end of slavery by violent means. Third—a more broadly cast version of the second—abolition of slavery would have occurred no matter what action the slaves had taken. The first two, and probably the third as well, are correct, yet it is hard not to question the thrust of this work despite the fact that it is always useful to question the more extreme assertions of those who see abolitionism as having achieved little.

The idea that abolitionism is peculiar to western societies is not new. Orlando Patterson has argued that "[b]y the end the Middle Ages, Europe had been not only formed as a cultural unity but, in the process of its creation, infused body and soul, with the value of freedom"—at least for other Europeans—in contrast to non-Western societies that had also had long experiences of slavery. That abolition evolved only in the West was the main theme of David Davis' Pulitzer Prize winning book, and Davis' more recent work has tracked the earliest references of the possibility that slavery should not exist to the Roman Justinian Code and an early Christian writer.[1] Extensive debates on slavery in Islamic societies appear to have centered on who should be a slave rather than whether or not the institution should exist. When slavery was discussed in non-western societies, the main preoccupation was either the question of eligibility for enslavement or the question of how slaves should be treated. It is perhaps only to be expected that the part of the world—Western Europe—that experienced more wars per century and killed more people than any other in the process of doing so, should institute the most efficient and exploitative form of chattel slavery in history. One of the major justifications of enslavement, especially for prisoners of war, has been that it is an alternative to death. But why such a violent collection of societies should then make the idea—that slavery for Europeans should not exist for those it is willing to kill, rape, and torture—a matter of public policy is at the very least a major paradox.[2]

Marques takes aim at an interpretation of abolition that is not as widely held as he implies. He separates out revolts from slave resistance, and restricts consideration of "revolts" to those involving 300 slaves or more. He does this on the grounds that only large revolts could threaten a slave system and thus match the impact of abolition. Recent historians of nineteenth century slavery have given increased emphasis to events in Haiti that "tautened the nerves of slaveholders from Maryland to Brazil."[3] But the number of historians that argue that revolts on this scale brought the system to an end is still rather limited. C.L.R. James, Beckles, and Hart give preeminence to violence in the ending of slavery, but most historians focus on a more broadly defined interpretation of slave resistance when attempting to explain the disappearance of coerced labor, a definition that includes day-to-day resistance, which does not seem to have been a very effective way of lowering productivity. Another element of this is slave flight, which Marques sees as no threat to the system because even when slaves did not return to the plantations, they formed or joined maroon communities that were never strong enough to (or even aimed to) overthrow the plantation regime. Indeed, they often reached agreement with colonial governments to return subsequent runaway slaves to the plantations. In addition, such communities perhaps acted as safety valves for discontented slaves, and, in any event, prior to 1789 were not committed to the ending of slavery itself, as Genovese pointed out three decades ago.[4] Yet slaves escaping to freedom certainly reduced the number of slaves and accelerated the demise of the system. About 30,000 slaves left with British and French forces when the latter withdrew from the mainland at the end of the War of Independence and in the British case, the War of 1812. In other parts of the world, many more fled to urban areas of southeast Brazil after 1885, and in colonial Africa—beginning with Sierra Leone in the mid nineteenth century—slaves escaped in sufficient numbers to areas where their free status would be recognized that colonial authorities feared social upheaval. Yet slave prices kept rising, so these incidents did not indicate the imminent decline of slavery as an institution.

The path to freedom for nine out of ten slaves in the Americas was laid down by five events: the Saint-Domingue rebellion; a British act of Parliament; the US Civil War; the Spanish Moret law of 1870; and its

Brazilian counterpart of the following year —the Rio Branco law. The emancipations where Marques concedes that slave resistance did play a role were Saint-Domingue, accounting for about ten percent of the slave population of the Americas in 1790, and in the British Caribbean case, resistance, he concedes, had an indirect role. The 1833 Abolition Act eventually freed a further 15 percent of the 1830 slave population.[5] In the other three cases mentioned by Marques, overt resistance was not a factor, but in Brazil flight did count for something. Here, the emancipation process was ended prematurely in part by slave flight. Slaves escaped to freedom in various other parts of the Americas, via enlistment in rebel armies and direct escape. Allowing for these suggests that a sizeable minority of the population left slavery in a way shaped in part by actions of the slaves themselves that are seen by most historians as forms of "resistance." As Marques notes, most of the remaining majority lived in societies in the US and Brazil where rebellion would have been suicidal—in other words, where there were large numbers of whites. Moreover, many of the abolitions he describes as occurring without active slave participation involved small numbers. Vermont's decision in 1777 to abolish slavery freed at most a total of nineteen people, and none of the other northern states that followed Vermont held significant shares of the bonded peoples of the Americas.[6] For the northern state with the largest slave population, New York, even a minor revolt in 1812 did have some limited impact on the abolition process.

These are quibbles, however, compared to the basic problem with the analysis. His description of the emergence of abolition goes beyond what even the abolitionists claimed in their interpretation of their own movement. Consistent with his earlier writings, Marques not only sees abolition as unique to the West, but also attributes it to "humanitarian feelings" that were restrained "by various forces, such as material interests" until the later eighteenth century. Before the abolitionist era, he argues, "[i]t is wrong to think that the peoples of the Western world were not sensitive to the iniquity and brutality of slavery."[7] After 1770, "new hopes for human progress" turned disapproval yet toleration of the slave trade into active opposition to the institution.

There can be no doubt that writings critical of slavery—and to a much lesser extent, the slave trade—appeared every few years from late Hellenic times down to the eighteenth century. Such criticisms are not confined to the West, and are frequently centered, at their roots, on the eligibility question. Both Christian and Islamic societies were concerned at the enslavement of members of their own communities, however "slave" was defined. But there was little evidence of humanitarian feelings, restrained or not, being expressed toward African slaves during the era that witnessed the establishment of the slave systems of the Americas. In the English Americas, slave societies were founded about the time that the English rebelled against their King, with the claim that he was enslaving them, and just prior to English Barbadians accusing Cromwell of doing the same thing when he tried to bring the royalist island into submission. It also coincided with a groundswell of protest against the Barbary pirates who enslaved the English and others, literally, and not just figuratively. Awareness of Europeans enslaved by Barbary powers might have been expected to raise general consciousness of enslavement, but it did not. Apart from rare voices such as Thomas Tryon, no one in England had sympathy for African slaves in the seventeenth and early eighteenth centuries. It was not something that ever occurred to any of them.

If we are to understand the emergence of abolition and the ending of slavery, a more useful approach is to see abolition in terms of the continual shrinking of the eligibility criteria for enslavement as well as major shifts in what was considered to be acceptable levels of cruelty. Both of these connect to violent resistance on the part of captives in a less obvious way than the hypothesis considered by Marques, Beckles, and others. On the first, if Western Europeans, by 1600, had come to see themselves as ineligible for slavery as a group, Africans by contrast had a more localized idea of who could be enslaved. The transatlantic slave trade was made possible by transactions between Africans and Western Europeans, both of whom viewed the captive as an outsider.[8] As Eltis has argued elsewhere, during the long coercive interlude of forced transatlantic migration, European and African conceptions of self and community (and eligibility for enslavement) did not remain static. And abolition is in one sense a widening of conceptions of ineligibility to the point where, at least for Europeans not living in plantation societies, slavery is regarded as inappropriate for anyone except convicted criminals.[9]

As for the shift in human sensibilities toward cruelty, acceptance of rules of war in conflicts between Western European powers—in the English case after the Norman Conquest—indicates some narrowing of limits on violence. An increasing concern with cruelty and brutality became more marked during the late medieval period and renaissance.[10] Intensive debates developed in Europe on what these limits should be by the time of the Thirty Years War and the British variants of these was fueled by a burgeoning print culture that may be tracked by the analysis of the content of titles of published works. Three topics in particular dominated the pamphlet literature between 1640 and 1700, the Civil War, rebellion in Ireland, and sectarian conflict between Protestants and Catholics.[11] Phillipe Rosenberg has argued that these issues provided "models for complaints" against other forms of violence, particularly in the domestic sphere (the jailing of debtors and captivity abroad, including slavery, which is of lesser concern). A rapidly expanding literature charts this pattern in Europe, much of it paying little or no attention to chattel slavery.[12] In fact, so broad-based was the impact of shifting attitudes to cruelty and violence, that its manifestation in other European countries affected issues quite different from slavery. The treatment of prisoners, military personnel, animals, the rights of citizens before the state, and many other issues received attention first. Scholars who wonder why Britain was exceptional in its pursuit of suppression of the slave trade and abolition of slavery, might consider this broader picture and reflect that such prominence in the British case could have been a simple function of the British having the most productive slave empire. In any event, the behavior of slave owners in the Americas toward their slaves had not seemed out of line with the treatment of criminals and the poor in the seventeenth century. But by the onset of the half century often termed the Age of Revolution, the shift in human sensibilities had progressed to the point where this same behavior often provoked outrage, even though the whipping of sailors continued into the mid nineteenth century in both the US and Britain.

Concern with shipboard slave revolts helped ensure that British manifestations of the shift in sensibilities between the seventeenth and the nineteenth centuries focused first on the abolition of the slave trade. Slave uprisings on the voyage to the Americas shaped the direction of the traffic and helped determine its volume, but of course were never sufficient to bring the slave trade to an end.[13] They nevertheless made a critical contribution to abolition for quite a different reason. They were both more frequent and more likely to be successful in the second half of the eighteenth century than earlier. This increase coincided with the rapid growth of an extraordinarily rich newspaper culture in Britain and what later became the US. For three centuries after ocean-going contact was established, Africa and Europe remained insulated from each other and their chief point of contact—the slave trade—was a specialized business that received about as much public attention as the whale fisheries or the fur trade.[14] The great broadsheet, pamphlet, and eventually newspaper culture that exploded in England during the seventeenth century and a little later in New England took almost no notice of either the establishment of the slave colonies or the trade in people that sustained them. In the eighteenth century, the number of newspapers increased—by the 1750s, there were seventeen daily, tri-weekly, and weekly newspapers circulating in London alone and another 40 in the provinces—and stories from the slave colonies and from slave voyages began to form the subject matter of their columns in a way that commerce in long-distance non-human commodities never had. Like the advent of television in the mid twentieth century, there was now suddenly a medium for the dissemination of information about the interaction of Africans and Europeans that had never existed before.[15]

Newspaper interest in such matters began in the 1720s. Some record of 579 rebellions or attacks on the slave ship and its auxiliary boats are now available. Almost four out of five of these are recorded as occurring in the period of 1726 to 1800. Part of this concentration is explained by patterns in the slave trade itself.[16] But an important part of the explanation stems from changing patterns in the reporting of revolts during the eighteenth century, which made it more probable that a record of such events would survive. In short, there may have been more slave ship revolts in this period, but those incidents were also more likely to have been reported—particularly in the published record. The interests and preoccupation of the literate public had changed.

For much of the history of the slave trade, as also for slavery itself, the resistance of slaves, while feared, was not unexpected, or regarded by the larger society as exceptional and even worthy of report, unless on a large enough scale. A preliminary tracking of newspaper coverage of violent incidents over the last two centuries of the transatlantic traffic shows that, initially, such incidents were rarely the subject of press or pamphlet coverage. Violent crime and military violence was much more likely to be reported—the former in the form of street crime, public punishments, and shaming. In the English and North American press, relative indifference to slave ship and plantation violence lasted into the 1720s, when a second phase of coverage may be discerned, marked by a new willingness to report resistance in the colonies, conflicts on the African coast, and violence at sea, including piracy—the latter no doubt triggered by the upswing in piracy in the aftermath of the Treaty of Utrecht. There follows eighty years when violence in the Atlantic slave system was regularly before the reading public, culminating of course in the Saint-Domingue revolution and intense public discussion of the abolition of the slave trade. While we do not know much about the readership for these publications (though they were part of the coffee house culture in the capital) and their impact on anti-slavery attitudes, these sources may have provided knowledge for what slavery and the slave trade meant and thus influenced attitudes of specific groups. It may be that the concern with shipboard conditions in the slave trade, as reflected in Parliamentary regulation from 1788, helped reduce the number of revolts in the late eighteenth century. After 1807, a third phase of coverage of the slave trade in British and US newspapers is apparent. Attention shifted sharply away from revolts and toward the detention of foreign slave vessels. In the US case, the internal slave trade from the Old to the New South became a major preoccupation. More central to the present argument is the second of these three phases, but the very long-term pattern of these phases is also of interest.

The entry of slave revolts into the public record can be shown with some precision. In the sixteenth and seventeenth centuries, violent incidents on slave vessels whether within the crew, among slaves, or between crew and slaves, appear in private correspondence, logbooks, and occasionally in court records, but not generally in the nascent newspapers of the period. A slave rebellion was a misfortune of business, but not a matter of public interest. In fact, newspapers did not exist in Brazil (where over forty percent of slaves arrived) until the nineteenth century, or in most ports around the Atlantic from which vessels cleared for slaving expeditions. A complete run of the *Lloyd's List* shipping newspaper exists for 1702–1704, a period for which other sources tell us that five instances of slave revolts on English vessels occurred. Not one of these revolts was reported in *Lloyd's List*. By 1742, when continuous runs of the publication once more become available, reports are frequent. In other newspapers, the first references to violent resistance by slaves is in 1726 and are extremely cryptic—phrases such as "cut-off" or "slaves rose," and little else. In the first quarter of the eighteenth century, there was far more interest in the attacks of Barbary corsairs, the resulting enslavement of English sailors, and, of course at this time, violence involving pirates—including that of the violence of pirates against slaves. Sources other than the newspapers in France as well as England make it clear that the resistance of captives was taking its toll of slaving ventures in these years, yet the incidents are not seen as worthy of publication.

Beginning in the late 1720s, public interest in the English Atlantic (but not as far as we can tell in the non-English Atlantic) apparently increased and more detail is provided on the incidents themselves.[17] By the 1730s, the dramatic story of the Rhode Island sloop, the "Little George," attracted wide attention on both sides of the Atlantic and has frequently been reported by several historians from different sources.[18] The *Daily Post Boy* published it in full, giving over more than a column of its four pages to the story. The depth of coverage here and in other newspapers constitutes a watershed. For land-based incidents, the rebellion on St. John in the Danish West Indies in 1733, where slaves took control of the whole island, was given similar coverage in the London press, as were the later revolts in Suriname and Jamaica. Thereafter, slave revolts, but particularly those on slave ships, where they were most common, are reported systematically in the English language press on both sides of the Atlantic. The vessels concerned were mainly English, but what we know of rebellions on French, Dutch, and Danish vessels also often comes from such newspapers.

The tone of the reports was matter of fact, though the rebels were occasionally termed "barbarous." The tone is similar to that used for public executions or disasters or street crimes often found on the same page. There is a strong sense of placing the reader at the scene and being involved in the horrors of the events. A sense of sharing is the same as making the reader feel what those present must have felt, and while the captives are sometimes cast as the villains, this is not always the case. For decades there is no hint of an anti-slave trade sentiment, or links to issues of rights. Eric Slauter has tracked mentions of "natural rights," "rights of man," "human rights," and the "slave trade" in three major electronic collections of eighteenth century publications—the *Goldsmith-Kress Library of Economic Literature* (for 1750–1849), *Eighteenth Century Collections Online*, and *American Imprints, 1700–1819*. "Human Rights" comes into use slowly only in the nineteenth century, and prior to the late 1780s, as we might expect, usage of "Rights of Man" is fairly rare. An upward trend in mentions of "Natural Rights," however, is apparent from the 1720s, well before a modest increase in the trend line for "slave trade" begins in the 1760s. Unfortunately, the collections he consults do not include any newspapers. While the latter never link the topics of natural rights and the slave trade before the second half of the eighteenth century, it seems clear that awareness of both topics increases at about the same time, albeit in different branches of the print media.[19] By the 1760s and 1770s, when reports of slave revolts in newspapers are at their most frequent (and the incidence of revolts in the slave colonies is relatively low), references to natural rights are already at half or more of the level of usage attained during the 1780s, 1790s, and early 1800s. This probably accounts in part for the abolitionists making the slave trade their first target rather than focusing on slavery itself.[20]

Would the slave trade have been abolished in the absence of slave ship revolts? Given the strength and breadth of the shift in attitudes toward eligibility for enslavement, and, more generally, the cruelty described above, the answer must be yes. Did the pattern of slave resistance have a major effect on the timing of abolition of the slave trade (or the timing of abolition of slavery itself in the British Caribbean)? Quite possibly, though the specific timing may be more a reflection of British legislative priorities. Abolition of the slave trade did not have to be the first of the major reforms instituted in nineteenth century Britain. More fundamentally, do we increase our understanding of abolition by counterposing slaves and abolitionists as the lead agents in the process? Probably not. Forcing scholars to choose between slaves and abolitionists as the major agents of the legislated repudiation of coerced labor that began to take effect in the late eighteenth century risks undermining our understanding of how slaves and abolitionists influenced each other. And the simple choice between slaves and British citizens ignores the differences within these groups. The debates in parliament and in the press about abolition clearly demonstrate the divisions in British society over slavery and the slave trade. Divisions also existed among New World blacks. The maroons desired their freedom, but not the end of slavery as a system, while free persons of color owned slaves and often treated them no differently than did white masters. The split between the metropolitan centers and the slave colonies in what levels of violence constituted cruelty provided an environment in which major slave revolts were more likely to happen. In the seventeenth and most of the eighteenth century, no such split existed. The persistence of violence could, of course, lead to a more negative attitude toward Africans, and a hardening of pro-slavery sentiments. Yet this is not what happened prior to the mid nineteenth century.

Notes

1. Orlando Patterson, *Freedom*, 2 vols. (New York, 1991–); vol. 1, *Freedom in the Making of Western Culture*, xvi–xv. David Brion Davis, *The Problem of Slavery in Western Culture* (Ithaca, 1967). More recently see David Brion Davis, *Inhuman Bondage: The Rise and Fall of Slavery in the New World* (New York, 2006), 21, 34–35, 42–43, 55.
2. Between 1500 and 1815, nations in Europe were at war more than 50 percent of the time and 10 million people died in those wars—about three percent of the population in 1700 (Wim Klooster (ed.), *Migration, Trade and Slavery in an Expanding World: Essays in Honor of Pieter Emmer* (Leiden, 2009), pp. 9–43).

3. David Brion Davis, *The Problem of Slavery in the Age of Revolution, 1770–1823* (Ithaca, NY, 1975), 557.

4. Eugene Genovese, *From Rebellion to Revolution: Afro-American Slave Revolts in the Making of the Modern World* (Baton Rouge, 1979).

5. For the British case, the best analysis of the interaction between slaves and abolitionists in the last two decades of British slavery is Gelien Matthew's recent book, which Marques does not cite (*Caribbean Slave Revolts And The British Abolitionist Movement* (Baton Rouge, 2006)).

6. Stanley L. Engerman, "Slavery after the Abolition of the Slave Trade: The United States and the British West Indies" (forthcoming).

7. See Marques text above.

8. Nathan Irvin Huggins, *Black Odyssey: The Afro-American Ordeal in Slavery* (New York, 1977), 20.

9. The 13th amendment of US constitution 18 December 1865 states that:
   1. Neither slavery nor involuntary servitude, except as a punishment for crime whereof the party shall have been duly convicted, shall exist within the United States, or any place subject to their jurisdiction.
   2. Congress shall have power to enforce this article by appropriate legislation.
   And article 6 of the Northwest Ordinance of 13 July 1787 states: "There shall be neither slavery nor involuntary servitude in the said territory, otherwise than in the punishment of crimes whereof the party should have been duly convicted. Provided, always, That any person escaping into the same, from whom labor or service is lawfully claimed in any one of the original states, such fugitive may be lawfully reclaimed and conveyed to the person claiming his or her labor or service as aforesaid."

10. Renato Rosaldo, *Culture and Truth: The Remaking of Social Analysis* (Boston, 1989), ch. 4.

11. Phillipe Rosenberg, *Negative Enlightenment: The Polemics of Brutality and the Cultivation of Restraint in the British Isles (1640–1700)* (forthcoming). We thank Dr. Rosenberg for generously allowing us to read and cite his manuscript in advance of publication.

12. See for example Lynn Hunt, *Inventing Human Rights: A History* (New York, 2007).

13. Stephen D. Behrendt, David Eltis, and David Richardson, "The Costs of Coercion: African Agency in the History of the Atlantic World," *Economic History Review*, 54 (2001): 454–476.

14. The Netherlands, for example, sent far more vessels and men between 1680 and 1720 to hunt whales than to carry slaves from Africa.

15. The most convenient way to track the distinctive time profile of reports of slave ship revolts in newspapers is at www.slavevoyages.org or the appendix in Eric Robert Taylor, *'If we must die': Shipboard Insurrections in the Era of the Atlantic Slave Trade* (Baton Rouge, 2006), 179–213. For newspapers see Jeremy Black, *The English Press in the Eighteenth Century* (London, 1987).

16. A fuller version of the next five paragraphs along with the supporting references can be found in David Eltis, "Abolition and Identity in the Very Long Run," in Wim Klooster (ed.), *Migration, Trade and Slavery in an Expanding World: Essays in Honor of Pieter Emmer* (Leiden, 2009), pp. 227–257.

17. There was no counterpart to the newspaper culture of the English-speaking Atlantic in the areas held by other slave trading powers, so comparisons across national boundaries are not possible. Paradoxically, the slave-trading country with the most complete record of slave ship rebellions is France. The paradox arises from the fact that captains of ships on ocean-going voyages were required to submit detailed reports of their completed voyages to the port authorities upon their return, and in the case of Nantes, these reports have largely survived. These remained part of the official record, but never formed part of a published record.

18. The ninety-six captives gained control of the vessel south of Sierra Leone. The captain, three crew, and a boy were trapped in the cabin under the quarterdeck while the captives managed to make their escape. The account in the *Daily Post Boy*, 25 June 1731, was written by a survivor.

19. Eric Slauter, Commentary, presented to the "The Bloody Writing is forever Torn," a Conference on the Abolition of the Slave Trade, held at Elmina, Ghana, August 2007.

20. Thomas Clarkson was quite explicit about the reasons for moving against the slave trade before slavery itself. There were fewer slave owners involved, international commerce was relatively easy to regulate compared to waging war on property rights, the campaign would prevent people from being wrested from their homes, there would be greater benefits for African societies, and there would be no need to deal with large numbers of freed "savages." (Engerman, "Slavery after the Abolition of the Slave Trade"). For comments by abolitionists on slave ship uprisings see Thomas Clarkson, *The Substance of the Evidence of Sundry Persons on the Slave Trade* (London, 1789), 199–209, 220–221; Great Britain, Parliament, *An Abstract of the Evidence Delivered Before the Select Committee of the House of Commons in the Years 1790, 1791; on the Part of Petitioners for the Abolition of the Slave Trade*, 43–44 (we thank Seymour Drescher for this reference), and Taylor, '*If we must die*,' 1–14, which summarizes the work of earlier historians on this topic.

Bibliography

Behrendt, Steven D., Eltis, David, and Richardson, David, "The Costs of Coercion: African Agency in the History of the Atlantic World," *Economic History Review*, 54 (2001): 454–476

Black, Jeremy, *The English Press in the Eighteenth Century* (London, 1987).

Clarkson, Thomas, *The Substance of the Evidence of Sundry Persons on the Slave Trade* (London, 1789).

Davis, David Brion, *The Problem of Slavery in Western Culture* (Ithaca, 1967).

——, *The Problem of Slavery in the Age of Revolution, 1770–1823* (Ithaca, 1975)

——, *Inhuman Bondage: The Rise and Fall of Slavery in the New World* (New York, 2006).

Eltis, David, "Abolition and Identity in the Very Long Run," in Wim Klooster (ed.), *Migration, Trade, and Slavery in an Expanding World: Essays in Honor of Pieter Emmer* (Leiden, 2009), pp. 227–257.

Engerman, Stanley L, "War, Colonization, and Migration over Five Centuries," in Wim Klooster (ed.), *Migration, Trade and Slavery in an Expanding World: Essays in Honor of Pieter Emmer* (Leiden, 2009), pp. 9–43.

——, "Slavery after the Abolition of the Slave Trade" The United States and the British West Indies," in Marcel van der Linden (ed.), forthcoming.

Genovese, Eugene, *From Rebellion to Revolution: Afro-American Slave Revolts in the Making of the Modern World* (Baton Rouge, 1979).

Huggins, Nathan Irvin, *Black Odyssey: The Afro-American Ordeal in Slavery* (New York, 1977).

Hunt, Lynn, *Inventing Human Rights: A History* (New York, 2007).

Matthews, Gelien, *Caribbean Slave Revolts and the British Abolitionist Movement* (Baton Rouge, 2006).

Patterson, Orlando, *Freedom*, vol.1 *Freedom in the Making of Western Culture* (New York, 1991).

Resaldo, Renato, *Culture and Truth: The Remaking of Social Analysis* (Boston, 1989)

Rosenberg, Phillipe, *Negative Enlightenment: The Polemics of Brutality and the Cultivation of Restraint in the British Isles (1640–1700)* forthcoming.

Taylor, Eric Robert '*If we must die*': *Shipboard Insurrections in the Era of the Atlantic Slave Trade* (Baton Rouge, 2006).

–7–

SLAVE RESISTANCE AND ABOLITIONISM: A MULTIFACETED ISSUE

Olivier Pétré-Grenouilleau

At first sight, it seems logical to think that slave resistance is as old as slavery itself and that slaves resisted in all slave systems, all epochs, and regions of the world where slavery existed. That said, many problems remain to be discussed. Can we precisely define these types of resistance as well as the effects and consequences they had on slave systems and analyze the goals of the rebellious slaves? Did slave resistance always occur widely or, on the contrary, was resistance usually dependent upon more specific and contingent events and contexts? More important yet is the core problem discussed in this volume by J. Pedro Marques, that is to say, that of the nature of the links that one might ultimately establish between slave resistance and abolitionism. To tackle this issue, I shall discuss some elements of its historiography before focusing upon the variety, importance, and limits of slave resistance so as to address, in the last part of this paper, the very problematic nature of the links between slave resistances and abolitionism.

When viewing the historiography of the topic, one quickly arrives at the conclusion that during the last century, we have moved from one cliché to another, from the myth of the docile slave to that of the ever-rebellious slave.[1] In 1918, in his *American Negro Slavery*, Ulrich B. Philips presented the plantation world of the American Old South as something quite idyllic, peopled by paternalist planters and docile slaves. We had to wait until the middle of the twentieth century to see this traditional view gradually criticized and refuted, thanks to authors such as H. Aptheker, K. Stampp or F. Tannenbaum. Moving from his *The World the Slaveholders*

Made (1968), to his *The World the Slaves Made* (1974), and then to his *From Rebellion to Revolution* (1979), E.D. Genovese contributed to another shift in historiography: a growing interest in slave resistance. From the 1970s onward, this subject became a widening and autonomous field of research. This trend was strengthened by the "third world movement," by Marxist historiography devoted to the study of the exploited and their "struggles," by a *Nouvelle Histoire*, largely dedicated to cultural facts and realities, and by *micro-history*. Gender studies also weighed in with the study of the role of women in slave resistance. Each approach contributed to this renewal and to what one can define as a logical and legitimate "rehabilitation" of the image of the slave.

Meanwhile, other works, initially rare but now more frequent, tended to use the information unearthed by slave resistance studies to paint a portrait of the ever-rebellious slave, using any occasion to fight against his master, and, if possible, to escape from his or her condition. Undoubtedly, one cannot resist a system without contesting it. Consequently, some authors concluded that resistance equaled abolitionism and that, in the American colonial world, the slaves liberated themselves from the hell of slavery. Thereafter, these authors challenge and sometimes even nullify the role played by the abolitionists' movements within Europe and the Americas. This kind of school of thought is not represented broadly in the academic world. (A notable exception is France, where specialists on slave resistance were few and often linked to non-academic circles like the Church, the colonial administration, and social movements.) Now, however, this kind of discourse, is more widely diffused among international institutions such as UNESCO and associations of slave descendants. As a result, it is increasingly permeating public discourse and opinion. In most cases, it is grounded on a simple syllogism: slaves always resisted and slave resistance means a contestation of slavery, therefore slave resistance equals a slave abolitionism that independently explains why slavery happily disappeared from the Americas. Let us examine these assumptions.

Did slaves always resist? Answering this question requires defining resistance. Explicitly or not, scholars often make a distinction between two types of resistance. The first is called "passive" and the second "active." This differentiation reflects—as I have tried to show elsewhere[2]—the classical and Marxist distinction between *revolution* (collective and violent forms of resistance), and *contestation* (individual and less violent, and so *passive* resistance). I am personally not convinced of the relevance of this distinction. Some apparently "passive" resistance, like petty "*marronnage*" (flight), could be more dangerous to the economic efficiency of a slave system than large-scale revolts, which generally failed. I emphasize that any form of resistance reflects at least the beginning of liberation from the ideological fetters imposed by slavery. This is why I think that "passive" forms of resistance should not be devalued compared with those called "active." All forms have to be taken into account.

The meaning of resistance can also be interpreted in the light of the issue of slave agency and can be extended to actions not usually linked to the notion of direct challenge. I am thinking, above all, about the process of recreating a common slave culture through numerous and various mediations: familial, religious, and "folkloric" (e.g., dance). These rites and practices enabled the enslaved to escape, at least partially, from slave discipline, to reinforce their autonomy as actors in their own lives, and to recover life after the "social death" (O. Patterson) entailed in their introduction into slavery. However, since masters also encouraged their slaves to develop such practices through "paternalistic" policies designed to reduce internal tensions within slave society, this extension of a kind of slave resistance impels us to point out its limits. In this way, one can emphasize that, along the boundaries of slave resistance, actions capable of subverting slave systems and those facilitating its reproduction are sometimes relatively closely related.

Much might also be said about enfranchisement and resistance. Manumission is still often viewed through a lens inherited from the masters' ideology. Enfranchisement is presented as a legal and definitive sanction issuing only from an owner's will and motivated only by religious and/ or philanthropic goals. In reality, the enfranchised slave was generally someone close to his or her master: a woman who gave him a child; that same child; or, someone who maintained a certain familiarity with his master. Consequently, enfranchisement appears to have been the result of the close ties that the slave maintained with the slaveholder. In this case, the slave played a role in a process of enfranchisement that was not controlled totally by the master. Let us add that enfranchisement often benefited the master. This occurred especially when the slave bought his freedom. When freed, the former slave sometimes remained a client of his former master. Sought by the slave and allowed by the master, enfranchisement was both the result of a negotiation (and thus indicative of the slave's agency and "resistance") and an instrument of domination for the master. Rebellious slaves, of course, could be punished or sold, while "good" ones were sometimes enfranchised. Enfranchisement—present in all slave systems—thus encouraged slaves to accept the slave order. This is why I refer to "exits" from slave systems through enfranchisement as "systemic exits." They did not call the existence of a given slave system into question -, rather, they sometimes enabled its reproduction.[3] Once again, slave resistance and slaveholders' interests seem to play hide and seek.

The fact that slave resistance is recorded, to one degree or another, in all historical systems,[4] and that the concept of resistance has to be apprehended in this larger sense, does not imply that all slaves were resisting nor that they resisted all of the time. It is not very easy, unfortunately, to know how slaves viewed slavery. Nobody ever really asked them what they thought. The ones who got the opportunity to express their views were generally those already enfranchised by their masters. It is only through the prism of their new free condition that they provided their testimonies. With the exception of a few words or phrases on Roman gravestones, we have no testimonies from Ancient and Medieval times. At the end of the eighteenth century, some narratives written by former Atlantic-American slaves, were published. Examples are that of Olaudah Equiano or the lesser-known Mahommah Gardo Baquaqua.[5] The only large-scale biographical survey ever compiled was the one launched in the USA during the 1930s. It was a collection of the memories of people born as slaves, which were gathered sixty-five years after the abolition of slavery (1865). The oldest of those people surveyed were often only children during their servitude. With the exception of some documents—like letters from slaves, artistic artifacts or testimonies from former slaves—it is generally only through indirect means that one can hope to understand what the slaves thought about slavery.

Another alternative is to reconstruct the ideas of slaves not by what they said, but by what they did. Here, one discovers that while some slaves were resisting, others were quite faithful to their masters. According to various criteria and modalities measured though time and space, many slaves preferred to accommodate themselves to slavery rather than to contest it. They did so either because they could not imagine any alternative as the result of brutal treatment, or because it was in their interest to serve their masters well. Deprived of legal descendants by their status, slaves could not be seen as attempting to challenge their masters. All that they normally had or could get was achieved at the discretion of their owners. Those who enjoyed special treatment were entirely dependent upon their masters' wealth and will. This is why—even if it is surprising for us, today—many slaves were considered and used by theirs masters as trusted allies: bodyguards, members of private militias, soldiers, and even public servants. Others, attached to their masters' families as nurses, helped their owners to escape during slave rebellions. Cases of this kind are documented for slave systems as wide-ranging as those in Ancient China, the Medieval and Modern Muslim world, Sub-Saharan Black Africa, the ancient Roman world, the Indians of the Northwest Coast of America, and the peoples of the Celebes Islands. Freed slaves were sometimes slaveholders themselves. Such was Toussaint-Louverture, the most famous leader of the great slave rebellion in *Saint-Domingue* (1791–1804).

We are tempted too often to analyze past events and past actors of history in the light of our own contemporary values and in a world where slavery and many other forms of dependency and exploitation have been abolished or overwhelmingly condemned by moral opinion. I do not think that slavery was ever regarded as something "natural," even by those who theorized the concept of "natural slavery." This was simply because you do not have to legitimate something that does not cause you any discomfort. In times when slavery was widespread, well-integrated into many cultures, and apparently impossible to destroy, it was very difficult for slaves to even imagine a society without slavery. The Zendjs, who rebelled in the region of southern Mesopotamia between 869 and 883, attempted to install a new order for their own benefit, shifting themselves from the status of slaves to that of masters.[6] It seems that Spartacus and his troops obliged some of their own prisoners to fight to the death, imitating the circus games in which they themselves had been the designated victims. *The Two Princes of Calabar,* tells us the story of two African princes from "Old Town" (nowadays Nigeria), who, captured by English slave traders, became slaves in America. They recovered their freedom, sailed to the British Islands, converted to Protestantism, and associated with abolitionists' circles. Then, returning to Africa, they reverted to their traditional business of slave trading. All of this serves to remind us that slaves, like other people, had varying attitudes toward the institution of slavery.

This leads us to the fact that slave resistance did not always or mechanically lead to the end of slavery. Nelly Schmidt may list all of the slave revolts recorded over four centuries in the history of slavery in the Americas, but most of them were very small affairs. As early as 1980, Moses Finley noted that, of approximately 250 registered slave revolts in the history of the United States, even the most important remained generally local affairs involving no more than a few hundred slaves. Their total resistance endured from just a few months to individual struggles lasting no longer than a few days.[7] By comparison, European serf revolts were more numerous than were slave uprisings. This was because serfs constituted true communities, while it was in the nature of a slave system to block the crystallization of class or group consciousness. In the entire history of slavery, only three great revolts endangered large slave systems. We have already noted those of the Zendjs and Spartacus. That of *Saint-Domingue* was the only one to succeed. Definitive escapes (known as *"grand marronnage"*) were more common within the colonial Americas. Sometimes, as in the case of Dutch Suriname, they led to important conflicts involving regular soldiers. But all enduring maroon societies had to come to terms with the colonial world in order to secure supplies of products and of women. Sometimes, as in the case of the "Blue Negroes" of Jamaica, maroons helped to maintain the colonial order in exchange for their own guaranteed autonomy.

This is not to say that there are no links between slave resistance and abolitionism. Much depends on how we also define abolitionism. For thousands of years, critics of slavery, relevant as they might be for historians, never undermined the good conscience of pro-slavers. Before abolitionism, some tried to ameliorate the daily life of the slave (which was not contradictory to the interests of owners because amelioration could reduce tensions intrinsically linked to the existence of the institution and consequently enable the continued reproduction of the slave system). Sometimes states interfered in master/slave relations, so as not to yield too much of their power to the masters. Indeed, slavery introduces a peculiar situation in which some people may dispose of others with much more arbitrary power than the sovereign had over his free subjects. And so, the intrusion of rulers into slavery (for instance their tendency to establish slave codes) reflects an attitude that has led A. Testart to conclude that the daily life of slaves may have been better in despotic regimes than in democratic ones, where slaves were more completely at their masters disposal.[8] Before abolitionism, some arguments thereafter used by abolitionists were already forged. Some people facilitated enfranchisement. Others thought about how to reform slavery so as to reinforce its efficiency as well as to improve the condition of slaves. But before the second half of the eighteenth century, with rare, localized, and provisory exceptions (for instance, the Jewish sect of the Essenes during the second and first centuries B.C.E.), even the more advanced moralists accommodated themselves to slavery with all of its contradictions. Those contradictions were entailed in the very existence of slavery between religious principles or natural rights and the laws sustaining slavery. For centuries, commentators attempted to establish a balance of the pros and cons in their texts, including sometimes very convoluted arguments in order to arrive at a casuistic way to accommodate their own consciences to every slave system's dilemmas. All systems were difficult to totally legitimate, but all were perceived as impossible to eradicate.

From the second half of the eighteenth century this slowly changed. For the first time in human history, some people began to denounce not only the cruelty of slavery, but also its very existence. For the first time, the aim was no longer just to reform or ameliorate slavery, or to favor the exit of some slaves through enfranchisement,—now the goal it was to *abolish* slavery in its entirety. Grounded in universal principles, this new project was, from the outset, conceived of as a global task. First, it addressed European colonial territories; thereafter, it addressed the world. Abolitionism was therefore undoubtedly the first international and global fight for human rights. Another point to insist on is the fact that abolitionism emerged in a context that was unfavorable in certain respects. The American colonial slave system was just reaching its climax. The Atlantic slave trade was breaking all records. White prejudice against free people of color was being reinforced in the colonies. Racism was developing in some elite metropolitan circles, notably in France.[9] To eliminate a declining system would have been a much easier task. To attack an established, well-grounded, and dynamic institution was much more complicated. That is the reason why many abolitionists were initially denounced in their own countries as foreign agents and traitors to their nations. The revolutionary context of the so-called "Atlantic Revolution" did not always ease abolitionists' policies. It stimulated rebellion in *Saint-Domingue*, but it also reinforced the fear of change, and thus slowed down many abolitionist projects.

As we saw, many forms of slave resistance were not designed to put an end to the slave system. Some slaves probably dreamed about a world without slavery, but before the second half of the eighteenth century, their actions were mainly directed to extricate themselves from slavery. Even the citizens who declared the existence of the Black Haitian Republic in 1804 did not really try to liberate the slaves living in the surrounding islands of the region. Were some links thereafter woven between slave resistance and abolitionism? To answer the question is not easy, simply because historians mainly focus either on the abolitionist movement or on slave resistance, but often not simultaneously on both of them. What we can say with certainty is that most Europeans and Americans, thought about abolition without envisioning any consultation with slaves. Was not one of the most famous slogans of abolitionist propaganda, "Am I not a man and a brother?," uttered by a slave, kneeling before the (white) people at whom the image was directed?

On some occasions, abolitionists' activities were clearly deterred by slave resistance. That was the case during the insurrection in *Saint-Domingue*. It helped to portray abolitionists as dangerous and crazy agitators in France, in England but also in some Latin-American countries. Let us remember the words by Franciso de Miranda (1798), a leader of the independence movement in Venezuela, according to whom it would have been better for Latin America to remain under the "imbecile and barbarous Spanish oppression" for another century rather than to witness the flood of violence that had accompanied the slave rebellion in *Saint-Domingue*. In other cases, there is no doubt that abolitionists were helped and encouraged by former slaves who became fervent abolitionists themselves. Olaudah Equiano, whose autobiography was published in 1789, was famous in his time. Before the US Civil War, African Americans played key roles in the organization of the Underground Railroad, which aided the flight of slaves from Southern States to the "free soil" North. Some historians also argue that slave revolts evolved during the abolitionist era. Indeed, according to M. Schuler, some revolts tended to draw slaves toward abolitionist agendas, or to exert pressure on the abolitionist movement and thus to accelerate abolition.[10]

To conclude, I would say that: (1) Slave resistance has been legitimately rehabilitated by academic research during the last quarter century. Its historiography has retrieved many significant forms of action. The concept of resistance can be extended into some domains where we have not been accustomed to see it; (2) On the other hand, slaves did not resist all of the time. Some were faithful and, while implicitly challenging slavery, slave resistance did not unequivocally lead to its destruction; (3) Abolitionism means the will to put an end to slavery *as a system*, wherever it may exist; (4) Slave resistance cannot be linked always and simply to abolitionism, much less confused with it; (5) That said, many complex and sometimes contradictory links might be establish between them. Their relationship needs to be better studied as processes. Sometimes slave resistance was unrelated to any abolitionist project and even acted against abolition. Sometimes the two processes really converged and reinforced each other.

Notes

1. On these issues (as well as on some others developed here—like the opposition between systemic and non-systemic exists in slave systems), see my "Processes of exiting the slave systems: a typology," in *Slave Systems, Ancient and Modern*, eds. E. Del Lago and C. Katsari (Cambridge: Cambridge University Press, 2008), 9, 233–264.
2. See note 1.
3. See note 1.
4. See note 1.
5. R. Law, and P. Lovejoy, eds., *The Biography of Mahommah Gardo Baquaqua* (Princeton: Markus Wiener Publishers, 2001).
6. A. Popovic, *The revolt of African Slaves in Iraq in the IIIrd–IXth Century* (Princeton: Princeton University Press, 1998).
7. M.I. Finley, *Ancient Slavery and Modern Ideology* (1980), 2nd ed. (Princeton: Princeton University Press, 1998), 153.
8. A. Testart, *L'esclave, la dette et le pouvoir: études de sociologie comparative* (Paris: Errance, 2001).
9. See P. Boulle, *Race et esclavage dans la France d'Ancien Régime* (Paris: Perrin, 2007).
10. M. Schuler, "Akan Slave Rebellions in the British Caribbean," in *Caribbean Slave Society and Economy*, ed. H. Beckles (New York: New Press, 1973), 373–386. On this question, and more generally concerning slave resistance during the revolutionary era, see our *Les traites négrières* (Paris: Gallimard, 2004), ch. 5, and "Révoltes et révolution. Le prisme de l'esclavage colonial," in *Le bouleversement de l'ordre du monde. Révoltes et révolutions en Europe et aux Amériques à la fin du XVIIIe siècle*, ed. J.-P. Poussou (Paris: SEDES, 2004), 253–294.

Bibliography

Beckles, H. (ed.), *Caribbean Slave Society and Economy* (New York: New Press, 1973).

Boulle, P., *Race et esclavage dans la France d'Ancien Régime* (Paris: Perrin, 2007).

Del Lago, E. and C. Katsari, *Slave Systems, Ancient and Modern* (Cambridge: Cambridge University Press, 2008).

Finley, M.I., *Ancient Slavery and Modern Ideology* (1980), 2nd ed. (Princeton: Princeton University Press, 1998).

Law, R. and P. Lovejoy, eds., *The Biography of Mahommah Gardo Baquaqua* (Princeton: Markus Wiener Publishers, 2001).

Pétré-Grenouilleau, O., *Les traites négrières* (Paris: Gallimard, 2004).

Popovic, A., *The revolt of African Slaves in Iraq in the IIIrd–IXth Century* (Princeton: Princeton University Press, 1998).

Poussou, J.P. (ed.), *Le bouleversement de l'ordre du monde. Révoltes et révolutions en Europe et aux Amériques à la fin du XVIIIe siècle*, ed. J.-P. Poussou (Paris: SEDES, 2004).

8

SLAVE REVOLTS AND ABOLITIONISM

David Brion Davis

୧>୦

I can well understand the appeal of the argument that slave emancipation in the New World resulted mainly from continuing slave resistance
and slave revolts and not from the efforts of the Wilberforces and Garrisons. While the white abolitionists deserve much praise and respect for
their virtually unprecedented moral efforts, they inevitably tended to be
condescending to both slaves and free blacks. This point is dramatically
symbolized by the most famous anti-slavery icon, the figure of a kneeling, grateful slave, pleading, "Am I Not a Man and a Brother?" (When
President Lincoln entered the Confederate capital of Richmond, toward
the end of the Civil War, he had to implore some freed slaves *not* to kneel
to him).[1]

Partly because of widespread white fears of the violent behavior of
blacks when freed from the discipline of slavery—a political problem not
aided by slave revolts, which were repeatedly *blamed* on abolitionists from
the Haitian Revolution onward—abolitionists often emphasized the docility of slaves, while predicting a meek, pious, cheerful, and dutiful population of freedpeople. If abolitionism provided whites with the internal
spiritual liberty to champion the cause of the downtrodden, the *objects* of
emancipation externally could be freed only if they gave evidence of a
continuing internal bondage to the benefactor race. In the early twenty-
first century, this is a very disturbing message.

The expectation of black gratitude and "civilized behavior" is perhaps most vividly portrayed in a British anti-slavery anthology of 1834
commemorating the abolition of British colonial slavery. One author con-
ducts us on a trip to Jamaica in May 1934. On the bay where the author

lands, the descendants of the slaves have erected a magnificent statue of Wilberforce, who even in marble exudes a "holy, kindly air." In this thoroughly Christianized Elysium, the blacks seem to spend most of their time singing hymns, praising everything English, and expressing their eternal gratitude to Wilberforce, Brougham, and Clarkson. They are especially keen on sending missionaries to Borneo. No less striking, racial amalgamation has now eliminated the "Negroid" dilated nose, thick lips, receding brow, and other features, so that the freedpeople's physiognomy *now* exhibits "the image of man's Creator." Even so, the white governor, who in 1934 addresses a mostly dark-skinned senate and assembly, is an English peer.[2] Fortunately, this kind of information has not (at least not yet) infected the kind of ignorant and superficial anti-abolitionist prejudice that has curiously dominated the popular media from pro-slavery days to Steven Spielberg's film, *Amistad*.

Far more serious than the media's caricatures of abolitionists, with respect to historical accuracy, has been the appalling expansion of anti-intellectualism in US life since Richard Hofstadter's 1963 Pulitzer Prize-winning book on the subject. Thanks in part to historians such as Hofstadter, intellectual (and cultural) history made great gains in the 1950s and 1960s, even if the word "intellectual" was probably an unfortunate choice. The term referred not only to ideas and concepts, but also to assumptions, feelings, intuitions, basic attitudes, a worldview—the entire life of the mind (would "history of ideas" have been better?). "Ideology" helped to remove the elitist implications of "intellectual," but often suggested a biased mind or even what some Marxists called "false consciousness." In any event, as disdain increased for "intellectuals," many people assumed that "intellectual history" pertained only to a very small number of elite white males, as if ordinary folk were deprived of ideas or were wholly encased in an ideology dictated from above as they pursued their tedious daily tasks.

As it happened, with respect to the abolition of slavery, the hundreds of thousands of Britons and Americans who signed anti-slavery petitions surely had ideas and strong feelings that drew on the history of ideas. In both Britain and the US, women played a central and indispensable role in promoting the cause; so too did free blacks. In short, the international history of anti-slavery is still much misunderstood.

The most fundamental point, perhaps, is that chattel slavery appeared for millennia in almost every human society, but that abolitionism did not arise until the late eighteenth century and was then for a time limited to North America, Britain, and France. The emergence of anti-slavery and then abolitionism can only be explained in terms of intellectual and cultural history, beginning with radical religious sects in the seventeenth-century English civil wars and extending on, partly via Quakers, to the Enlightenment. The great British abolitionist Thomas Clarkson understood this progression and was basically right when he imagined "streams" of religious and intellectual thought converging into a great reform movement. This involved what I have termed a momentous "change in moral perception":

> In one sense slavery stood as the starting point for a divine quest. It was from slavery that the Hebrews were delivered and from which they acquired their unique mission. It was slavery to desire and social convention that Cynics and Stoics sought to overcome by self-discipline and indifference to the world. And it was from slavery to the corrupted flesh of Adam that Christ redeemed mankind.
>
> For some two thousand years men thought of sin as a kind of slavery. One day they would come to think of slavery as sin.[3]

There was, of course, a very long history of slave resistance, including the tens of thousands of Roman slaves whom the famous gladiator Spartacus led in revolt in the late 70s B.C.E. (many of them then hung crucified along many miles of Roman roads); the thousands of black African slaves, or Zanj, led by Ali b. Muhammad, who in 871 C.E. captured Basra, in modern Iraq, killing thousands of Arab men and enslaving the women and children; the thousands of black slaves in seventeenth-century Brazil, who fled to the mountainous maroon "republic" of Palmares, defending their independence for nearly a century until the Portuguese exterminated them in 1695; and the countless smaller groups of New World blacks who fled to shorter-lived maroon communities or, like Tacky's thousands of Coromantees in Jamaica, discovered in 1760 that insurrection was suicidal.

But none of these slaves were abolitionists. By work slowdowns, sabotage, stealing, running away, and other forms of resistance, slaves throughout history were able to exert some pressure that could lead to bargaining, the winning of some space, and slight modifications in their relations with overseers and masters. But since slaves were human and since slavery itself was relatively unquestioned, freed slaves not infrequently aspired to become masters (in the nineteenth century Congo, even at times the *masters* of former masters). Jamaican maroons long cooperated with the government in hunting down and returning fugitives. The crucial point is that, over millennia of time, even massive slave resistance failed to undermine the institution or, despite the frequency of revolts in the eighteenth century Caribbean, keep it from flourishing and expanding in the New World. During the American Revolution, the southern states lost more than twenty thousand slaves, the majority of whom were freed after escaping behind British lines. This flight to freedom can well be seen as the most momentous act of slave resistance in North America before the Civil War. Yet, slavery in the South was clearly stronger and more prosperous in 1800 than it had been in 1775, when the Revolution began.[4]

It was not until the Haitian Revolution of 1791–1804 that a small number of rebel leaders absorbed anti-slavery ideology. But this was because the French Revolution's theories of the rights of man provided many of the free coloreds in Saint-Domingue with an intellectual basis for challenging the white racist treatment that had worsened greatly since the Seven Years' War. Toussaint Louverture, a former privileged black slave who then became a slave owner during his prosperous years of freedom, eventually internalized this anti-slavery ideology—thus giving some substance to the slaveholders' new claims that abolitionists were responsible for slave insurrections.[5]

Slaveholders had long been accustomed to slave resistance and had devised effective ways of crushing even major revolts. But abolitionism presented a wholly new threat, from governments as well as from the slaves themselves. This point becomes very clear in the almost hysterical response of representatives from the deep South to two moderate anti-slavery petitions in the First US Congress of 1790; in the widespread conviction that the French *Amis des noir* helped to incite the Haitian Revolution; and in the evidence of similar anti-slavery knowledge associated with Gabriel's well-planned Virginia conspiracy of 1800, with the Barbadian insurrection of 1816, and with the Denmark Vesey conspiracy of 1822. Yet, amazingly, from Nat Turner's bizarre and bloody uprising in 1831 to the end of the Civil War in 1865, there were no slave revolts in the US, despite all of the dire predictions and despite the unprecedented increase in anti-slavery propaganda and power.

Let me now emphasize that I have chosen to devote a long chapter on the impact of the Haitian Revolution as the opening event, defining "the Age of Emancipation," in my forthcoming book, *The Problem of Slavery in the Age of Emancipation*. The slaves' rebellion in Saint-Domingue represented a crucial, unprecedented, and almost unthinkable example of slaves overthrowing their masters and then defeating the armies of Spain, Britain, and France. The initial uprising led fairly quickly to France's radical and unprecedented attempt in 1794 to emancipate all of the slaves in French colonies. No doubt the Haitian Revolution originally dealt a major setback to anti-slavery in America and especially Britain, where even conservative opponents of the slave trade were tarred with the stigma of being "Jacobins." It was Napoleon's restoration of both slavery and the French slave trade in 1802, and the fact that the victorious Haitian rebels became virtual British allies against French despotism, which finally mitigated the highly negative links between anti-slavery and the French Revolution. The subsequent history of Haiti presented serious problems for abolitionists, but the blacks' military triumphs helped to inspire numerous other conspiracies and revolts throughout the hemisphere. Even more important, the rise of anti-slavery changed the nature and meaning of many subsequent slave revolts, especially those in Barbados in 1816, Demerara in 1823, and Jamaica in 1831.

Of these three major British West Indian uprisings, only the Jamaicans seem to have had a positive effect in helping to hasten slave emancipation (the Barbados revolt was clearly a setback for British abolitionists).

Nevertheless, I have recently made the somewhat controversial argument that the incredibly low white mortality in all three insurrections shows that the slaves' leaders were aware of a growing sympathetic public in Britain and were remarkably self-disciplined in preventing the killing of whites, despite the huge number of blacks who were shot during the revolt or then executed. If there had been massacres of whites, as in Saint-Domingue and some eighteenth century revolts (and in Nat Turner's escapade), emancipation might well have been significantly delayed.[6]

In short, it was the rise and development of anti-slavery ideas that made the difference. If there had been no abolitionist movements, there would have been no end to the New World slave systems in the nineteenth century.

Notes

1. James M. McPherson, *Battle Cry of Freedom: The Civil War Era* (New York, 1988), 846–847. Crowds of freed slaves in Richmond hailed Lincoln as "The great Messiah!" Lincoln said to one black man who fell on his knees before him: "Don't kneel to me. That is not right. You must kneel to God only, and thank Him for the liberty you will enjoy hereafter."
2. *The Bow in the Cloud: or, The Negro's Memorial* (London, 1834), 321–361. Discussed in more detail in David Brion Davis, *Slavery and Human Progress* (New York: Oxford University Press, 1984), 125–126.
3. Davis, *The Problem of Slavery in Western Culture* (paperback ed., New York: Oxford University Press, 1988), 90.
4. Davis, *Inhuman Bondage: The Rise and Fall of Slavery in the New World* (New York: Oxford University Press, 2006), 141–156. I continue to draw on this book in my subsequent paragraphs. See also Cassandra Pybus, "Jefferson's Faulty Math: The Question of Slave Defections in the American Revolution," *William and Mary Quarterly* 62:2 (April 2005): 243–264.
5. Madison Smartt Bell, *Toussaint Louverture: A Biography* (New York: Pantheon, 2007).
6. Davis, *Inhuman Bondage*, 205–230.

Bibliography

Bell, Madison Smartt. *Toussaint Louverture: A Biography.* New York: Pantheon, 2007.

The Bow in the Cloud: or, the Negro's Memorial. London: 1834.

Davis, David Brion. *Slavery and Human Progress.* New York: Oxford University Press, 1984.

———. *The Problem of Slavery in Western Culture.* (paperback ed.) New York: Oxford University Press, 1988.

———. *Inhuman Bondage: The Rise and Fall of Slavery in the New World.* New York: Oxford University Press, 2006.

McPherson, James M. *Battle Cry of Freedom: The Civil War Era.* New York, 1988.

Pybus, Cassandra. "Jefferson's Faulty Math: the Question of Slave Defections in the American Revolution." *William and Mary Quarterly* 62:2 (April 2005), 243–264.

9

THE ROLE OF SLAVE RESISTANCE
IN SLAVE EMANCIPATION

Robin Blackburn

ențo

Reassessing the contribution of slave resistance in the destruction of the New World slave systems is worthwhile partly because, as João Pedro Marques notes, of the wealth of new information that has been unearthed in recent decades. However he does not mention that much of this more recent scholarship was provoked by an earlier neglect. Standard early- and mid-twentieth century histories of abolition in Britain, France, and the United States dwelt on the role of Wilberforce, Clarkson, Gregoire, Schoelcher, Garrison, Phillips, Tappan, and Stowe, with little or no mention of black abolitionism or slave resistance and revolt. British abolitionism was seen as normative and even general histories gave little or no space to Haiti. Such a vital source as the key slave narratives were out of print.

This began to change in the 1960s but the tendency to portray abolitionism as a white phenomenon lingered. For example, in an otherwise valuable work, The Rise and Fall of Black Slavery (1976), the distinguished Oxford historian Duncan Rice despatched the memorable defeat of the slave owners in Saint Domingue and Haiti in little more than a paragraph. In the 1980s the *American Historical Review* published a very stimulating exchange on the nature and origins of abolitionism by half a dozen contributors, which almost completely ignored any contribution made by slave resistance and black protest (these important exchanges were published in book form as *The Antislavery Debate* in 1992, edited by the outstanding intellectual historian Thomas Bender). It is also notable that benchmark histories of the French revolution by Francois Furet and

Simon Schama in the 1980s managed to pass over in silence a slave uprising that disrupted the French economy, radicalized the Jacobins, and
was to become the only example of a successful large scale slave revolt in
world history.[1] These eminent historians offered important insights and
arguments but nevertheless show how unconscious blinkers—or "ideological" blinkers, as Marques might put it—can lead to indefensible ex-
clusions. Yet the challenge to the aporia of the received view came from a
tiny minority of dissidents.

The task of recovering and registering the voice of black anti-slavery
was left to Caribbean writers or to historians at the margins of, or sometimes even quite outside, the academic study of history—not just C.L.R.
James, Eric Williams, and W. E. B. Du Bois, but Philip Foner, Marion Starling, and Yves Benot, each of whom made an outstanding contribution.[2]
The failure of mainstream historiography to register the importance of
slave resistance and black witness produced a flawed portrait of abolitionism since the latter, at its best, owed something vital to such figures
as Equiano, Cogoano, Toussaint Louverture, Sam Sharpe, Bissette, Frederick Douglass, Wells Brown, Luis Gama, and so many others. Clarkson,
Wilberforce, Buxton, Schoelcher, Garrison, Gerrit Smith, and Wendell
Philips all paid tribute to slave resistance and to the evidence of the slave
narratives.[3] Marques himself has little to say about this formative influence on anti-slavery. His references to "Western" or "white" abolitionism
fail to grasp racial egalitarianism found in the more radical currents of
abolitionism.

Slave resistance is cited in many early attacks on slavery—from Ger-
mantown in 1688 to Raynal's *Histoire des Deux Mondes* in 1770—because
it contradicted slaveholder claims concerning the happiness, good for-
tune, and docility of their slaves. Even the strong pacifist current in anti-
slavery, embodied by the Quakers and Garrisonians, pointed to slave
revolts and their suppression as proofs of the violence inherent in slavery.

Although his argument has gaps, Marques is right to observe that
slave resistance is only one strand in the make up of anti-slavery, and
sometimes a quite subordinate one. Drawing on the impressive work of
Michael Craton, David Geggus, Laurent Dubois, Mary Turner, Emilia
Viotta da Costa, Mary Prince, and others, Marques produces an account of
the uneven advance of French and British anti-slavery that improves on the
previous received account. This is welcome. But Marques is by no means
the first to notice that slave resistance often did not aim at a general destruction of slavery. Eugene Genovese, in *From Rebellion to Revolution* (1979),
a much reprinted work, argued that slave resistance aimed mainly at the
restoration of African forms until it was generalized in Saint Domingue
in the 1790s in the course of a 'bourgeois democratic' revolution radicalized by slave revolt and the sans cullottes. Less schematically, Craton and
the others, while not necessarily using this concept, observed both the
initial limitations on slave resistance and its gradual politicization under
the impact of a wider crisis of the slave regime and colonial order.

One way of understanding the impact of democratic revolution on the Atlantic world is to identify the way in which the "rights of man" proclaimed by propertied white men were claimed and transformed by those with little or no property, or living in the colonies, or by women or people of color. The original "rights of man" did not totally ignore women or slaves, but subsumed them in the household of their husband/owner. In claiming the "rights of man" for themselves, the excluded or oppressed also expanded the meaning and content of those rights, as Lynn Hunt has explained. Marques's account at points argues that only the most Westernized or creole slave rebels made a contribution, and allows for little or no influence running in the other direction.

Yet recent work by John Thornton, David Geggus, Laurent Dubois, and Caroline Fick stresses that Saint Domingue was a colony with an African-born majority within the slave population.[4] At certain crucial junctures, radicalization of the anti-slavery struggle was marked by a specifically African contribution. This may have been the case in July and August 1793 when Louis Pierrot, most of whose followers were African-born, encouraged Sonthonax to raise the standard of general liberty in his effort to overcome Governor General Galbaud and the pro-slavery forces. Indeed, the very first call for general emancipation was made at a mass meeting of the Commune of Le Cap on 26 August 1793, a few days prior to the appeals made by Toussaint and Sonthonax. Ten years later the generality of creole military leaders, whether black or mulatto, were initially willing to serve under General Leclerc. The standard of resistance was held aloft by grass-roots rebels who were largely African-born. By this time it is reasonable to suppose that such resistance was against slavery as such, not just an attempt to preserve their own liberty. (While I still hold to the account I presented in *The Overthrow of Colonial Slavery*, my own blinkers led me to insufficient attention to this African element in the story).

Marques has an implicit argument for the "Western" character of anti-slavery that, it might seem, can scarcely be denied since it is tautological. This line of argument insists that, strictly speaking, the term abolitionism should only be applied to acts or movements that aim at a quite comprehensive outlawing of slavery. Prior to the foundation of modern states in Europe polities were not structured by a legal-rational order. Indeed, even these states—whether absolutist or constitutional—were only just beginning to experiment with the idea of national legislation. Absolutist states were characterized by "parcellized sovereignty," so that decrees of the Paris parliament did not apply in Guyene, let alone in Saint-Domingue.[5] European monarchs sought to impose their edicts on their colonies but—since their administration and courts were riddled with special interests and jurisdictions—with very indifferent success, hence the frequent reiteration of the same instruction and variations on the theme that *se obedece pero no se cumple* (we obey but do not comply).[6] The federal structure of the Netherlands or antebellum United States also virtually ruled out general legislation against slavery, which is why Garrison—contrary to the claim of Marques—refused the path of legal reform and, instead, condemned the Constitution and advocated disunion.

While there is a case for limiting the term abolitionism to thinkers and movements aiming at a general emancipation, we should remain attentive to variety in abolitionist sentiment, drawing on religious and political radicalism, slave aspirations, and the "free air" doctrine. A narrow-minded approach to abolitionism using this criterion would have to exclude much "white" as well as black anti-slavery. Measured against the declaration of the republic of Haiti in 1804 many "abolitionists" settled for half-measures or worse. Many white "abolitionists" did not support the immediate freeing of the slaves, but instead satisfied themselves with slave trade bans or free womb laws (contrary to what Marques states such laws did not immediately free children born to slave mothers, but only promised them freedom in twenty or thirty years time). To be severe on maroon or rebel compromises while overlooking those of the white abolitionists is not only inconsistent, but also risks obscuring half-formed and hybrid impulses of resistance that educated the anti-slavery radicals. And does it make sense to deny that large-scale revolts, which utterly disrupt the plantation economy, had something to do with "anti-slavery"?

The Haitian constitution not only proclaimed the illegality of slavery but also offered safe haven to those fleeing bondage. By contrast, Pennsylvania's "emancipation" law postponed freedom for decades and the state was soon, like Massachusetts and other "free states," yoked to a federal Constitution which privileged slave owners with extra representation and required the return of fugitive slaves. Marques notes that Haitian leaders tried to restore draconian labor controls, but—he might have added—such plans invariably foundered due to the combined resistance of free lance *piquets* and the Haitian peasantry.

While Marques furnishes a broadly chronological account of French and British emancipation he elsewhere elects for an analytical structure that gives chronology little importance. Yet there was a cumulative character to anti-slavery in the "age of abolition," albeit that slave revolts could have quite different short-term and long-term impacts, as horror at rebel atrocities was succeeded by the growing conviction that slavery was inimical to enduring peace and prosperity.

Marques's discussion could have benefited from a clearer identification of the major turning points. The first controversies over slavery drew significance from inter- and intra-imperial conflicts, with recent books by Cassandra Pybus and Simon Schama, drawing attention to the interesting evolution of former American slaves who escaped their masters in the course of the Revolution.[7] The variety of decrees and judicial decisions that suppressed slavery in Europe and North America helped to clear the way for attacks on slavery where it really counted—in the plantation zone. As far as plantation slavery is concerned there were three decisive turning points: Franco-Haitian emancipation, British abolition and emancipation, and US emancipation. These major upheavals sealed the fate of slavery in the New World. Other emancipations—especially those in Spanish America and Brazil—have an interest and importance since they seem to show the comprehensive and irresistible advance of anti-slavery at this time.

However Whiggish notions of progress leave out the real drama. The succeeding waves of abolition may have been cumulative but they confronted another, seemingly implacable, force—the appetites of consumer capitalism. While one can narrate the steady rise of abolitionism, in successive steps from 1780 onward, so too can one chart the inexorable growth of the output of slave-grown sugar, coffee, and cotton—by the latter half of the nineteenth century slavery tails off but is often replaced by oppressive contract labor and colonial labor regimes. There are many times more unfree laborers in the world today than there were slaves in the Americas in 1860.

Despite some omissions, Marques's account of French and British emancipation can scarcely be read as marginalizing the general and cumulative impact of slave revolt. The willingness of British proprietors to settle for compensated emancipation was certainly informed by the awareness of the increasingly politicized pattern of slave revolt, culminating in the "Baptist War" of 1831–2. In its turn, the generally peaceful outcome of British emancipation, combined with the significant improvement in the condition of the former slave population, made it easier for abolitionism to become respectable in the US North. We should also consider whether the slave owners of the South would have opted for the huge gamble of secession unless they had been gripped by fears of a revolutionary threat if they stayed in the Union. As it turned out, they simply accelerated the revolution, albeit in the form of a "revolution from above," accompanied by secondary impulses "from below." The more or less revolutionary ending of US slavery, and the growing isolation of Cuban, Puerto Rican, and Brazilian elites, was a powerful factor in the "free womb" laws that were soon adopted in these territories. Haiti, British abolition, and US emancipation should not be seen as happening tidily within borders. They were events with complex but ultimately negative implications for slavery throughout the Americas.

In the US case Marques urges that emancipation can be subsumed under the category of lawful "reform." I myself would see the Civil War and Reconstruction rather in terms of a "second American revolution," albeit an "unfinished revolution," as explained by Eric Foner and Barrington Moore.[8] Lincoln's Emancipation Proclamation was not the product of a legislative process but an emergency decision taken by the President alone invoking his war powers. And the rebel states were obliged to sign up to the Thirteenth and Fourteenth Amendments if they wished to regain their existence and rejoin the Union. Marques rightly emphasizes the role of black soldiers in the Union Army. However he does not properly examine the claim that the Confederacy was weakened in the last stages of the war by slaves downing tools, or even sabotaging production. While the notion of a slave "general strike" was over-pitched, it deserves some attention.

Ultimately Marques is, of course, right to argue that the emancipation process was often not dominated by slaves. But he remains rather vague in identifying the other major strands in the equation. Radical abolitionists, whether white or colored, had to reckon with elites they did not control and a public opinion that was not always responsive. Each of the major turning points and most of the less far-reaching anti-slavery acts depended on a host of special conditions. Sometimes these can be broadly grasped by the notion of democratic revolution, but motives were not consistently high-minded. There were significant sectors of both elite and popular opinion which endorsed emancipation not for its own sake, but to punish the slave owners' crimes against the nation. Abolition first arose in Britain in the reaction to the North American colonial insurgency. It triumphed in France in 1794 at a time when most planters were seen as traitors and in the United States because slave owners had provoked a bloody war of secession.

Marques does not explore whether the limits on the slave contribution weakened and distorted the emancipation process. In Haiti and Jamaica, where slave resistance had been important, the condition of the former slaves improved significantly, at least for a while. In the United States the ending of one system of racial oppression was followed, after a brief interval, by the elaboration of another. If the weight of the colored population in the emancipatory process had been greater, then Jim Crow would have been harder to establish. For example, Reconstruction would have been less vulnerable if those 200,000 black soldiers had been stationed in the South rather than disbanded—or sent to fight the Indian nations.

By the standards of their time, the abolitionists opposed the most degrading stereotypes of the slaves. But the consistency of their abolitionism was weakened by continuing doubts about the capacity of the slaves to handle freedom or power. Thus Condorcet—one of the best of the early anti-slavery thinkers—poured withering scorn on the apologetics of the slave order. But he still thought that the degradation imposed by slavery made the newly freed slave unsuitable for freedom or citizenship. He was also acutely aware that emancipation would simply destroy France's colonial labor force. So he proposed a "free womb" law instead of emancipation. Under his scheme the children of slave mothers would only become free at the age of thirty-five. Taking into account the children born to children of slave mothers, the institution would survive for another seventy years. De Tocqueville and Lincoln also supported excruciatingly slow schemes of emancipation. Slave revolts and slave "contrabands" (as runaways were called in the US Civil War) exercised a wholly positive influence on such timid abolitionism and deserves a more handsome tribute than they receive here.

The US Anti-slavery Society decided to wind itself up in 1865, notwithstanding the threat of new types of racial oppression. Official French and British abolitionism endorsed racially defined colonial projects and practices, including both forced labor and the widespread survival of slavery itself.

Notwithstanding its very mixed results, the banishing of slavery from the New World was both a very positive and highly original achievement. It was the result of a complex class struggle embracing religious and secular radicals, bourgeois social reformers, slave rebels, and protagonists of the free labor doctrine. New World plantations and their attendant slave trades brought slavery to a new scale and intensity, provoking a variety of hostile reactions. These reactions reflected the contradictory impulses of early capitalism and colonialism, on the one hand, and democratic revolution and colonial reform on the other. Slave witness and rebellion made an essential contribution but should not be exaggerated—in part because this would also be to overlook emancipation's often very incomplete or botched character.

Marques describes the claims of Hilary Beckles in his essay "Caribbean Anti-Slavery: the Self-Liberation Ethos of Enslaved Blacks" (*Journal of Caribbean History,* 1988) as "tainted by ideology." Hilary Beckles has published a series of notable studies of slavery and slave resistance in the British West Indies. The essay cited should not be dismissed in this way—it is thoughtful, complex, and nuanced, if also sometimes awkward and spiky. It explores the wider meanings of slave resistance and of the rebel or revolutionary black contribution to anti-slavery. For example, he notes a "proliferation of acts of 'day to day' resistance," which were not designed "to overthrow the slave system." He acknowledges that "the more informed slaves saw their anti-slavery as articulated to those of metropolitan lobbyists." He also makes the elementary but often neglected point that the actions and thoughts of slave rebels were marked by "deep-rooted conceptual heterogeneity." Fundamental to his argument is that slaves did have minds of their own and that they were well-informed as to their own oppression—by contrast, one might add, most white abolitionists had no direct experience of the workings of the slave system and often harbored stereotyped conceptions of the slave. Beckles claims the evidence of slave resistance shows that most slaves did not recognize the "legitimacy" of their enslavement and sought to escape it when the opportunity presented itself. But in normal times slave society was successfully organized to divide, weaken, and repress the slave community and escape or resistance was very difficult and dangerous. According to Beckles, the slave rebels elaborated an "ethos of self-liberation." As I read him this ethos was distinct from metropolitan abolitionism and—Haiti aside—generally did not prevail in the historical process of emancipation. He argues, for example, that slave rebels may have wished to become free peasants, but that this did not mean that they accepted the planter hegemony that—again Haiti excepted—still characterized post-emancipation societies.

Some of Beckles' claims concerning slave resistance may be too sweeping, but Marques himself notes the problem of finding evidence for slave mentalities. Since 1988 more light has been shed on evidence for the survival of African customs and beliefs in the Americas. However, Africa itself was marked by great heterogeneity of culture, political forms, religion, and language.[9] This fact may have meant that Africans spoke more languages than Europeans, and were less exclusive in their religious and political allegiances. African captives were usually familiar with slavery as an institution, but that does not mean that they accepted it as rightly applying to themselves. Once in the New World they encountered a slavery that was more permanent and racialized than traditional African slavery, which may well have further encouraged an ethos of rejection. As we study the patois and creole languages, burial practices and land inheritance within the slave community, further light will be shed on slave mentalities. There is also the evidence of slave narratives and of various types of trial. The outlook of slaves was very often also inflected by the different national and religious cultures of the colonial powers and American states. Both Beckles and Marques note the interaction between abolitionism and slave resistance. This should be acknowledged without making the dubious claim that slave rebels conceived of their struggle in legalistic terms. Beckles does not consider the creolization of African ideas and, in a critique of Michael Craton, Beckles seems to discount the evidence that slaves often fought very tangibly for the control of land, time, and labor rather than legal formulas.

In that essay twenty years ago, Hilary Beckles addressed issues with which historians are still dealing and proposed some interesting hypotheses. Some of his observations are excessive, in my view. But they are not *tainted* by ideology. Rather we should be grateful that this author brings a West Indian sensibility to bear on the interpretation of slave resistance. It has widened the horizon of scholarly debate. Marques might have noted that the title of Beckles' article was "Caribbean Anti-slavery" and its argument might not apply without modification to the United States and Brazil. However, despite some gaps, Marques helpfully registers that resistance made a contribution. Today the argument is more familiar than it was in 1988, but we still need to push for greater precision and comprehensiveness in defining that contribution.

Notes

1. Simon Schama, *Citizens* (London 1988); Francois Furet, *Interpreting the French Revolution* (Cambridge 1981). For a critique of the marginalization or "banalization" of the Haitian Revolution see Michel-Rolph Trouillot, *Silencing the Past: Power and the Production of History* (Boston, MA 1995), pp. 88–107.

2. Marion Wilson Starling, *The Slave Narrative: Its Place in American History* (New York 1949); Philip Foner, *Frederick Douglass* (New York 1945), *The Black Voice* (New York 1956), *Frederick Douglass: Speeches and Writings* (New York 1971); and (a posthumous collection with a full bibliography) Yves Benot, *Les Lumières, l'esclavage, la Colonisation* (Paris, 2006).

3. There is now a considerable literature on all this. Recent examples would include James Oakes, *The Radical and the Republican: Frederick Douglass, Abraham Lincoln and the Triumph of Anti-Slavery* (New York, 2006); John Stauffer, *The Black Hearts of Men: Radical Abolitionists and the Transformation of Race* (Cambridge, MA, 2001); and Florence Guathier, *L'aristocratie de l'épiderme* (Paris, 2007).

4. John Thornton, *Africa and Africans in the Making of the Atlantic World, 1400–1800*, 2nd ed (Cambridge 1998, pp. 303 et seq); Laurent Dubois, *Avengers of the New World* (New York 2004); David Geggus, *Haitian Studies* (Oxford 2002); Carolyn Fick, *The Making of the Haitian Revolution* (Knoxville, TE 1990); see also David Geggus and Norman Fiering, eds., *The World of the Haitian Revolution* (South Bend, IN 2008).

5. See Perry Anderson, *Lineages of the Absolutist State* (London, 1974), 15–59.

6. J.H. Elliott, *Empires of the Atlantic World* (New Haven, 2006), 131–132.

7. Cassandra Pybus, *Epic Journeys of Freedom* (Boston, MA, 2006); Simon Schama, *Rough Crossings*, (London 2006).

8. Eric Foner, *Reconstruction: America's Unfinished Revolution, 1863–1877* (New York 1988); Barrington Moore, Jr., *The Social Origins of Dictatorship and Democracy* (New York, 1964).

9. Thornton, *Africa and Africans in the Making of the Atlantic World*, documents both African contributions to the New World and Africa's diversity.

Bibliography

Anderson, Perry. *Lineages of the Absolutist State*. London: N. L. B., 1974.

Beckles, Hilary McD. "Caribbean Anti-Slavery: the Self-Liberation Ethos of Enslaved Blacks," *Journal of Caribbean History* vol. 22: 1 and 2 (1988), 1–19.

Bender, Thomas. *The Antislavery Debate: Capitalism and Antislavery as a Problem in Historical Interpretation*. Berkeley: University of California Press, 1992.

Dubois, Laurent. *Avengers of the New World*. Cambridge MA: Harvard University Press, 2004.

Elliot, J. H. *Empires of the Atlantic World: Britain and Spain in America, 1492–1830*. New Haven: Yale University Press, 2006.

Fick, Carolyn. *The Making of Haiti*. Knoxville TE: University of Tennessee Press, 1990.

Foner, Eric. *Reconstruction: America's unfinished Revolution, 1863–1877*. New York: Perennial Classics, 2002.

Foner, Philip. *Frederick Douglass: Speeches and Writings*. New York: 1945.

Foner, Philip. *Frederick Douglass: Speeches and Writings*. New York: 1971.

Geggus, David and Norman Fiering, eds. *The World of the Haitian Revolution*. Bloomington: Indiana University Press, 2009.

Geggus, David. *Haitian Revolutionary Studies*. Bloomington: Indiana University Press, 2002.

Gautier, Florence. *L'aristocratie de l'épiderme*. Paris: CNRS 2007.

Hunt, Lynn. *Inventing Human Rights: A History*. New York: W. W. Norton, 2007.

Moore, Barrington. *Social Origins of Dictatorship and Democracy*. Boston, Beacon Press, 1966.

Oakes, James. *Radical and the Republican: Frederick Douglass, Abraham Lincoln and the Triumph of Antislavery Politics.* New York: W. W. Norton, 2007.

Pybus, Cassandra, *Epic Journeys of Freedom: Runaway Slaves of the American Revolution.* Boston: Beacon Press, 2006.

Rice, Duncan. *The Rise and Fall of Black Slavery.* New York: Harper and Row, 1975.

Schama, Simon. *Citizens: A Chronicle of the French Revolution.* New York: Knopf 1989.

Starling Marion Wilson. *The Slave Narrative: Its Place in American History.* Boston: G. K. Hall, 1981.

Stauffer, John. *The Black Hearts of Men: Radical Abolitionists and the Transformation of Race.* Cambridge: Harvard University Press, 2001.

Thornton, John. *Africa and the Africans in the Making of the Atlantic World, 1400–1800.* Cambridge: Cambridge University Press, 1998.

Trouillot, Michel-Rolf. *Silencing the Past.* Boston: Beacon Press, 1995.

Yves Benot, *Les Lumières, l'esclavage, la colonization.* Paris: 2006.

10

João Pedro Marques, Slave Revolts and the Abolition of Slavery: A Misinterpretation

Hilary McD. Beckles

❧❦❧

Despite the excellent work published in recent decades detailing the anti-slavery politics of enslaved communities in the Atlantic World, we continue to experience what can best be described as attempts at conceptual reversals disguised as research based revisions. The central flaw of João Pedro Marques' analysis is its refusal to accept that enslaved Africans in the Atlantic World were a modern people. This is where Marques rests his case, whether it is stated explicitly or otherwise. From this position, all of his other arguments, secondary by classification, should be read and could be understood.

Marques' assertions lack conceptual sophistication, and as a result, he cannot see clearly the relations between resistance postures and possibilities, and the "politics" of anti-slavery. Scholars have granted modern people the right to have "politics" built around the complexity of their reality. They are expected to "read" their political condition, assess what actions it can bear, when and how, and craft rational responses within an ideological framework that speaks to notions of self-interests and philosophies about self, society, and spiritual being. Marques does not see the enslaved African people in this way. It is pertinent that he does not see them as "free" persons who have been "enslaved," but rather as "slaves," a term laden with notions of mindlessness and ideas about an inability to reason and respond with reference to time and space.

This inability or refusal to grant the enslaved communities a modern mentality, and hence a modern, ideas-based politics, connects to earlier racist notions about the cultural and intellectual inferiority of enslaved Africans, which underpinned and gave energy to the most extreme versions of the pro-slavery ideology as articulated best by eighteenth century political narrators as well as plantation managers. The consequence of this is that we are presented with an analysis that begins with the following statement:

> The African slave has often been represented as someone always ready to revolt against slavery, but it is wrong to think that the inherent injustices and violence of servile institutions—of Africans and other peoples—necessarily or frequently gave rise to such rebellious outburst.

My opinion of this statement reveals all that I think is wrong and weak with this analysis.

I know of no work, by any academic of slavery, which takes the position that the enslaved in the Americas were always ready to revolt against slavery. This is simply not true. Most scholars begin with the concept of survival as a primary response, a posture that lends to multiple forms of behavior, of which revolt is but one. It has not been argued that men, women, children, and the elderly were possessed of a common social consciousness that gave vent to militant machinations. On the contrary, the common argument has been that most persons lived in fear, were intimidated by the violence of the system, and that the brave few who provided the leadership struggled to recruit and build armies for militant combat.

In addition, traditions of scholarship have converged around the notion that armed rebels were in the minority, though the potential always existed for these minorities to be transformed into majorities, in some places, at specific times. The numbers game, on a plantation, a slave ship, or in a colony, was an expression of political readings and evolving consciousness that took into consideration several variables. That is, the making of the revolutionary mind within the enslaved community is a subject that has engaged social science models of human behavior, but remains elusive on account of the extraordinary complexity of African and Afro-creole inter-relations within the criminal and institutional inhumanity of enslavement.

The concept of injustice in early modernity requires very careful treatment. Where Marques has failed is in his inability to look closely at three separate issues, namely, the idea of class, race, or ethnic oppression internal to African societies; the historic varieties of institutional social and labor subordination of which African enslavement was a part; and the peculiar features of race-based European enslavement of Africans that took shape in the institution of chattel bondage across the Americas. Enough has been said about these matters, but it is important to reiterate that it is folly to compare domestic domination in pre-Atlantic slave trade West Africa, or medieval Europe/Asia, with chattel slavery in the Caribbean,

Brazil, and the US south. It is equally unhelpful to compare the behavior of the enslaved in these communities with other persons so classified as "slaves," such as in ancient Europe.

It remains a reasonable proposition that most enslaved Africans in the Atlantic carried an anti-slavery consciousness. That is, they preferred not to live as enslaved persons and anticipated a future in which they and/or their children could live as the white people did. From this base line, a political culture of resistance emerged, ranging from war against the system to accommodation to its demands for survival. Within this network of postures, we must account for those who were psychologically broken and traumatized. Those who were prepared to fight to the death, in the face of almost certain death, should not be located too far away from those whose minds were crippled with fear and concern for the well being of their children and families. Human awareness presented daily predicaments that centered on the reality of sacrifice. You could sacrifice your life, or you could save it in order to preserve the existence of others. There were hard political choices, and we read of them each time the anatomy of a rebellion is presented, or the provisions of a maroon treaty with slave owners are set out. These choices are fundamentally no different today in places like the Middle East, where groups of persons are prepared to become suicide bombers against Euro-Americans, while others from the same community see Euro-Americans as their allies and saviors. Many enslaved persons were "suicide" rebels, but there were those who saw their improvement in terms of closer relations with the dominant power of the enslavers.

The details of each maroon treaty, in which leaders sought to protect their "freedom" by forming alliances with slave owners, should serve as early expressions, for example, of the reasons for Soviet-Sino differences in relation to the West. Also, the ideological conflict between Trotsky and Stalin with respect to how the Soviet revolution should proceed. The former was in favor of "permanent" revolution, while the latter preferred, like the maroons, to consolidate in one place, and form alliances with the "oppressors." Stalin's politics of isolated socialist survival, in this regard, was not far removed from Cudjoe's in mid 18th Jamaica. We know, of course, that the politics of the Haitian revolution show clearly the extent to which leaders were aware of internal and external political forces and features, and sought to craft their leadership within the matrix of multiple possibilities.

We have come a very long way in dealing with the many forms and varying intensities of anti-slavery. On the ground, so to speak, in the slave societies, were persons who were free—black, brown, and white—who participated in the politics of rebellion and the culture of anti-slavery. They provided the enslaved with ideas, information, weapons, moral support, as well as with leadership. The politics of anti-slavery, then, did not belong exclusively to the enslaved. It was, at its height, a popular front requiring serious intellectual analysis for comprehension. Much of this is lost in the superficial assertions of Marques, a not surprising but unfortunate circumstance since this work represents a retreat from depth and detail.

Part III

Afterthoughts

João Pedro Marques

Afterthoughts

João Pedro Marques

෴

In the last decades, the role of the slaves in the abolition of slavery has been overemphasized. Sometimes it extends to the point of claiming that slaves were the first fighters for the abolition of slavery and that they virtually emancipated themselves by their rebellions. In my opinion, this is quite excessive. I have tried to demonstrate that, with rare exceptions, it is not possible to establish a necessary and sufficient causal connection between slave resistance—or, more specifically, slave rebellion—and the emancipation laws enacted in the West. This demonstration originated a small book, originally published in Lisbon in 2006. The comments of several fellow historians are now appended in its English version.

Prior to clarifying factual or circumscribed questions, it may be useful to ask of these historians: have their comments reinforced or weakened my main thesis, i.e., that the abolition of slavery was not the outcome of slave resistance, but rather a result of the emergence of a new factor—abolitionism?

Slaves Did Not Abolish Slavery

John Thornton agrees that slave revolts had "limited aims" and that "it is only our own romantic interpretation" of those events that leads us to expect more from rebellious and runaway slaves. Thornton does not reject the possibility that slave resistance may have indirectly contributed to the suppression of slavery in the last decades of the New World slave regime. Nothing, however, indicates that slaves were seeking to put an end to slavery in a "global or institutional sense," when they resisted or revolted. This was not the goal of the slaves. Of course they disliked being slaves, but "those who are exploited are likely to respond to the conditions of exploitation, by trying to reduce or eliminate exploitation, and not necessarily the legal and political system that underlies it." Therefore, as Thornton notes, in accord with my thesis, slaves could escape plantation slavery and then build social organizations that included slaves, as is exemplified in Palmares.

There is a subtle difference between being against one's individual or one's group bondage—and so trying to escape or soften it—and developing an attitude tending to suppress that bondage on a wider scale. Aiming at this wider scale would imply knowledge of the world and a level of utopia that apparently were not common among the slaves. I would like to stress that this very level of utopia inspired abolitionism. This is the most significant difference between the majority of slave actions against their conditions and the systematic actions of humanitarians, politicians, and military men to eradicate slavery. This is the fundamental difference that I tried to underline in my argument and that Thornton also stresses in his comments.

The utopian dimension—or the lack of it—is also emphasized by Pieter C. Emmer as he states that the slaves "even ever questioned the principles of unfree labor. And why should they? Except for a few slaves who accompanied their masters to Europe, no African or Caribbean slave had any experience of what a society without slaves looked like." Emmer, who analyses the Dutch Caribbean case, stresses that slave resistance could be propelled by an "ideology of liberation" (which did not inhibit the rebels from owning slaves, if the occasion presented itself), but not by an ideology aimed at ending slavery, i.e, not by abolitionism. As he says, "none of the acts of slave resistance were started in order to get rid of the *system* of slavery, but in order to put pressure on the slave owners and plantation management to force them to make changes *within* that system."

David B. Davis shares this point of view. In his words, "if there had been no abolitionist movements, there would have been no end to the New World slave systems in the nineteenth century." It is true that before the advent of abolitionism, slaves had already revolted and escaped on a massive scale. Yet, as Davis says, none of those slaves were abolitionists and their actions did not prevent the slave institution from thriving and expanding in the New World. It was the theory of the rights of man, conveyed by the French Revolution, and "the rise of anti-slavery" that "changed the nature and meaning of many subsequent slave revolts." Even so, the impact of the rebellions occurring after 1789 had a reduced effect on the final decision of abolishing slavery. In the English case, Davis states that only the Jamaica rebellion, starting in the end of 1831 "seem(s) to have had a positive effect in helping to hasten slave emancipation (the Barbados revolt was clearly a setback for British abolitionists)."

It is therefore wrong to consider that emancipation in the Americas resulted "mainly from continuing slave resistance and slave revolts"—a judgment to which I obviously subscribe. But Davis also explains that the origin of this mistaken theory lies on the paternalist and tutelary attitude of the liberators toward slaves and free blacks. This attitude is already shown, for instance, on the "most famous anti-slavery icon," the cameo seal by Josiah Wedgwood representing a kneeling slave asking, "Am I not a man and a Brother?" I add that the image of the thankful or imploring slave is a typical representation found in the abolitionist, or would-be abolitionist, iconography. Although this representation is not a mere fiction—Davis reminds us that when Lincoln entered Richmond "he had to implore some freed slaves *not* to kneel to him"—the fact is that it conveys a message of dependence, docility, and thankful humility, which gratified and tranquilized the benefactors, but which is hardly acceptable nowadays. Summing it all up, Davis solved, simply and brilliantly, the problem of the complex relation between ideology and history I dealt with in chapter 4 of my text.

David P. Geggus also points out that the "eagerness to redress the distorted interpretations of previous generations has often caused contemporary historians to inflate the incidence and importance of slaves' resistance to slavery." However, slave resistance, although undoubtedly a factor among many others that led to abolition, had "an essential and preponderant role" only in two cases. Geggus focus on one of these cases, i.e., the revolt of Saint-Domingue, and he raises some objections to my way of dealing with this subject (I shall comment on his objections later). Nonetheless, Geggus considers that "the general thrust" of my argument "is both sound and salutary."

David Eltis and Stanley L. Engerman have a different opinion. Although they say that my main thesis is correct, they add that, "it is hard not to question the thrust of (my) work." Robin Blackburn's comment—although he also finds my main thesis basically correct—apparently follows the same path.

Cumulative Conceptions of Slave Agency

With Blackburn's and Eltis and Engerman's comments we are led to focus our attention not so much on slave revolts, but on wider categories like slave activism or slave resistance. This is the result of a cumulative and teleological conception, one that lumps together revolts, conspiracies, homicides, and escapes, and then concludes that all of this combined contributed to the undermining of the slave system, weakening it, and leading to or aiding in its ruin. In my book I tried to refute this perspective, but, as it emerged in some of the comments, I believe it is important to say something more in this respect.

Eltis and Engerman state that only a few historians maintain that revolts led to the end of slavery. On the other hand, there are many who argue that resistance, "broadly defined," played a role in abolition. By focusing essentially on the major revolts, I have undervalued that role, they claim. That would be a mistake, as one could easily see by my own text.

In fact, based on my own statements and examples, Eltis and Engerman try to show that slave resistance was important for abolition. They consider that in Brazil "flight did count for something," as it contributed to the anticipation of the emancipation process. So, bearing in mind the number of slaves escaping to freedom in various other parts of the Americas, we would have to conclude that, "a sizeable minority of the population left slavery in a way shaped in part by actions of the slaves themselves."

Eltis and Engerman think that flights "certainly reduced the number of slaves and accelerated the demise of the system." They exemplify this assertion with the fact that thousands of slaves fled to the English and the French during the American Revolution, and eventually left the new nation. This same example is used by David B. Davis, to demonstrate precisely the opposite, i.e., that before the political emergence of abolitionism, "even massive slave resistance failed to undermine the institution." As Davis says, "during the American Revolution, the southern states lost more than twenty thousand slaves ... This flight to freedom can well be seen as the most momentous act of slave resistance in North America before the Civil War. Yet, slavery in the South was clearly stronger and more prosperous in 1800 than it had been in 1775, when the Revolution began." I share Davis' point of view, but I think it is important to underline that Eltis and Engerman seem to be making recurrent and persistent confusing statements. "Leaving slavery" is not the same as "abolishing slavery." To anticipate abolition is not a synonym of agitating for or decreeing abolition. Historians should, of course, take into account that the French slaves' demonstrations in Martinique hastened the enforcement of the 27 April 1848 emancipation decree in the island, but they must not forget that abolition had been decided in Paris before those demonstrations had occurred. That is precisely the point at issue here: *abolition*, not anticipation. Stressing the importance that slave revolts may have had in the timing of abolition, as various commentators do, is to displace the problem at stake.

I do not mean to say that slaves played no role in emancipation. I say exactly the opposite, as some commentators—like Blackburn, for instance—noted and emphasized. But I also say that, with rare exceptions, that participation was not decisive. Having a positive impact on the thing is not the same as causing the thing. The issue here is one of historical causes and, mainly, of strategic variables.[1] As I tried to show, the strategic variable in this case was clearly abolitionism (and to a lesser extent, the spirit of independence which arose in certain American regions), a new factor that turned the scales of colonial balance upside down. Slave resistance and rebellions, on the contrary, were a constant and, using Drescher's words in this book, "you cannot explain a variable by a constant."

The use of cumulative conceptualization leads us to the comments of Peter Blanchard and Olivier Pétré-Grenouilleau. Blanchard does not discuss the issue of slave revolts. He focuses his attention on slave activism and particularly on slaves' participation in the armies of belligerents. Although he recognizes that "there is little to suggest that the wars caused the slaves to press for abolition decrees," Blanchard considers that armed conflicts, which led to the death of the Spanish American Empire, created "unprecedented opportunities for the slave population to act, and their resulting initiatives seriously undermined slavery in the new states." Pétré-Grenouilleau also chooses to underline slave resistance rather than slaves' revolts: "some apparently 'passive' resistance, like petty marronage (flight), could be more dangerous to the economic efficiency of a slave system than large-scale revolts, which generally failed." Pétré-Grenouilleau states that "slave resistance did not always or mechanically lead to the end of slavery," which implies that sometimes it did. Blanchard has a similar idea. Yet, neither of the two authors mentioned concrete examples. Therefore, we cannot discuss real cases as evidence for or against their hypotheses.

Nevertheless, we may look at these problems in terms of comparative history. If we do, we find that in the Greco-roman world, slavery lasted for centuries despite marronage and various forms of passive resistance. The same can be said in respect of the three first centuries of the system of slavery in the Americas. Those who claim that slave resistance played a major role in the abolition of slavery have not explained clearly why that resistance had no anti-slavery effect in any part of the world before the end of the eighteenth century. If this reasoning holds for New World resistance in general, it is also valid for Blanchard's cases of military activism. Ever since the Antiquity, there were slaves fighting in armies. Those slaves could obtain freedom on an individual basis. That did not, however, endanger the *peculiar institution*. This happened in nineteenth-century Spanish America because the wars in which slaves participated were fought in a republican and abolitionist context. This was the new and decisive element—the strategic variable. That variable was not the incorporation of slaves or ex-slaves into the armies, which had always been a common practice in times of crises.

Speaking of resistance rather than revolt refers not just to cumulative conceptions, but also to a persistent conceptual maze. As Geggus notes, when slaves' reactive attitude is discussed, there is a tendency to mix all manners of resistance (conspiracies are sometimes called revolts and so on). Slaves' actions, like most human actions, are complex processes that can change their nature and purpose. It is therefore important that the concepts used are as accurate as possible to avoid misunderstandings as to the different forms of resistance, their motivations, and their aims. This is not always easy. As I noted in my text, there are unavoidable juxtaposed zones. Many revolts began by flights, which then escalated into something else. Various so-called revolts were mere projects that never went beyond the conspiracy phase. Some revolts were mixed social movements where it is hard to see the boundaries between who was a slave and who was not. For instance, was the Venezuelan revolt of 1811, which Blanchard mentions, a slave movement with some free *pardos* joining in, or the other way around? We can ask the same question in relation to various revolts in Cuba, in Brazil, and in other American regions. In this field, great efforts of clarification are needed. I hope this book may be an encouragement in that direction.

Is There a Central Flaw in My Reasoning?

Seymour Drescher states that "slave rebellion was not synonymous with anti-slavery, either in intention or impact" and he advises us against "over-evaluating the power of either revolts or threatened revolts to determine the actual terms of entry into full legal freedom." This is perhaps not enough to allow me to conclude that Drescher fully supports my thesis, although it is obvious that he does not reject it.

On the contrary, Hilary Beckles strongly opposes my views. He regrets that in spite of the good work carried out in the last decades on "anti-slavery politics of enslaved communities in the Atlantic world," there are still "attempts of conceptual reversals disguised as research based revision." My book is presumably an example of such attempts and disguises. According to Beckles, I could not—or would not—recognize that African slaves were men with a modern mentality and, hence, a modern ideas-based politics. Besides linking my reasoning to eighteenth-century pro-slavery ideology and to racist affirmations of the cultural and intellectual inferiority of African slaves, an alleged incapacity to see the Africans as modern beings would be the essential flaw of my argument. As Beckles puts it: "the central flaw of João Pedro Marques' analysis is its refusal to accept that enslaved Africans in the Atlantic World were a modern people. This is where Marques rests his case, whether it is stated explicitly or otherwise. From this position, all of his other arguments ... should be read and could be understood."

Nowhere did I suggest that Africans were different from any other people. However, Beckles supposes I did and bases this supposition on the fact that I use terms like "slave" instead of "enslaved Africans." According to him this means that I did not see them as free people who had been enslaved, but rather as mentally impaired people who would not be able to reason and respond with reference to time and place. Actually, those who read my work carefully and with an open mind are aware that I wrote that Africans easily adjusted to what was blowing in the wind. They reasoned and responded very quickly to new ideas and changing circumstances. Hence, the term "slave" does not imply any judgment on the intellectual and cognitive abilities to those it refers. When historians use this term, it usually means a status—a relation of total juridical and economical subordination—and not any condition of mental inferiority. Moreover, if we look at the texts of the other commentators, we can see that the expression "enslaved Africans" is seldom used, with all of them (Beckles excepted) employing the term "slaves."

Obviously, when I use the word slave, I am not trying to "conceal" or imply any message of superiority or inferiority, of modernity or backwardness. If we bear in mind that we usually use the term "slave" when referring to servile status in Classical Antiquity or the Middle Ages, we readily understand that the word does not carry that meaning at all.

Beckles does not approve of that kind of historical comparison. He defends the exclusiveness of the Atlantic slave system. He thinks it is "folly" to compare domestic domination in the pre-Atlantic slave trade in West Africa or Medieval Europe/Asia with chattel slavery in the Caribbean, Brazil, and the US south. He also believes one should not compare the behavior of the enslaved in these communities with persons classified as "slaves" in ancient Europe and elsewhere. In my book, I try to show that this is a mode of argument that tries to elude conceptual difficulties. We cannot bypass the central dilemma with terms such as "folly," "error" or "lack of conceptual sophistication": either we recognize that resistance to slavery and the corresponding anti-slavery consciousness had their origins in ancient times (and then we must explain why that anti-slavery consciousness had no long-term practical effect on the institution in those distant days), or we must consider that revolts, conspiracies, and flights occurring before the sixteenth century implied no anti-slavery consciousness. In the latter case, we must explain why it did not.

In the last part of his comment, Beckles compares the New World's rebellious slaves with contemporary Middle Eastern suicide bombers, and the conciliatory actions of Cudjoe—the leader of the Jamaican maroons—with Stalin's political alliances with the oppressors. I shall not pursue these comparisons. I would just like to point out that, for someone who considered the comparison of slavery in Medieval Europe with chattel slavery in America to be a "folly," such arguments seems rather incoherent.

Amidst his challenges and conjectures, Beckles reaffirms his well-known thesis, i.e, that "most enslaved Africans in the Atlantic carried an anti-slavery consciousness" meaning that "they preferred not to live as enslaved persons and anticipated a future in which they and/or their children could live as the white people did." But this is of no consequence to our discussion here. It is self-evident that people usually prefer not to be enslaved. Still, I continue to think that this preference is neither anti-slavery nor a way of thinking that inevitably led to the project of universally abolishing slavery.

To sum it all up, it seems clear that the majority of the commentators confirm—or at least do not refute—my main thesis, i.e., that rebellious slaves were not aiming at the abolition of slavery and that, with rare exceptions, it was not their resistance that put an end to slavery, but rather the emergence of a new factor: abolitionism. I do not mean to imply that the commentators fully agree with all of my arguments, descriptions or secondary theories. Some of them do point out errors or gaps that should be explained or addressed (if this is the case).

Haiti

Criticism by the contributors focuses mainly on my description and interpretation of the Haitian Revolution and its impact. Geggus thinks that I undervalued or failed to recognize the role of French commissioner Sonthonax as the leading hand of abolitionism in Saint-Domingue. Instead, I turned Toussaint into the key figure, and I weakened my main argument by doing so.

There is some weight to Geggus' remark. But, in a historical perspective, the main interest lies on what is uncommon or unexpected. In this case, the more significant fact was that Toussaint was aware of Raynal's theories, rather than that, 13 years earlier, Sonthonax had written a newspaper article in favor of abolition, or that he was aware of what was happening and of what was being said in France. Would it be necessary to say that Sonthonax was influenced by the French Revolution? The reader takes it for granted. On the other hand, it should be emphasized that I did not mean to remove the African slaves or ex-slaves from the abolitionist equation. My purpose was to reach a balanced view of the role that those slaves and ex-slaves played in the course of events. Was Sonthonax more important than Toussaint from an abolitionist point of view? I did not look at the issue in that way. In my opinion, the significant fact was that Toussaint was able to grasp the circulating rumors and ideas and turn them into an anti-slavery stance. Geggus himself implicitly recognizes the importance of Toussaint when he says that Sonthonax's first, limited, abolition proclamation failed to win over many black insurgents. In August 1793, Toussaint first associated himself with liberty and equality. From then on, insurgents gradually rallied to the French Republic.

Geggus also raises a question that is hard to answer, namely: what was the motivation of the slaves when they rebelled in 1791? It is often said they just wanted to improve their living conditions. I share this view with various historians, namely, with Thornton, who in his comments concludes that "it was probably true that even in the Haitian Revolution, the participants were not thinking about overthrowing slavery as much as winning a few extra free days and a less harsh disciplinary regime." Geggus states that after having studied this subject for thirty years, he still has not reached a definite conclusion about the real purpose of the majority of the insurgents. But it seems to him unlikely that the slaves would have killed and destroyed on such a massive scale, unless they were expecting to live afterwards free from the possibility of French revenge. I agree that this is a reasonable conjecture.

Seymour Drescher does not follow my views on the impact of the Haitian Revolution in Britain. Drescher thinks that stating, as I do, that this revolution was "influential" in the abolition of the slave trade in 1807 is an "overstatement."

According to Drescher, with exception of a brief remark by Wilberforce, the risk of slave revolts was never considered "in the period just preceding British abolition." What should we understand by the statement "period just preceding British abolition"? Drescher went back in his commentary as far as 1805 and left 1804 out completely. Now, 1804 is exactly the year of the Haitian independence and the one I focused on in my book, referring to a text by David P. Geggus: in 1804, "all abolitionists agreed" that Haitian events signified a "grave danger" to the British West Indies, and "brought new urgency to the abolitionist question." The abolition committee re-assembled after a hiatus of eight years, and Wilberforce pressed for "immediate abolition" in the Commons. The bill he introduced passed in June, with large majorities, but was withdrawn.[2] In later writings, Geggus echoed the conclusions of Seymour Drescher and considered that the Haitian Revolution had no decisive or long-lasting influence on British abolitionist campaign. He repeats that idea in these very pages, stating that the Haitian Revolution was not a significant issue in the Parliamentary debates.

The underlying question is the following: can we consider that the specter of Haiti played a major role in the revival of abolitionism in 1804, but played no role at all in the approval of the Abolition Act in March 1807? I believe that we cannot cut the flow of pro-abolitionist ideas into impermeable sections. Of course, slave violence usually caused no more than transitory alarms. In 1835, after the Malê's revolt, the Brazilians proposed to the Portuguese government the formation of Luso-Brazilian mixed commissions to try the arrested slave ships. However, when the alarm began to fade away, the idea was abandoned due to the lack of initiative by both parties.[3] Yet, the revolt of Saint-Domingue had a unique and very lasting impact. I think it is very plausible that, although not often verbalized, the thoughts that were in full blossom in 1804 influenced what happened two and a half years later, in March 1807.

In my opinion, this is precisely the only case in which the spectre of Haiti and the fear of slave revolts had an influence in the passing of abolition laws. This is the exception that seems to confirm the major rule of non-influence. Anyway, if I am wrong in this evaluation and if Drescher is right, then that will strengthen my main thesis even further, because in that case it would prove that the Haitian Revolution had even less significance for the abolition process than I admit it had.

Humanitarian Feelings in Europe

Eltis and Engerman characterize Western Europe as that part of the world that "experienced more wars per century and killed more people than any other in the process of doing so." Thus, they add, "it is perhaps only to be expected (that Europe) ... should institute the most efficient and exploitative form of chattel slavery in history," the paradox being that "such a violent collection of (European) societies" decided to ban slavery. According to Eltis and Engerman, this paradox would be explained by "the continual shrinking of the eligibility criteria for enslavement as well as major shifts in what was considered to be accepted levels of cruelty."

Not having considered this paradox would be "a basic problem" of my analysis, in the opinion of both authors. Going beyond what the abolitionists themselves thought, I stated that the "humanitarian feelings" long pre-existed abolitionism. Accordingly, I considered that, in the Western World, people were sensitive to the iniquity and brutality of slavery, but those feelings had been stifled by various forces. Eltis and Engerman completely disagree with my view. As they say, "there was little evidence of humanitarian feelings, restrained or not, being expressed toward African slaves during the era that witnessed the establishment of the slave system in the Americas."

This is not so. It is true that a strong aversion to slavery developed in the course of the eighteenth century, and that was new. But most of the basic humanitarian feelings were already in place. Let us consider Zurara's description of the first disembarkation of slaves in Lagos, in southern Portugal (1444). Zurara was deeply moved by the forced separation of parents and their children. In accordance, he cried "pitifully" for the "pain" of those people. If even the animals with their "beastly feelings" reacted to the injuries done to their own, how much more should he, with his "human nature," be moved by the anguish of those sons of "Adam"?[4] In 1633, Father António Vieira confessed, in the last of his sermons to the black slaves of Bahia, that he was appalled with the cruel and iniquitous slave trade—"Oh inhuman trade whose goods are men!"—and by the way African captives were treated. He was saddened by the sight of ships full of slaves coming in from Angola; he was stirred by the contrast between the humility of the famished, helpless, and naked slave, and the master's arrogance, opulence, and brutality.[5] I chose these two figures of Portuguese history because they are accessible to the reading public in English. They show that Eltis and Engerman are mistaken when they say that, in the era of discoveries and of the colonization of the Americas, the Western World had no humanitarian feelings toward the African slaves.

But their misconception has its origin in the definition of Europe as the most warlike and aggressive of worlds. According to Eltis and Engerman, between 1500 and 1810, nations in Europe were at war 50 percent of the time and 10 million people died in those wars—about 3 percent of the population in 1700. These figures are, undoubtedly, impressive, but they become less striking when compared with what we know from other periods and other parts of the world. Unfortunately, horror is not exclusively European and one example should be enough to illustrate the point. In the end of the twelfth century, the Mongols started the fast conquest of what would become their vast empire. It is hard to tell the exact toll of deaths, but it is certain that the Mongol military actions were far more destructive—either in lives or in properties—than the above mentioned three centuries of war in Europe. Northern China had 50 million inhabitants in the end of the twelfth century; 40 years later, after the Mongol raids, it contained fewer than 9 million.[6] This balance refers to a limited period of time and also to a limited geographical area. It should be reminded that the bloody relation the Mongols had to the sedentary world happened along the almost continuous strip of steppe that extends from Manchuria to Hungary. Within a few decades, the Mongol war machine also reached Korea, Central and Eastern Europe, and had assaulted the Islamic world with all of its strength. During a long part of the thirteenth century, that world, from the north of India to Turkey and Gaza, was under the attack of the Mongols. They destroyed dozens of cities and methodically slaughtered the urban and rural populations.

Taking the above into account, Europe certainly will look no more cruel and violent, and the creation of their brutal slave system will not appear so predetermined and unavoidable.

On Abolitionism

In my book, I tried to show that British emancipation, for instance, and the Saint-Domingue revolt correspond to two different ways of abolishing slavery. Saint-Domingue inaugurated a revolutionary path that was never repeated in full. On the other hand, British emancipation was often reproduced in the Western World and it is part of a reformist tradition that clearly diverges from, or is opposed to, the revolutionary way. As I wrote, the two pathways and traditions rarely converged.

Robin Blackburn does not directly attack the fundaments of this thesis, but he actively tries to associate both traditions, suggesting that the Saint-Domingue revolt converged with British and US emancipation, as the "three major upheavals that sealed the fate of slavery in the New World." This is a distorted view, in my opinion.

There were abolitionists who evoked the British, US or other cases to promote abolitionism in their national parliaments. Even the liberation of the Russian serfs in 1861 served as an example to be followed. Yet, as far as I know, the Haitian example was never used as a model or an incentive to the emancipations in the nineteenth century. While British emancipation was an example that the Western World governments should follow—"the world will be shamed into imitation," as it was said in a sermon held in 1834[7]—the case of Haiti pointed in the opposite direction. These two cases do not make part of the same series nor do they converge. It is possible, as Blackburn says that "three is a cumulative character to anti-slavery," since an event would influence the subsequent ones. But this influence could be exerted in different directions and the parts cannot be added up as if it were an algebra operation. The tendency to do so is evident in Blackburn's comment and leads, in my view, to a teleological judgment that results from the blending or the fusion of opposing trends.

This fusion implies a very wide notion of abolitionism. Blackburn is a critic of "mainstream historiography," which, in his opinion, undervalues the importance of slave resistance and black witness. This produces a flawed portrait of abolitionism that, in his opinion, owes "something vital" to such figures as Equiano, Cogoano, Toussaint Louverture, and many others of African descent. To support this point, Blackburn adds that Clarkson, Wilberforce, and other abolitionists "paid tribute to slave resistance." Let us discard the idea that abolitionism owes "something vital" to men such as Equiano or Cogoano—which is a clear overstatement—and let us focus our attention on the statement that a man like Clarkson "paid tribute to slave resistance." What does "paying tribute," in this context, really mean? Could this mean that Clarkson thought of the slave rebels as pioneers in the road that led to abolition? The answer is negative, as Clarkson's river of ideas clearly shows. The author of the first history of abolition, in 1808, names those he thinks were the forerunners and coadjutors in the great cause of abolition, but he does not mention Toussaint Louverture or any other rebel leader.[8]

This was not a flawed perspective from the first wave of abolitionists to be corrected later on by their successors. In his forced retirement in London in 1883, Joaquim Nabuco, the great Brazilian abolitionist, looked in retrospect at a century of anti-slavery history and analyzed the relation between slave violence and emancipation. According to Nabuco, the only consequence of a possible slave revolt in Brazil would be "an aggravation of slaves' captivity"; those who promoted that possible revolt would commit a crime and would sign the death sentence of "Wilberforce's abolitionism," opening the door to the methods of "Spartacus or John Brown," which lead nowhere as history had repeatedly shown. So he foretold:

> Slavery in Brazil will not be suppressed by a slave war, and even less by insurrections or local rebellions.... Emancipation shall be reached, among us, by a law with all external and internal requirements such as any other. Thus, it shall be in Parliament, not in the plantations or in the outback quilombos, nor on the streets and squares of our cities, that the cause of liberty shall be gained or lost.[9]

The men who proposed and decreed abolitions in the governments or the Parliaments of the Western World did not consider that slave revolts converged with the abolitionist cause. For many of them, emancipation from below or emancipation from above were two different and incompatible things.

On the contrary, Blackburn considers that slave revolts exerted a wholly positive influence on the timid abolitionism of people such as Lincoln, Tocqueville or Condorcet. We do not know—and Blackburn does not say—which specific slave revolts had that alleged influence in the spirits of these three men (Tocqueville, as is well known, praised British emancipation because it was obtained through the enlightened will of the Masters and not by the daggers of a black Spartacus). It is also hard to understand why Blackburn chose these examples and not those of less timid abolitionists. Why Condorcet and not Granville Sharp? Why Tocqueville and not Schöelcher? Blackburn is not unaware that, alongside what he calls "timid abolitionism," there was a more daring kind. It was the latter, and not Tocqueville's or Condorcet's, which lead to the liberation of the majority of slaves. To think that the liberation of those slaves had in most cases a relation, albeit an indirect one, with slave revolts is an article of faith that Blackburn has left unproved.

Blackburn criticizes my alleged narrow-minded approach to abolitionism, which, were it rigorously applied, would exclude much white as well as black anti-slavery. Blackburn concludes that, in my frame of reference, for me "the term abolitionism should only be applied to acts or movements that aim at a quite comprehensive outlawing of slavery." He then suggests that this is absurd, since at that time there were no political and legal conditions available to allow such a goal to be implemented in Europe. But Blackburn fails to grasp my more precise notion of abolitionism, which leads him to several misunderstandings. Abolitionism, as I defined it, would be an attitude aiming at the immediate or short-term abolition of the slave trade and, in the medium term, of slavery itself. In the British case, the goal of abolitionism was also a cumulative process, envisioning the end of slavery on a universal scale.[10] Actually, due to the political and administrative structure of many states at the time, it was difficult uniformly and simultaneously to apply the legislative measures. Blackburn confuses legislation and law enforcement and confuses the application of particular laws with the underlying philosophy. Many abolitionist measures were incomplete and circumscribed, but they were abolitionist measures nevertheless.

However, using either a broader or a restricted notion of abolitionism, the fact remains that an action aimed at one's liberty but otherwise accepting the slavery of others cannot be considered as a form of anti-slavery or abolitionism. Thus, contrary to what Blackburn thinks, it sometimes makes perfect sense to deny that large-scale slave revolts, "which utterly disrupt the plantation economy, had something to do with 'anti-slavery'." We must bear in mind that many rebels intended to perpetuate slavery (as it happened in Palmares); these were not anti-slavery actions.

Brief Clarifications

Finally, I must rectify some misunderstandings or misreadings of my text. Some passages attributed to me do not correspond to what I wrote. For instance, it is not true, as Eltis and Engerman say, that "many of the abolitions (I) describe as occurring without active slave participation involved small numbers." We can consider, for example, that the Portuguese and Dutch abolitions were effected without active slave participation. Yet, there were around 120,000 slaves in the Portuguese colonies in Africa and around 45,000 in the Dutch colonies in America, which can hardly be considered "small numbers."

I did not exactly state that rebellion would be suicidal in Brazil or in the US, i.e., where there were large numbers of whites. This is an idea shared by various authors, including Eugene Genovese, but not by me. I stated that, considering the disparity of forces and logistic support, slave revolts would have been useless and suicidal, "unless, as it happened in Saint-Domingue, that society was involved in a revolution and civil war dividing the slave owners themselves."

Neither do I consider—as Blackburn claims—that free womb laws granted immediate freedom. On the contrary, as I wrote in respect to the case of the US: "as was usual in the case of free womb laws, the newly born would only attain full freedom as adults (between 15 and 30 years of age)." The same applies, as I wrote, to the cases of Portugal, Spain, Venezuela, Brazil, and other American countries.

I wrote that, "the African slave has been often represented as someone always ready to revolt against slavery." Hilary Beckles thinks "this is simply not true" and adds that he is not aware of any work "by any academic of slavery" affirming that the slaves were always ready to rebel. Nevertheless, such works exist. I referred to some of them, and Pétré-Grenouilleau reminds us here that the image of the ever-rebellious slave is still very much alive, mainly in French historiography. Anyway, it is important to stress that the image of the slave as someone ever ready to rebel is to be found not only in the work of some historians of slavery, but also in popular historiography and in society at large. This was just what I meant when I said that slaves were often represented as people always ready to rebel.

Conclusion: the Opening of a Debate

To conclude, the Portuguese original text was written to oppose the theory that slave resistance was a major cause of abolition, a cause even more important than the efforts of the abolitionists.

Perhaps it would have been easier to accept a mixed solution, i.e., that both the rebellious slaves and the abolitionists had contributed to put an end to slavery. Eltis and Engerman wrote that forcing scholars to choose between slaves and abolitionists as the major agents of the legislated repudiation of coerced labor that began to occur in the late eighteenth century, "risks undermining our understanding of how slaves and abolitionists influenced each other." Yet the aim of this whole collective discussion is not to force people to take sides, but to distinguish the essential from the accessory, and to try to discover, in the blurred images of the past, what really made people follow a certain path. As Seymour Drescher and Pieter C. Emmer observe in the foreword of this book, a mixed solution could be comfortable but would leave many questions unanswered. The fact that my original text is now combined with a set of valuable comments allowed for the opening of a debate on these questions. This is an ongoing conversation and I hope that this debate will become even wider and richer.

Notes

1. For the idea of strategic variable see Paul Veyne, "L'histoire conceptualisante," in *Faire l'histoire, Nouveaux problèmes*, eds. Jacques Le Goff and Pierre Nora (Gallimard, 1974), 66.
2. David P. Geggus "Haiti and the Abolitionists: Opinion, propaganda and International Politics in Britain and France, 1804–1838," in *Abolition and its Aftermath*, ed. David Richardson (London: Frank Cass, 1985), 116.
3. Palmela to Sérgio Teixeira de Macedo, 7th July and 12th November 1835, Arquivo Nacional da Torre do Tombo (MNE), L° 592.
4. *Crónica da Guiné*, XXV.
5. António Vieira, "Sermão vigésimo sétimo," in *Sermões, problemas raciais e políticos do Brasil*, ed. Cultrix (São Paulo, 1975), 57–58.
6. Thomas J. Barfield, *The Perilous Frontier. Nomadic Empires and China* (Oxford: Basil Blackwell, 1989), 204.
7. Ralph Wardlaw (in a sermon held in Glasgow in 1834), quoted in David B. Davis, *Slavery and Human Progress* (Oxford and New York: Oxford University Press, 1984), 121.
8. Thomas Clarkson, *History of the Rise, Progress, and Accomplishment of the Abolition of the African Slave Trade by the British Parliament* (London, 1839; 1st ed.,1808), 49.
9. Joaquim Nabuco, *O Abolicionismo*, ed. Nova Fronteira (Rio de Janeiro, 1999; 1st ed., London, 1883), 29–30.
10. João Pedro Marques, *The Sounds of Silence. Nineteenth-century Portugal and the Abolition of the Slave Trade* (New York and Oxford: Berghan Books, 2006), 1–3.

Bibliography

Barfield, Thomas J. *The Perilous Frontier. Nomadic Empires and China*. Oxford: Basil Blackwell, 1989.

Clarkson, Thomas. *History of the Rise, Progress, and Accomplishment of the Abolition of the African Slave Trade by the British Parliament*. London, 1839; 1st ed., 1808.

Crónica da Guiné, XXV.

Geggus, David Patrick. "Haiti and the Abolitionists: Opinion, Propaganda and International Politics in Britain and France, 1804–1838." In *Abolition and its Aftermath: The Historical Context, 1790–1916*, edited by David Richardson. London: Frank Cass, 1985.

Marques, João Pedro. *The Sounds of Silence. Nineteenth-century Portugal and the Abolition of the Slave Trade*. New York and Oxford: Berghahn Books, 2006.

Nabuco, Joaquim. *O Abolicionismo*. Edited by Nova Fronteira. Rio de Janeiro, 1999; 1st ed., London, 1883.

Palmela to Sérgio Teixeira de Macedo, 7th July and 12th November 1835, Arquivo Nacional da Torre do Tombo (MNE), L° 592.

Veyne, Paul. "L'histoire conceptualisante." In *Faire l'histoire, Nouveaux problèmes*, edited by Jacques Le Goff and Pierre Nora, 66. Gallimard, 1974.

Vieira, António. "Sermão vigésimo sétimo." In *Sermões, problemas raciais e políticos do Brasil*, edited by Cultrix, 57–58. São Paulo, 1975.

Wardlaw, Ralph. Sermon held in Glasgow in 1834. In *Slavery and Human Progress*, by David B. Davis. New York and Oxford: Oxford University Press, 1984.

CONTRIBUTORS

Sir Hilary Beckles is professor of Social and Economic History and Principal and Pro Vice-Chancellor, Cave Hill Campus, University of the West Indies, Barbados. He has written widely on various aspects of the history of slavery in the Caribbean as well as on cricket. Among his many publications are *Natural Rebels: A Social History of Enslaved Black Women in Barbados, 1680-1838* (Rutgers University Press/Zed Books, 1989), (with Verene Shepherd) *Liberties Lost: Slave Systems in the Caribbean* (Cambridge University Press, 2004), and *Freedoms Won: Emancipation, Identity and Nationhood in the Caribbean* (Cambridge University Press, 2006).

Robin Blackburn teaches at the New School for Social Research in New York and the University of Essex, in the UK. He is the author of *The Making of New World Slavery: From the Baroque to the Modern, 1492–1800* and *The Overthrow of Colonial Slavery, 1776–1848*.

Peter Blanchard is Professor of Latin American history at the University of Toronto. His publications include *Slavery and Abolition in Early Republican Peru* (Wilmington, DE: Scholarly Resources Inc., 1992) and *Under the Flags of Freedom: Slave Soldiers and the Wars of Independence in Spanish South America* (Pittsburgh, PA: University of Pittsburgh Press, 2008).

David Brion Davis is Sterling Professor of History Emeritus at Yale University and Director Emeritus of the Gilder Lehrman Center for the Study of Slavery, Resistance, and Abolition. His books include *The Problem of Slavery in Western Culture* (Ithaca: Cornell University Press, 1966; rev. 1988); *The Problem of Slavery in the Age of Revolution, 1770–1823* (Ithaca, NY: Cornell University Press, 1975), and *Inhuman Bondage: The Rise and Fall of Slavery in the New World* (New York: Oxford University Press, 2006).

Seymour Drescher is Distinguished University Professor of History and Sociology at the University of Pittsburgh. Among his publications are *Econocide: British Slavery in the Era of Abolition* (Pittsburgh: The University of Pittsburgh Press, 1977), *Capitalism and Antislavery* (New York: Oxford University Press, 1986), *The Mighty Experiment: Free Labor versus Slavery in British Emancipation* (New York: Oxford University Press, 2002), and *Abo-*

lition: A History of Slavery and Antislavery (New York: Cambridge University Press, 2009).

David Eltis is Robert W. Woodruff Professor of History at Emory University. He received his PhD from the University of Rochester in 1979. He is author of *The Rise of African Slavery in the Americas* (Cambridge: Cambridge University Press, 2000), co-compiler of *The Transatlantic Slave Trade: A Database on CD-ROM* (Cambridge: Cambridge University Press, 1999), and its successor on www.slavevoyages.org, and author of numerous articles on slavery and migration, most recently with Philip Morgan and David Richardson, "Agency and Diaspora in Atlantic History: Reassessing the African Contribution to Rice Cultivation in the Americas," *The American Historical Review* 112/4 (December 2007): 1329–1358.

Pieter C. Emmer is Professor of the History of European Expansion, University of Leiden, the Netherlands. His publications in English include *The Dutch in the Atlantic Economy, 1580–1880: Trade, Slavery and Emancipation* (Aldershot: Ashgate, 1998) and *The Dutch Slave Trade, 1500–1850* (New York/Oxford: Berghahn Books, 2006).

Stanley L. Engerman is John H. Munro Professor of Economics and Professor of History at the University of Rochester. Among his publications are *Time on the Cross: The Economics of American Negro Slavery* (co-authored with Robert W. Fogel, Boston: Little, Brown and Company, 1974) and *Slavery, Emancipation, and Freedom: Comparative Perspectives* (Baton Rouge: Louisiana State University Press, 2007).

David Geggus teaches history at the University of Florida, Gainesville. His most recent books are *Haitian Revolutionary Studies* (Bloomington: Indiana University Press, 2002) and (with Norman Fiering) *The World of the Haitian Revolution* (Bloomington: Indiana University Press, 2009).

João Pedro Marques is a researcher at the Instituto de Investigação Científica Tropical (Lisbon). He has published dozens of works on the subjects of slavery, abolition, and other colonial issues, including *The Sounds of Silence. Nineteenth-century Portugal and the Abolition of the Slave Trade* (New York and Oxford: Berghahn Books, 2006).

Olivier Pétré-Grenouilleau is Professor of History at the Institute of Political Sciences of Paris and member of the Academia Europaea. He has published a dozen books, mainly related to European maritime expansion, slave trade, and slavery.

John Thornton teaches African History at Boston University. His publications in this field include *Africa and Africans in the Making of the Atlantic World, 1400–1800*, 2nd ed. (Cambridge: Cambridge University Press, 1998).

INDEX

www.ingramcontent.com/pod-product-compliance
Lightning Source LLC
Chambersburg PA
CBHW070926030426
42336CB00014BA/2551